Security and Territoriality in the Persian Gulf

Security and Territoriality in the Persian Gulf

A Maritime Political Geography

Pirouz Mojtahed-Zadeh

CURZON

First Published in 1999
by Curzon Press
15 The Quadrant, Richmond
Surrey, TW9 1BP

© 1999 Pirouz Mojtahed-Zadeh

Typeset in Sabon by LaserScript Ltd, Mitcham, Surrey
Printed and bound in Great Britain by
TJ International, Padstow, Cornwall

British Library Cataloguing in Publication Data
A catalogue record of this book is available from the British Library

Library of Congress Cataloguing in Publication Data
A catalogue record for this book has been requested

ISBN 0–7007–1098–1

Contents

Preface

There are many areas of border dispute in the region of the Persian Gulf as potentially explosive as that of the Kuwait crisis of 1990–91.

Ten years have gone by since the ceasefire put an end to the Iran–Iraq war and the two countries have not been able to settle their border differences; Iraq has only grudgingly suspended claims of sovereignty over Kuwait in spite of the bitter lesson the country was taught in January 1991; whereas Saudi Arabia's claims to the islands of Qaruh and Umm al-Maradim, currently controlled by Kuwait, have been kept at a low profile, they are not to be taken lightly.

Though Bahrain and Qatar have agreed to refer their disputes over the issue of the Hawar archipelago, the shoals of Dibal and Jaradah, and the related seabed, to the International Court of Justice, an adjudication not satisfactory to both parties could renew serious conflict. Saudi Arabia, on the other hand, has proved that it is prepared eventually to allow the force of arms to be the judge of its territorial differences with Qatar.

Saudi Arabia's broad-based and rather inconclusive border arrangement of 1974 with Abu Dhabi concerning Al-Liwa and Khor al-Udayd, which also embraces border differences with Qatar, is too vague and too unreliable to support the idea that territorial and border disputes between Saudi Arabia and the United Arab Emirates have been resolved in full.

The United Arab Emirates has revived claims to the islands of Greater Tunb, Lesser Tunb and Abu Musa and entered into open dispute with Iran on the issue of sovereignty over these islands. The Sultanate of Oman has, in the course of little more than 15 years, delimited her boundaries with Iran, the United Arab Emirates, Saudi

Arabia and the Yemen. Nevertheless, Oman has territorial differences with the United Arab Emirates over areas in the Diba region.

None of the territorial and border disputes in the Persian Gulf region is a new phenomenon. These disputes have existed for decades without seriously threatening peace and security in the region.

The changing world order, which manifested itself most tangibly in 1991 with the demise of the Soviet Union and the success of the unprecedented military operation of the US-led coalition in the Gulf, introduced a new dimension to territorial and border disputes in a new era of security uncertainties in that region. The highlighted vulnerabilities of these changed circumstances in the Gulf region necessitate a more thorough study of the areas of territorial and boundary differences in that region.

Yet, as territorial and boundary disputes in the inland areas of the Persian Gulf have been studied quite extensively in many works of scholarly standing, attempts are made in this book to restrict the study of territoriality and boundary differences to the maritime areas only. In this context, there are two major areas of difference which need to be studied in more detail. These are Iran–UAE differences on the ownership of three islands and the Qatar–Bahrain differences on a number of islands and shoals. On the other hand, since arguments of ownership of any geographical space rely heavily on historical foundations of territoriality in that geographical space, prominence has been given throughout this book to the history of the emergence of the states involved in the territorial disputes under study as well as dealing with the historical background to all these disputed geographical localities.

In this book, attempts will be made first to introduce the background to the historical and geographical settings in the Persian Gulf, and to the instances of settled continental shelf boundaries in the region (Sections I and II). Secondly, the two most complicated and fiercely contested instances of maritime territory and boundary issues of the region will be examined (Sections III and IV).

These four sections are designed to represent the story of successes and failures of the treatment of security matters pertaining to territorial and boundary affairs in the maritime areas of the Persian Gulf only. This in turn, I hope, will present an example of the study of the impact of territoriality on global-wide maritime security.

Pirouz Mojtahed-Zadeh
London

Acknowledgements

This work was partly prepared in 1986 in the form of a research project. Early versions have appeared in various publications both in English and Persian. It was completed in its present form in June 1994 and was amended in July 1998.

Late Professor Jean Gottmann, an internationally respected political geographer of our time, under whom I studied at Oxford in the late 1970s, was very generous in advising me on a number of concepts discussed in this work in its early stages. I owe him an immense debt of gratitude.

Dr Najib Naeimi, Qatar's Minister of Justice, and Mr Karim Al-Shakar, former Ambassador of the State of Bahrain in London, were very kind in reading parts of the early versions of this book without making any suggestion. Nevertheless, I owe them both much gratitude.

Former Iranian Minister of Foreign Affairs, Mr Amir Khosro Afshar, who was personally involved in the development of some stages of the affairs related to Iran's former claim to Bahrain and their withdrawal, and to Iran's seizure of the islands of Tunbs and Abu Musa in the early 1970s, was very kind in providing me with his personal knowledge of these developments. I am most grateful to him for his generosity.

Dr Parviz Mina, formerly in charge of the National Iranian Oil Company's international relations, who negotiated and signed many of Iran's continental shelf boundary agreements in the Persian Gulf in late 1960s and early 1970s, has been generous in sharing with me his personal notes and memoirs of these agreements. I owe him much gratitude. My sincere thanks are also due to Mr Heshmat Mina for his constant encouragement of my academic work and for facilitating my interview with his brother Dr Parviz Mina.

I am most grateful to Mr Abbas Maleki, former Deputy Minister of Foreign Affairs of the Islamic Republic of Iran for Research and Education for assisting me in studying Iranian Foreign Ministry documents. Similarly, Mr Haj-Husseini, former director of the Institute of Political and International Studies (IPIS) of the Ministry of Foreign Affairs, Mr Kavousi, head of the document centre of the IPIS, and Mr Abdollahi, head of the document centre and exhibition of the Foreign Ministry were most helpful in making it possible for me to see the documents of Iranian Foreign Ministry on the special permission of former minister of foreign affairs, Dr Ali-Akbar Velayati.

Mr Shams and his colleagues at the National Document Organisation of Iran and Mr Kalateh and his colleagues at the document centre of the Contemporary Historical Studies Centre generously assisted me in sifting through the documents of their establishments. My sincere thanks are due to them.

During the course of my research for this book I exchanged views with and received information from a number of academics and government officials in the United Kingdom, Iran, France and the Arab states of the Persian Gulf. Similarly, a number of academics and interested friends have seen this book in its evolutionary stages and have made a number of valuable suggestions which undoubtedly improved the text. I am very grateful to all of them especially HE A. H. Khozeime Alam, Dr Alinaghi Alikhani and Professor K S McLachlan. My sincere thanks are due also to Miss Margaret Davis, secretary of the Urosevic Research Foundation, and Miss Pamela Davis, treasurer of the same Foundation, for their assistance in editing the text.

Similarly, I am most grateful to the controllers of the India Office Library and Records, the Public Record Office, the Library of the School of Oriental and African Studies, and the UN Office and Library in London who have been very kind in permitting me to use and helping me to find and photocopy masses of relevant documents. Others who have assisted me in my quest for documented fact and evidence relevant to the subjects discussed in this book are Dr Hassan Kiudeh and Mr Hamid-Reza Malek-Mohammadi Nouri. I owe them both much gratitude. I am also grateful to Mr Arash Salarian of Fara Pardaz Company of Tehran and his colleague Mr Pouyan Dadvand for their assistance in drawing or re-drawing the maps appearing in this book; a fine work of art worthy of admiration.

Last, but by no means least, I am most grateful to Ms Norma Edwards and to my wife, Nahid Mojtahed-Zadeh, for the outstanding help they have given me in preparing the text.

List of Illustrations

Introduction

GLOBALIST IDEAS AND REGIONAL REALITIES

The collapse of the Soviet Union and former Warsaw Pact, which resulted in the demise of the bi-polar global system, gave rise, in some Western quarters, to the idea that a vacuum had occurred in global geopolitics. The unprecedented success of the US-led Western response to the Kuwait crisis of 1990–91 seems to have encouraged some US politicians to proclaim the New World Order of a single-polar system in the form of a pyramid of hierarchy of powers with the United States at its top playing the role of ultimate global arbiter. Some of these men have openly advocated US military domination of the globe as the only way of ensuring global stability. Charles Krauthammer, for instance, contended, in the early 1990s, that the best hope for global safety and security lay 'in American strength and will – the strength and will to lead a uni-polar world, unashamedly laying down the rules of world order and being prepared to enforce it'.[1]

In their endeavour to fashion this single-polar global system, these American politicians base their thoughts on medieval notions of the categorisation of mankind according to religious and racial divides, totally ignoring the speed at which information technology is bringing our divided world together in a harmonious 'human community'. New meanings have been devised by ultra-right groups to terminologies such as 'civilisation' so as to give a new façade to the old hegemonical desires. A new class of US political visionaries, represented by men like Newton Gingrich is hard at work to enforce the idea of the revival of American civilisation. This ultra-nationalistic

1

idea which is seeking confrontation with racial and religious elements classed as 'non-American' is based on the definition of the term 'civilisation' as offered by a class of US academic visionaries represented by men like Samuel Huntington.[2] The scope of their concept of the term does not go beyond the limits of religious and racial divisions. Art, literature, science, technology and other cultural aspects of the human environment are not included in this peculiar definition of the term, for, if they were, the term could no longer be used to show divisions among the children of Adam.

Other American thinkers, however, disagree with the entire idea of a US global hegemonical endeavour. A distinguished US and Western thinker Russell Kirk, denounces all attempts to establish a New World Order. 'Soviet hegemony should not be succeeded by American hegemony', Kirk observes in his *Politics of Prudence*. 'Our prospects in the world of the twenty-first century are bright – supposing we Americans do not swagger about the globe, proclaiming our omniscience and our omnipotence.' Kirk predicts that any American New World Order will likely cause the United States to be more detested – beginning with the Arab peoples – than the Soviet Union ever was.[3] Furthermore, an American Conservative thinker of Michigan University, Dr Antony T. Sullivan even equates the idea of New World Order with eighteenth-century British imperialism in India.[4]

Moreover, the end of the Cold War coincided with increased economic competition between North America, Europe and South East Asia. Economic success of the European Union encouraged other powers to form economic groupings of their own. The United States joined forces with Canada and Mexico and created the North American Free Trade Area (NAFTA), while seven economies of South East Asia created the Association of South East Asian Nations (ASEAN), with Japan as its feared competitor of today and its potentially leading partner of the future. Although Russia's Commonwealth of Independent States (CIS), including the Slavic and Islamic nations of the former Soviet Union, may not succeed in its present form, it nevertheless represents a new form of grouping in that part of the world. This *Changing World Order* of the 1990s has deeply influenced the global system, and in spite of endeavours in Washington to create the concept of a *New World Order* with a single-polar system with the United States at the top of the pyramid of a global hierarchy system of power, the world is rapidly heading towards an unprecedented geopolitical order of economic competition in a multi-polar system which could, in time, lead to a kind of economic cold war between groups of economic giants.

The survival of other nations in this emerging geopolitical order will undoubtedly depend on their grasp of this situation and their ability to create economic groupings of their own in their particular regions. Formation of new economic groupings depends, above all, on defining a spatial arena based on the geographic concept of 'region'. Nations in such an arena are normally partners in some aspects of a common cultural, historical and economic life. In short, a 'region' is a geographical arena with some homogeneity of environments – the objects which constitute geopolitical regions.

SOME THEORETICAL BACKGROUNDS

Geography and politics are intertwined where and when a group thinks of using or influencing the geographical arena for the purpose of stating or elevating their standing among their fellow men or in comparison with them. There are times when geography is the initiating force in this interaction, and that is when such a group thinks of using their environment to better their position among their peers. Furthermore, there are times when politics are the initiating force in dividing the space for a group to state its spatial identity (territory).

Clearly, we are dealing here with two different approaches to one subject: the approach in which a group causes division in the space accessible to it to define its political position among others – known as *political geography*; and the approach in which geography plays the role of enhancing and elevating a group's power and influence among their fellow men – known as *geopolitics*.

At its simplest, geopolitics deals with the geographical dispersion of power in the world and the study of structural relations among them. In other words, it is the study of the role of geography in the dynamism of global politics. Geopolitics has also been considered as a part of the realist tradition in international relations as opposed to the idealism of a liberal doctrine that attempts to place international relations on a firm 'constitutional' basis.[5]

Political geography, by contrast, deals with political partitions in the space accessible to a particular group. If the earth's surface was level like the polished surface of the ping-pong ball, such matters as political geography and international relations would not exist.[6] In short, political geography deals with political divisions in the

3

geographical arena: it deals with such concepts as 'country and boundary', 'state and territory', 'movement and centre-periphery relationships', 'region and government'.

TERRITORY AND BOUNDARY IN POLITICAL GEOGRAPHY

Territory is the horizontal or spatial dimension of the legally organised structure known as 'state'. In other words, territory is the spatial manifestation of a 'state', while the latter is the organiser of the former.[7] Politically organised units have, in the past, been translated into a territorial state, later, into a nation state, which is one of the units forming the political map of the world. The basic elements of the geographical theory of 'state', as we are reminded by Peter Taylor (1989) were developed in the early 1950s by Gottmann (1951–2), Hartshorne (1950), and Jones (1954).[8]

Jean Gottmann has analysed the concept of 'territory' in relation to the notion of 'state'. In his 'evolution of the concept of territory', while acknowledging that the concept of territory is undergoing a substantial modification in our time, Gottmann argues that:

> Territory is a political as well as a geographical concept because geographical space is both partitioned and organised through political process.[9]

Having said this, Gottmann quotes Aristotle's remark in his 'Physics' that 'what is nowhere does not exist', and for that reason he submits that the definition of territory offered by him be accepted. He described the concept as follows:

> Territory is a portion of geographical space that coincides with the spatial extent of a government's jurisdiction. It is the physical container and support of the body politic organised under a governmental structure. It describes the spatial arena of the political system developed within a national state or part thereof endowed with some authority.[10]

This, a far more practical definition than others before it, leaves little doubt about the inseparability of the concept of state with that of territory. Nevertheless, it is noteworthy that while territory is more of a physical nature, state is more of a political one. Political partitioning of territories is normally demonstrated by 'boundaries'. Hence, boundary can be described as a line in space drawn to manifest the ultimate peripheries of the state and or a line in space to show the ultimate limitations of the territory.

4

Whereas man was preoccupied, in the ancient world, with the idea of establishing the 'frontiers' of his realm, modern man's main concern regarding the peripheries of his dominion is to define its 'boundaries'. Boundary in the modern sense of the word, did not exist until the nineteenth century. Ancient man considered the end of his conquest as the frontier. Frontier is, therefore, ancient and boundary is new. Endeavouring to distinguish frontiers from boundaries, geographers have used various etymologies. Having quoted Kristof (1959) that the etymology of each term determines their essential difference; that frontier comes from the notion of 'in front' as the 'spearhead of the civilisation', boundary comes from 'bounds' implying territorial limits, Taylor (1989) observes that:

> Frontier is therefore outward-oriented and boundary inward-oriented. Whereas a boundary is a definite line of separation, a frontier is a zone of contact.[11]

A frontier, therefore, functioned in ancient times as a zone of contact between two socially and politically united entities on its two extremes and can safely be described as the embodiment of the outer limits of a state's power and influence, and/or it can be described as the embodiment of the edges of political push of one power against another. Boundaries in the Persian Gulf are, on the whole, the manifestation of political push early on between the Persian and Ottoman empires and later, between British and Iranian powers in the nineteenth and twentieth centuries. Good examples of frontier zones in the ancient world were those between the Persian and Roman empires in the areas now known as Iraq and Syria.

On the northwestern corner of the Gulf, where the Sassanid and Roman empires' frontiers met, the vassal kingdom of Hirah was created on the river Tigris not far from the Sassanid capital Ctisphone, in the sixth century AD. This frontier-keeping state, paid for and defended by the Iranians, played the role of a buffer state or a zone of contact for Iran defusing pressure from the Romans who, in a similar move, created the vassal kingdom of Ghassan in the region now known as Syria, to play the same role for the Roman empire.[12] Nevertheless, it is noteworthy that Ferdosi (d.1020 AD), the most famous Iranian epic poet, speaks in his *Shahameh* (book of kings) of boundary pillars between Iran and Turan (now comprising the Republic of Turkmanistan and parts of Kazakhstan and Uzbekistan) at the time of Bahram Gur (420–438 AD) the Sassanid emperor of Iran.[13] Not only is there no indication that these boundary pillars were part of a wider zone of contact between the two powers at the time, but one could probably be safe in assuming that these boundary pillars were the earliest form of what constituted in the nineteenth century theEuropean concept of 'boundary'. Furthermore, Ferdosi speaks, in the same document, of the river boundary between Iran and Turan being put in the middle of River Oxus.

With the emergence of the world-economy in the nineteenth century, which in turn was caused by the development of imperialism, the global aspirations of the earlier periods, and the development of the inherent structural phenomena of the new world economic order such as trade and communication systems, the need for defining precise points of contact between states, through their political and economic agents, and establishing customs houses, gave birth to the idea of creating border lines or 'boundaries'. The new borderlines were defined first in North America, Europe, Australia, South Africa and in the neighbourhood of the Persian Gulf (boundaries between Iran and British India – now Pakistan).

THE CONCEPT OF GEOPOLITICAL REGIONS

Of all geopoliticians, Saul B. Cohen has provided perhaps the most comprehensible account of the global hierarchy system. Cohen moves away from Mackinder's Heartland-Rimland theory and sees the world in terms of 'geostrategic' and 'geopolitical' regions, which will form the basis for our discussion here.

In his *Geography and Politics in a World Divided*[14] Cohen bases his argument on exposing the global 'unity myth' that has, according to him, misled previous geopoliticians. He believes that the space is not united strategically, but a fundamentally divided world is a composition of a number of separate areas. He bases his approach to this method on the traditional geographical concept of 'region'. He, thus, identifies a hierarchy of two types of regions depending on their scope, being either global or regional. These two types are 'geostrategic regions' which are functionally defined and express the interrelations of a large section of the globe; and geopolitical regions which are subdivisions of each 'geostrategic region', and tend to be relatively homogenous in terms of one or more criteria of culture, economics and politics.

The geostrategic regions are two semi-hemispheric political regions; each dominated by one of the great powers. Cohen terms them, 'the Trade-Dependant Maritime World' and 'the Eurasian

Continental World'. This description of the two geostrategic regions is similar to the traditional geographical models. But by subdividing each of the two geostrategic regions into five and two geopolitical regions respectively he takes a step forward in recognising new geographical realities. In addition, Cohen recognises South Asia as a potential geostrategic region.

Between the two geostrategic regions, Cohen defines two distinct geopolitical regions which are referred to as the 'shatterbelts' – the Middle East and South-East Asia. These two geopolitical regions, according to him, are politically fragmented with both geostrategic regions having 'footholds' there.

In his 1982 revision of this thesis, Cohen designated Africa, south of the Sahara, as a third shatterbelt region and put more emphasis on the emergence of 'second order' powers in the world hierarchy system. In this revised model, Japan, China and Europe emerge as new world powers, joining the USA and the USSR. Other emerging regional powers are categorised as second order powers which dominate their region, such as Iran, India, Brazil, Nigeria and 24 others which have the potential for spreading influence beyond their boundaries.

The overall picture of the geopolitical world that he provides is a multiple power-node world with many overlapping areas of influence which make it much more dynamic than the old model of a bi-polarised world. Though the recent changes in Eastern Europe have resulted in the break up of the Warsaw Pact and the disintegration of the Soviet Union, the dynamic model of spatial structure that Cohen has provided has not been affected dramatically.

The fact remains that with the end of the Cold War, as a result of the break up of the Warsaw Pact and the Soviet Union, Russia alone has the potential for global aspirations. Though these changes have had a noticeable impact on the international hierarchy system, the process of evolution of a global spatial structure has not come to an end, so we cannot confidently speak of a 'new world order'. Rather, the changes are still at work for the creation of new and newer world orders. The old world of Cold War has ended, while economic competition between US, Japan and Europe has intensified in an unprecedented fashion which could lead to an economic cold war between the giants. While the new states of the former Soviet bloc may want to create an economic grouping of their own, China and South Asia have the potential to enter this competition.

None of these changes can undermine the basic principles that Cohen has identified in studying global hierarchical systems. In fact, he speaks of 'multiple great power nodes replacing the bi-nodal US–USSR competition'.

THE REGIONAL CONTEXT: A CONCEPTUAL APPROACH: IS THE MIDDLE EAST A REGION?

Notwithstanding the fact that Cohen's is an American view of the world, his world political hierarchy system provides a useful model on which more up to date studies of the spatial structure can be conducted. In his original model, Cohen identifies Iran, Turkey, Israel and Egypt as the 'second order' powers in the Middle East. At the same time, the fact is that the Middle East is a highly divided area of almost no strategic, political, economic or cultural homogeneity. Of the four second-order powers, Turkey, Egypt and Israel are Mediterranean countries with different areas of interest and influence. Turkey's main geopolitical objective is in Cyprus and her relations with Greece; however, her other interests include incorporation into the European Union. Egypt's overriding interests and influences are in North Africa and in her relations with the upper Nile countries, and in the oil fields of Libya, while Israel's main concern is with her immediate neighbours, especially Jordan, Syria, Lebanon and the Palestinians.

The remaining power, Iran, has no similarity of any kind in its views and concerns with the other three. Iran's traditional regions of paramount interest extends southwards to include the Persian Gulf, eastwards to include Pakistan and Afghanistan, and more recently, northwards to include the Muslim republics of former USSR.

None of these areas overlap with the areas of influence of Turkey, Egypt or Israel. In fact, Iran's main region of interest, the Persian Gulf, is a geopolitical region in its own right. This region share very little with the rest of what is generally known as the 'Middle East'.

The terms 'Middle East', 'Near East' and 'Near and Middle East' have been used in recent decades with great variation in the territories included. They have extended from North Africa to the Indian borders and from southern Russian boundaries to the Red Sea. This vast area lacks any obvious homogeneity, be it political, cultural, economical or any other criterion that would define a spatial structure worthy of the term 'region', and it therefore cannot be considered as a 'geopolitical region'. What is known as the 'Middle East' is, in fact, an amalgamation of several different environments such as 'the Persian Gulf,' 'the Levant' and 'the Maghrib', each of which is a region by merit of the homogeneity of objects that constitute an environment.

Faced with this great variation of characteristics, Cohen considers the 'Middle East' to be shatterbelt where great variations lead to great diversities in its character as a geopolitical region. The question is whether it is necessary to consider this vast area of great diversities as one geopolitical region. Cohen points out that neither geostrategic nor geopolitical regions are fixed or static. As second order powers emerge, they begin to fashion geopolitical regions in their own images. While often the regional boundaries are the same as those shaped by the impact of great powers, sometimes they are shaped by the action of second level nations. Moreover, two competing second order powers, located within the same geopolitical region, may shape the boundaries differently. The principle of regional boundaries, then, is not of a frame drawn first, within which objects of the system are fitted. Instead, the boundary is drawn last, after the relationship between the agent and objects is established. The Middle East as a geopolitical region, extending from North Africa to Afghanistan and Pakistan is, therefore, not applicable, and the term 'Middle East' is used conveniently in reference to the political environment that is shaped mainly by Arab–Israeli relations.

THE GEOPOLITICAL REGION OF THE PERSIAN GULF

Of the regions identifiable within the limits of the so-called Middle East, the Persian Gulf presents a unique model for a geopolitical region. While the southern half of the Persian Gulf could conveniently be considered as a sub-region of the wider 'Arab World', the geopolitical region of the Persian Gulf represents a homogeneous environment in its own right. This region includes nations varying in some cultural aspects, but with similarities of political, strategic and economic preoccupations. It includes Iran, Iraq, Saudi Arabia, Oman, Kuwait, the United Arab Emirates, Qatar and Bahrain.

With the migration of Arab tribes to the coasts of the Persian Gulf in the two centuries immediately preceding the advent of Islam, a great mixture of Arab–Iranian populations in the coastal areas of this sea began. As the new faith, Islam, overwhelmed variations in religions, the process of the emergence of a community particular to the Persian Gulf, north and south, began. Although Arabs and Iranians are of differing ethnic backgrounds and, notwithstanding the fact that the Iranians succeeded within two to three centuries of the Islamic era in reviving their national language, and their national identity and independence, the two continued their intermingled cultural activities in the cradle of Islam and, in that respect the two have become almost inseparable in the region of the Persian Gulf.

The increased trade exchange between the two shores created a situation in which the process of cultural conglomeration and language mixture strengthened the distinct community of the Persian Gulf, while continued migration from both Iran and the Arabian Peninsula to the region and their mixture has made it quite difficult even now to say who in the Persian Gulf is of true Iranian stock and who is of true Arab stock.

Geographical location, on the other hand, put the Persian Gulf at the heart of the old world as the great routes of the old world had to pass through this region, and this factor has given the region its importance since earliest times. An added factor which strengthened this region's character as a separate geopolitical region has been its strategic importance, to rival outside powers, since the end of the fifteenth century. The Portuguese, the Dutch, the French, the British and the Russians each found their domination of this region crucial to their colonial policies in the East. With the defeat of the French in the Napoleonic wars, the British, the Russians, the Ottomans, the Iranians and the Wahhabis became the main contestants in the region. The political environment created by each power, especially by the British, which lasted throughout most of the nineteenth and twentieth centuries, together with the economic life flourishing around pearl fishing and trade, which were replaced in the first half of the twentieth century by the oil economy, have all become objects of a distinct environment which can confidently be referred to as the 'geopolitical region of the Persian Gulf'.[15]

This distinct region with its common environment provides the best opportunity for the littoral nations to work together towards the creation of an economic grouping which is necessary for the economic survival of the regional countries in the emerging economically-oriented multi-polar world of geopolitics. Similarities of economic concern and related strategic issues, together with the global significance of the region with its enormous capacity for oil and gas production and export, with vast trade links to all economic groupings of the world, provide a unique opportunity for the creation of such an economic grouping which should not to be missed.

While involvement in the affairs of this region of extra-regional powers will inevitably add unnecessary complications to the political life of the region, inclusion of a regional nation like Iraq would inevitably make her more responsible towards the preservation of peace and the maintenance of the status quo in the region. Here it is worth examining the question of whether Iraq would behave so irresponsibly towards her two neighbours, Iran and Kuwait, should it be a member of a collective regional arrangement for security and cooperation.

Iraq's invasion and occupation of Kuwait, from this particular point of view, seems to be the fulfilment of Iran's prophesy of the early 1970s that the creation of an incomplete regional arrangement would be considered as a threat to the regional country or countries left out and would lead to insecurity. This warning came in the wake of the expression by Saudi Arabia of the desire for the formation of a cooperation arrangement in the Persian Gulf without the participation of Iran and Iraq,[16] a desire which was fulfilled in 1981 in the form of the Gulf Cooperation Council.

EVOLUTION OF THE CONCEPT OF 'BOUNDARY' IN THE PERSIAN GULF

The origin of 'boundary' in the Gulf can be traced to the pre-Islamic border pillars, mentioned in the *Shahnameh* of Ferdosi between Iran and Turan (present day Turkmanistan) and to the Sassanid tradition of frontier-keeping states.

The tradition of frontier-keeping states, however, was maintained by the Abbasid Caliphate of Baghdad (749–1258 AD). Several such states were created, the longest surviving of which was the Amirdom of Khozeimeh in Qohestan (Kuhestan), now known as Qaenat, Tabas and Birjand in the eastern borderlands of Iran.[17]

The Safavids (1501–1722) also revived the tradition of frontier-keeping states, but without endeavouring to modernise the idea by creating a clearer and more up-to-date system which would enhance the traditional relationships between the centre of the state and the peripheral autonomies, principalities and dependencies. This shortcoming began to show its impact at the time when the authority of the central government of Iran over the peripheries declined under the Qajars towards middle of the nineteenth century. This was the time when the British introduced European concepts of territoriality and boundary to the region of the Gulf. Intensification of the so-called 'great game' and clashes of Anglo–Russian territorial interests necessitated the creation of precise boundaries around Iran and in the Gulf.

Delimitation of the earliest examples of modern boundaries in the vicinity of the Gulf began in the 1870s (Baluchistan boundaries) when not only were Iran and others in the region totally unfamiliar with the legal implications and geographical sophistications of delimiting modern boundaries, but Iran's traditionally ill-defined relations between centre and periphery and her general weakness resulted in loss of territories in all directions. Out of these territories sprang more than ten independent countries now neighbouring Iran. Whenever claimed locally or by Britain and Russia that these peripheral dependencies were independent of Iran, Tehran failed legally and physically to prove the opposite.

By the end of the 1970s the most complicated and sensitive boundary issues in the region were settled which resulted in a significant decline in territorial and boundary disputes in the region. The collapse of the Soviet Union, which hastened changes in the world order, gave rise to the interest in defining or redefining territorial and boundary arrangements, or the lack of them, in the region. This substantial shift in the treatment of the political geography of the region was highlighted by Iraq's occupation of Kuwait in 1990; the US-led coalition's unprecedented military undertaking against Iraq in 1991; and the UN boundary delimitation and demarcation between Iraq and Kuwait in 1993–4. These developments once again revived interest in territorial and boundary contentions in the region: the United Arab Emirates demanded ownership of the islands of Tunbs and Abu Musa from Iran in 1992; Saudi Arabia clashed militarily with Qatar in the same year over border issues; Qatar and Bahrain referred their territorial and border disputes to the International Court of Justice and await adjudication; separatists in the Yemen, assisted by regional interests, endeavoured to recreate the former South Yemen in 1994; and a number of other territorial and border disputes in the region await full and final settlement.

A UNIQUE GEOPOLITICAL POSSIBILITY

The emerging geopolitical possibilities in the region seem to suggest that the increasing attention paid by the bigger powers to the Persian Gulf and the Caspian Sea as the two main sources of energy for the early decades of the twenty-first century, with Iran as the only country situated between them, will provide Iran with the advantage of turning this unique geographical location into an equally unique political power by allocating some of its many ports on the Persian

Gulf to the exclusive use of each of the land-locked states of the Caucasus, Caspian and Central Asia for a direct access to the open seas. By concluding a series of special treaties with the said states Iran can ensure that her full sovereignty rights remain intact. The UN convention of 1982 has paved the way for such arrangements. Articles 124 to 132 of the said convention provide for the 'Freedom of Transit' and 'Right of Access' to the open seas to be granted to the land-locked states. The same provisions provide, especially in paragraph three of article 25, that this 'right of access' will under no circumstance undermine the sovereignty of the state granting it. The UN Convention of 1982 has also noted the Islamic Republic of Iran's point of view that the 'right of assess' for the land-locked states is not an absolute right and that it is but an 'assistance' to the said states.

By granting each one of the land-locked states of the Caucasus, Caspian and Central Asia the exclusive right of use of one of its many ports on the Persian Gulf for access, not only will Iran connect the Caspian Sea to the Persian Gulf in a very effective way, and increase the number of the non-Arab states of the Persian Gulf from one to as many as ten or more, but she will also increase her geopolitical and geostrategic role as the most effective regional player with a global significance.

The Persian Gulf: security and territoriality

Chapter 1

The Persian Gulf

INTRODUCTION

With a surface area of about 29,500 square miles, the Persian Gulf possesses an estimated oil reserve of 565 billion barrels which counts for more than 63 per cent of the world's total known oil reserves estimated at 896.5 billion barrels.

This region's oil production, at present, does not exceed 21.9 per cent of the world total. It must not, however, be forgotten that this region's oil production has been declining since 1979 following the Iranian revolution and the outbreak of the Iran–Iraq war.

Oil consumption in the world, during the same period, had been declining. This decline reached its lowest in 1982. The trend began to recover from this decline and increases in consumption started again.

The energy-consuming world's oil import from the Persian Gulf was 10.3 million barrels per day in 1987. The region produced 13.1 million barrels per day in the same year which means, about 3 million barrels per day of oil produced in the region was consumed domestically, or exported in the form of refined products.

At present, though the world depends on the Persian Gulf for only about 41 per cent of its oil consumption, which is the lowest rate of dependency on this region's oil production during the past two decades, this situation is changing and as US Department of Energy has announced recently, the world will soon depend on oil importation from the Persian Gulf for 65 per cent of its oil needs.

Apart from oil, the Persian Gulf, with about 30.0 per cent of world's proven natural gas, is the second largest region of gas deposits in the world, only surpassed by the Russian Federation with a total deposit of 39.8 per cent of the world total gas reserves.

Other minerals discovered in Iran alone are: lead, zinc, salt, sulphur, manganese, nickel, gold, uranium, antimony, magnesite, barite, tin, tungsten, limestone, cobalt, fluorspar, borax, emerald, marble, alabaster, bauxite, topaz and sapphire.

> After five years of searching in the Saghand region of Yazd, experts have discovered uranium deposits of more than 3000 tons, and molybdenum of 4000 tons . . . . It was announced that so far, between 50 and 100 million dollars had been invested in the discovery of these mines and investment of a further 300 million dollars during the next year will make these mines ready for exploitation and exportation of products with a value estimated at 150 billion dollars . . .[1]

The Persian Gulf, with its enormous natural and mineral resources, is no longer significant only for playing the linking role of a trade highway between the east and west of the world. It is, at present, at one major extreme in world economic exchange. A situation as significant as this, and a strategic location as sensitive as the Persian Gulf has proved to be for future world's economic equilibrium, deserves every effort for better acquaintance from every point of view.

This region's main interaction is with the major energy-consuming industrial regions of the world, and its paramount concern is security of oil trade which is the lifeline of the region. Extra-regional powers who neither fit into the common cultural and social patterns of the region, nor are significant trade partners of the countries of the region, cannot be considered as partners to the objects of the environment of this region.

SECURITY SYSTEMS IN THE PERSIAN GULF

Security in the Persian Gulf has been and still is the overriding concern of both regional producers of oil and major consumers around the world. The idea of a regional pact for security is not new. In fact, it was Iran that, in the wake of the withdrawal of Pax-Britannica from the region, called for a regional arrangement for security in the Gulf. Iran's basic concern for this arrangement was that any security system that would exclude any littoral country not only is incomplete, but will be no more than a source of provocation against the country or countries left out. In fact, Iran issued a warning in the early 1970s that she would not tolerate any such incomplete arrangement in the region. Even when the American supported Gulf Cooperation Council (GCC) was formed in 1981, no claim of responsibility for the maintenance of security in the Persian Gulf was made and the GCC limited its aspiration to cooperation among the member states.

SECURITY CONCERNS

With the Kuwait crisis of 1990–91, the idea of a security system in the Persian Gulf was revived in Washington. While suggesting the idea, US leaders did not identify the sources of insecurity in the region. Yet, by encouraging Egypt and Syria to participate in a security system with the GCC countries, a system that would exclude Iran and Iraq, the sources of insecurity were identified by implication. The prospect of either Iran or Iraq being the cause of any insecurity in the Persian Gulf is, at present, unrealistic. Iraq can renew its outdated territorial ambitions against her neighbours only if she returns to her pre-crisis military power, a highly unlikely prospect in the foreseeable future.

Iran has not pursued any territorial claims since the settlement of the question of Bahrain and the three islands at the mouth of the Persian Gulf in 1970 and 1971 respectively. Iran's revolutionary call for returning to Islamic values has never had territorial or military implications against any country. The US initiative for a Persian Gulf security system with the participation of Egypt, Syria and the GCC countries is not, therefore, a necessity borne out of the strategic needs of the region. It has more to do with the Arab–Israeli relations. Washington made no secret of this by linking the two in one package for 'peace and security in the Middle East'. In other words, by suggesting that Syria and Egypt should maintain military forces in the Persian Gulf at the expense of the Arab governments of the region and hinting that Egypt and Syria could have a share in the oil wealth of the region, Washington wanted to entice Egypt and Syria into cooperation for seeking some kind of settlement between Israel and the Arabs. Otherwise, even Washington does not believe that Egypt, Syria and the GCC would be able to avert another threat to Kuwait's existence from a would-be strong Iraq. This is why the US signed separate defence treaties with Kuwait (July 1991) and other Arab states of the Gulf. Both Egypt and Syria are extra-regional powers with no real political and economic interests in the Persian Gulf. Neither Egypt nor Syria is a major consumer of oil and gas from the Persian Gulf. The overriding political concern in the region is security for the safe export of oil and gas, the lack of which can hardly pose any direct threat to the security of Egypt and Syria. Being aware of these facts, Egypt bases her argument on inter-Arab ties, as an Egyptian leader asserted:

> ... The overall relations among the region's countries are ... moving towards normalcy and (are) being governed by mutual trust, cooperation and collective interests, not any other principles ....
>
> Gulf security is primarily an Arab issue ... Egypt is the region's largest and most influential country. Pan-Arab security is an integral whole. What affects Gulf security necessarily affects the security of all Arab countries, notably Egypt. How then, can one imagine that security arrangements or structure can be established in the region without Egypt playing a role [and] indeed a prominent one?[2]

The Iranians, on the other hand, believe that an argument of this nature clearly lacks geographical compatibility. Firstly, it is not clear to which 'region' the Egyptian spokesman refers. The 'Middle East' as has already been discussed, is not a geopolitical region. More than anything else, the 'Middle East' is a term used conveniently by Americans on the basis of a presupposition that the place from where one speaks (in this case – the US) is in the west of the globe, and other parts of the globe are 'near', 'middle', or 'far' east in the order of their distances from that place. The Europeans frequently refer to the same area as the 'Near East'. That is to say, there is no unanimity even among the occidentals on the usage of this term of convenience. While there is no harm in the common usage of the term 'Middle East', analysts will note that the area concerned is, in fact, a collection of several geopolitical regions such as the region of the Persian Gulf. In this region, Egypt is not the largest and the most influential country but it is rather an outsider.

Secondly, the Egyptian official does not specify the manner in which what affects Persian Gulf security necessarily affects the security of the Maghrib and Egypt. Certainly, the Persian Gulf is not an exclusively Arab region. Iran's maritime boundaries include most of the Gulf. The Iranian coasts include the entire northern, northwestern and northeastern shores of the region, beginning from the opening of Fao and ending in the Indian Ocean. Iran is in control of the most sensitive strategic points in the Persian Gulf and the access routes to and from it. Iran is also the largest and most influential country of the region with the largest population and greatest economic, strategic and political potential. Persian is the most widely spoken language in the region and Shiism is the largest sect of Islam in the Persian Gulf. In addition to all this, Iran's economic life depends on the Persian Gulf. While Saudi Arabia and Iraq, the other two major countries of the region, can export part of their oil through pipelines to the coasts other than those of the Persian Gulf and can receive parts of their imports from coasts other than those of the Persian Gulf, Iran depends on the waterways of this sea for the bulk of its oil exports, the overwhelming part of its non-oil exports and also for the main bulk of its imports. When considering these undisputed factors, little doubt remains that security in the Persian Gulf is primarily an Iranian concern.

Thirdly, there is very little evidence supporting the claim that Pan-Arab security is an integral whole. Considering that Iraq, undeniably an Arab state, has invaded Kuwait, another Arab state; that Saudi Arabia with the help of Western armies, has invaded Iraq; that the Syrians invaded Lebanon; Libya's constant clashes with her neighbours; considering that Yemen (former South Yemen) invaded Omani territories; that history bears testimony to the fact that Arabs have always been the main source of insecurity for the Arabs, little credibility is left for the myth of Pan-Arabism and the claim that it is an 'integral whole'. Even if one is to consider the more realistic terminology 'the Arab World', one can hardly be oblivious to the fact that this term represents no geographical, economic or political structure on which the concept of 'an integral whole' could be argued. In other words, the 'Arab world' is not a geographical, economic or political region; it is, but a cultural environment with great geographical, economic and political diversity. It is a cultural arena for political rivalries which have been the main source of insecurity in the Arab Middle East in the post World War II period.

Egypt has, in a period of time, been able to display its ability in leading the Arab world. This was due to the coincidence of the Arab–Isreali conflict in the 1960s and a revolutionary leadership which appeared in the person of Colonel Nasser who was able to capture the idealistic imagination in the Arab world with his slogan of 'Arab unity'. The slogan lost its appeal soon after Nasser's defeat in the 1967 Arab–Isreali war, and with signing the Camp David accord, Egypt became totally isolated in the Arab world for over a decade. In other words, the coincidence of a particular political development and a particular political philosophy cannot be considered as a factor of permanence on the basis of which Egypt could claim the permanent leadership of the Arab world, and could therefore, argue for geographical or political legitimacy for presence in the Arab parts of the Persian Gulf.

What encouraged the United States to press for Egyptian and Syrian military involvement in the Persian Gulf were solely political considerations motivated by the want of bringing about a speedy settlement to the Arab–Isreali disputes in a way and at a time that would be most beneficial to Israel. To do so, the United States needs to pave the way for such a settlement, through promises of an arrangement which could give Arab states such as Syria and Egypt, both extra-regional states, access to the oil wealth of the Persian Gulf, as was stated in the Damascus Declaration of 6 March, 1991.

Notwithstanding Egypt's claims that security in the Persian Gulf is a Pan-Arab issue, and in spite of efforts to justify military involvement in this region, little progress has been made in realising the so-called 'Arab defence for the Gulf'. The main obstacles are, in fact, disunity among the Arab states. Not only do Saudi Arabia, Kuwait and the Emirates not have the same financial strength that they had in the 1970s and early 1980s, and thus cannot afford continued and limitless payments for the maintenance of foreign military forces in the region, but there are more important factors that prevent a lasting arrangement of the kind proposed. The most important of these factors are:

1 The Arab world has, since World War II, been suffering from rivalries between Egypt, Iraq, Saudi Arabia and Syria for the leadership of all Arabs. These rivalries intensified with Colonel Nasser's introduction of Pan-Arab ideas. Arab unity, thus, became a myth dominating the political environment and leading to a situation in which extremism of various kinds flourished and caused further political fragmentation in the Arab world. Thus, Arab unity, or Pan-Arabism for that matter, has failed, in about half a century, to take any shape or form other than a myth. Yet, the myth continues to nurture rivalry for the Arab leadership, the main source of insecurity in the Arab world.

   Saudi Arabia is one of the principal actors in this political rivalry for leadership in the Arab world. Saudi Arabia considers the Arabian Peninsula as its main geopolitical region. Military domination of this region by rival powers (ie Egypt and Syria) can hardly be acceptable to Saudi Arabia.

2 Saudi Arabia considers the small emirates of the Persian Gulf as its immediate region of influence, where regimes similar to that of

Saudi Arabia are viewed in Riyadh as vulnerable and in need of intense protection. Saudi Arabia sees in the downfall of these regimes a strong element of danger to its own survival. This view has led the Saudis to adopt a jealously protectionist policy towards these emirates, considering them as its sensitive areas. The surprisingly heavy-handed role that Saudi Arabia played in the Kuwait crisis of 1990–91, which involved great risk by inviting Western forces to be stationed on its soil during and after the crisis, bears testimony to the intense Saudi Arabian sensitivity towards the survival of the regimes in the small emirates. Moreover, the very myth of Pan-Arabism makes these sensitive areas of Saudi Arabia more susceptible to the influences of rival Arab governments than to the influence of non-Arab powers. Thus, military domination of the area by Arab powers such as Egypt and Syria can undermine Saudi Arabia's influence in its areas of sensitivity in a way that an Iranian presence, for instance, cannot match.

3 The fact that more than half of the Persian Gulf belongs to Iran, and that the most sensitive, strategic parts of the region are under Iranian control, together with the fact that Iran is the largest country of the region in terms of population and resources, makes Iran potentially the undisputed dominant power in the region. Furthermore, considering the fact that security in the Persian Gulf is necessary for the safe flow of oil in the region and the fact that Iran's dependence on the secure export and import of oil and other commodities via the Persian Gulf is vital, excluding Iran from a security system in the region will not amount to anything but an arrangement that will be the source of instability in the Persian Gulf. An arrangement that does not include Iran as the principal partner can only be for less than half of the Persian Gulf and, as a threat to Iran's lifeline, would be a source of insecurity in the region. Moreover, considering the vital dependence of Saudi Arabia, Oman, Kuwait and the Emirates on peace and stability in the region, these states cannot afford a needless gamble of tension with Iran which could involve their source of economic life.

Given the geographical, economic and strategic factors common to all countries of the Persian Gulf, the ideal arrangement for security in the region would be a system that includes all littoral states and excludes all extra-regional countries. Geographical and geostrategic factors in the region support such an arrangement to which any extra-regional military presence in the region is a very poor substitute, indeed, often causing instability in the region. The position of Iraq, of course, has to be determined after that country's compliance with all requirements laid down in the UN Security Council's resolutions concerning its two wars with Iran and Kuwait have been satisfactorily completed. An additional component of this arrangement will have to be the recognition of the oil-consuming world's natural interest in the region which cannot be but guarantee continued and safe supplies of oil and gas from the region, and the dialogue for which has to be channelled through the international energy markets.

Peaceful settlement of territorial and boundary disputes, on the other hand, is essential for preparing for the creation of economic grouping in the region, whereas unwarranted arguments aimed at reviving settled territorial and boundary disputes will gravely harm the prospect of the hugely important regional cooperation for collective economic rivalries in the emerging world.

ARAB–IRANIAN TERRITORIAL DIFFERENCES

There are a number of territorial disputes in the region of the Persian Gulf which, in general terms, can be classified into two categories: the inter-Arab territorial disputes; and the Arab–Iranian territorial differences. Of the first category the following instances are noteworthy. Territorial disputes between Iraq and Kuwait which are now supposed to be resolved; Kuwait and Saudi Arabia over Qaruh and Umm al-Maradim islands; Saudi Arabia and Qatar over their border areas; Qatar and Bahrain over the Hawar archipelago; Saudi Arabia and the United Arab Emirates (Abu Dhabi) over Buraimi and Liwa regions; and the United Arab Emirates' unsettled territorial problems with Oman over areas in the Diba region.

Although Bahrain, Kuwait, Oman, Qatar, Saudi Arabia and the United Arab Emirates have created the Gulf Cooperation Council (GCC) among themselves, real and effective cooperation among them is sometimes prevented by these territorial disputes. The best example of this was highlighted in recent years by the Qatar–Saudi Arabian border clashes of 1992, and disputes between Bahrain and Qatar which are to be considered at the International Court of Justice in 1998.

Of the second category, there are two major areas of territorial disputes between Iran and Arab states of the region: the Iran–Iraq border disputes and the issue of the United Arab Emirates' claims to Abu Musa and Tunb islands.

The Iran–Iraq Territorial Disputes

The Iran–Iraq territorial and border disputes began several centuries ago and ended in the eight-year war of the 1980s. These disputes have been used extensively for political purposes by both parties. While Iran used the issue of Iraqi Kurdish movements (a peripheral issue in the two countries' disputes) in the 1970s to establish her supremacy in the region, Iraq had been using the actual border disputes in the 1960s, 1970s and 1980s to forge a leadership role in the Arab world. It was in this context that Iraq planned and financed extensive propaganda warfare in the Arab world against Iran in the last 30 years or so. Seeing herself as one of the most eligible partners in the rivalry for Arab leadership in the said period (when hostility with Israel was the most effective determining factor in reaching the position of leadership in the Arab world) Iraqi leaders found their ambitions frustrated by countries situated on the front-line with Israel, such as Egypt. To turn this geographical deficiency into a geographical advantage exclusive to Iraq, in the Arab world, Iraqi leaders concluded that they needed to create a new common enemy for the Arabs with whom Iraq would be the only frontline Arab state. Not only was Iran the natural choice, but she was the only choice: a country with a long history of rivalries with the Arabs; a country suspected at times by some Arabs of political or economic cooperation with Israel; and a country with which Iraq's territorial and boundary disputes provided the best instrument or excuse for conflict. These disputes were presented to the Arabs as the symbol of Iran's ill-intentions towards Arab lands. Extensive planning of a propaganda campaign against Iran, which has absorbed huge sums of money in the past three decades, included attempts to change historic names of geographical features whereas Iran refused to seriously consider similar undertakings. The river separating Iran from Iraq is still referred to in Iran as Shatt al-Arab.

With the success of the Islamic revolution in Iran in February 1979, relations deteriorated initially with Arab neighbours. This was mainly because of the perception in the region of an acute threat to the security of the region arising from a direct undertaking either by the revolutionary government of Iran in the form of exporting Islamic revolution to the neighbouring countries, or as a result of an Islamic uprising in the countries of the region inspired by the Iranian revolutionaries.[3] These developments together with encouragements from the West enticed Iraq to unilaterally abrogate Algiers border agreements of 1975 with Iran, and to champion the slogan of 'defending the Gulf Arabs against Iran's revolutionary threats'.

Hoping for a quick victory over the Iranian army, largely dislodged by the revolution, Iraq waged a war of attrition against Iran which lasted from 1980 to 1988. Not only did Iraq fail to achieve its declared war aims, but Iraqi president Saddam Hussein wrote on 14 August 1990 to president Hashemi-Rafsanjani of the Islamic Republic of Iran confirming that Iraq was prepared to negotiate border and territorial settlements with Iran on the basis of the Algiers accord of 1975. Most of the land held by the Iraqis in Kurdistan and Khuzistan was also released to the Iranians as a result of the withdrawal of all Iraqi troops to the boundary pre-dating September 1980.

Quite apart from the fact that territorial and boundary differences with Iran have always been used by Baghdad as instruments of political manoeuvring for Arab leadership, the geographic and historical implications of these differences have been studied extensively and there is no need for them to be repeated here.

The Islands of Abu Musa and Tunb

Although attempts have been made in the past two years to politicise and internationalise the question of UAE claims to the islands of Tunb and Abu Musa, probably hoping to use the issue as an instrument of exerting pressure on the Islamic Republic of Iran, the nature of the claims could still be viewed as genuine, motivated by misunderstanding on the part of both sides of the 1992 incidents. This issue will be studied in detail in section IV of this book.

Chapter 2

The Strait of Hormuz

THE STRAIT OF HORMUZ AND ARAB–IRANIAN RELATIONS

The Strait of Hormuz, a narrow and curved channel, connecting the Persian Gulf to the Indian Ocean, is approximately 100 nautical miles long,[1] disrupting continuation of Iran's southern mountain range into the Musandam Peninsula. Thus, the Strait of Hormuz is a geological depression bounded by Iran to the north and the Musandam Peninsula to the south. The narrowest part of this Strait – 21 nautical miles – lies between the Iranian island of Larak and the Omani islet of Greater Quoin, both Iran and Oman claim 12 miles of territorial waters there, which overlap by a stretch of 15 miles. Here the two countries have agreed to define a median line.

Shipping in the Strait of Hormuz took the shortest route between the Little Quoin and the Musandam Peninsula until 1979 when Oman demanded that shipping in the Strait of Hormuz should take the lanes beyond the Quoin islands. This was to lessen the difficulties of ensuring safe passage of ships so close to these islands and the mainland. The new shipping lanes, generally used since 1979, are about one mile wide each and they are separated by a safety zone which is also about one mile wide. The new shipping lanes are also within Oman's territorial waters. This means that Oman takes official responsibility for the safety of shipping through these lanes. Shipping in the Straits of Hormuz is, however, not restricted to these particular channels. Although the Strait's depth decreases towards Iranian shores, there are still enough deep water channels for large tankers to approach within a few miles of the Iranian coast.

27

Figure 2.1 Iran–Oman territorial sea limits in the Strait of Hormuz

For the protection of the Strait of Hormuz against any foreign threats in the wake of the British withdrawal in early 1970s, Iran found herself better placed than any other country of the region. From the Iranian point of view, this was largely because, apart from possessing the strongest military of the region, the Strait could be better protected from strategically-situated ports alongside the waterway and the Iranian islands located favourably in the Strait of Hormuz and across the approach to it. Iran possesses a number of strategic islands at the entrance of the Persian Gulf, of which six islands of the so-called 'curved line' are of the greatest strategic significance. These are the islands of Hormuz, Larak, Qeshm, Hengam, Greater Tunb and Abu-Musa. As a top ranking officer of the Iranian Supreme Commander's staff under the Shah told this writer in 1978, Iran's perceived strategy was to utilise these islands' strategic value by maintaining a degree of defensive force there.

An imaginary line (the curved line) drawn alongside these islands, which are situated within relatively short distances of one another, makes it easy to appreciate how effectively the shipping lanes of the Strait of Hormuz would be covered by an Iranian defence power stationed on these islands, he said. Perhaps a relatively detailed study of the geographical situation of these islands would help better appreciation of this strategy.

The six islands are:

1 Island of Hormuz

Hormuz, 3 square miles, is situated 12 miles south of Bandar Abbas.[2] This island – referred to as the key to the Persian Gulf for centuries – has been regarded strategically so significant that the Strait of Hormuz was named after it. A glance at the historical sources suggests that Hormuz Island's strategic and commercial situation was highly valued by the local powers as well as those outside the region, over many centuries.

The Achaemenians used this island as a naval base,[3] it has also been used as a commercial centre for Indian, Chinese and other oriental goods and merchandise,[4] and by the Portuguese as a stronghold at the junction of the Persian Gulf and the Indian Ocean.[5]

In modern times, that is to say in the era of giant oil tankers which have to pass through the Strait of Hormuz, the island of Hormuz is still significant for its strategic sensitivity, albeit that it is situated at a relatively far distance from the deep water channels.

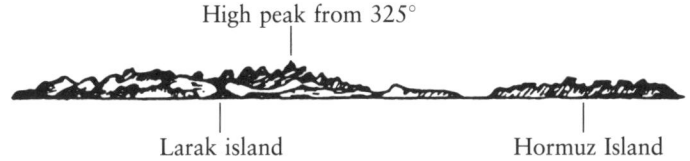

High peak from 325°

Larak island   Hormuz Island

Figure 2.2 Hormuz Island in contrast with Larak: profile from southwest (distance 8 miles)

Portuguese fort

old minaret

Figure 2.3 Hormuz Island profile from west (distance 9 miles)

2 Island of Larak

This island is situated at 25 miles south of Bandar Abbas, 12.5 miles southwest of the island of Hormuz and 7.5 miles east of Qeshm Island.[6]

Like Qeshm and Hengam, Larak is located very close to the deep water channels of the Strait of Hormuz normally used by supertankers. The island's surface is covered by hills with gentle slopes into open plains in the east of the island towards the Gulf of Oman.[7]

the cone shaped hill

Qeshm

Larak

Figure 2.4 Larak Island in contrast with Qeshm Island, profile from 302°
(distance 9 miles)

3 Qeshm Island

Qeshm, the largest island in the Persian Gulf, is situated 12.5 miles south of Bandar Abbas, 25 miles east of Bandar Lengeh and 19 miles northeast of the Greater Tunb.[8] The island is 87 miles long, and 25 miles wide at its widest points, while at its narrowest it is only 5 miles wide. Thus, the island's shape is similar to an arrowhead and this is why Qeshm is referred to as Kish Island in many old sources (*kish* is a Persian term for arrowhead),[9] whereas now Kish is the name of another island situated nearby.

Qeshm is a sand-desert island with some hills in the central part. The highest of these hills is Kuh-e Bukhu (1330 feet above sea level). The island's total population is estimated at 36,000[10] who live in its 68 villages, the largest of which is Basa'idu. Recent archaeological discoveries suggest that Qeshm's strategic values were known to the ancient empires, especially to the Achaemenians. Since then, Qeshm has been used by successive powers for strategic purposes.[11]

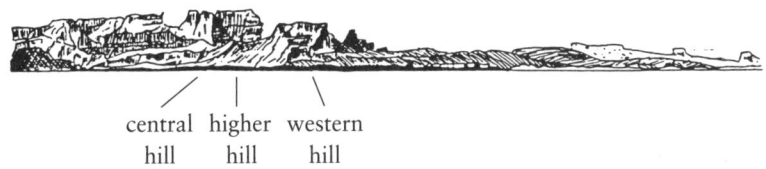

central higher western
hill   hill   hill

Figure 2.5 Qeshm Island: the three hills at the southwest of the island (westward view)

4 Hengam Island

Hengam, a small island – 2 miles south of Qeshm – like Larak, is situated on the edge of the deep water channels of the Strait of Hormuz. It is 37 miles from Larak; 31 miles from the Omani island of Al-Qanam,[12] and 2 miles from the Qeshm Island (see Figure 2.6). Hengam is 6 miles long and between 2 and 4 miles wide.[13]

Travellers have talked about the historical significance of this island.[14] The British established some military installations on this island, but gave them up during Reza Shah's rise into power.[15] Hengam's shores are more suitable for naval installations, and its deep offshore areas can be used as suitable harbours for warships and submarines.[16]

Tappeh Mitra

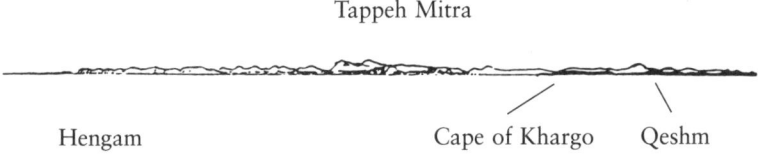

Hengam   Cape of Khargo   Qeshm

Figure 2.6 Hengam Island southwestern profile in contrast with Qeshm Island

31

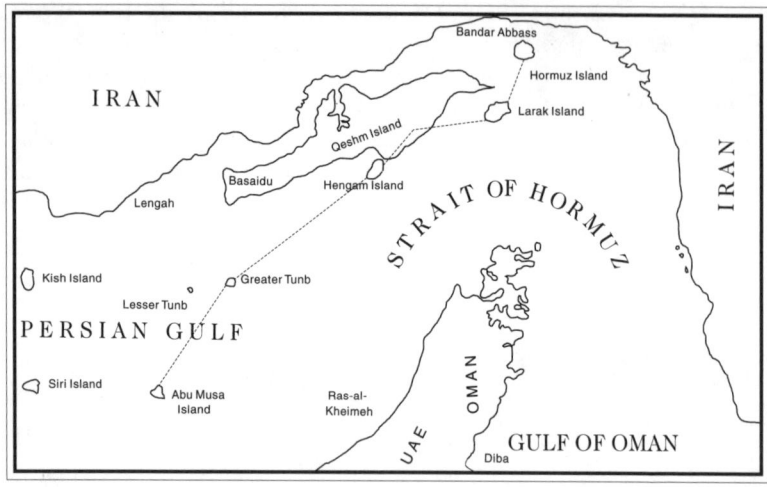

Figure 2.7 The six strategic islands of the curved line in the Straits of Hormuz

5 Greater Tunb will be studied in Chapter VII.
6 Island of Abu Musa will be studied in Chapter VII.

STRAIT OF HORMUZ AND IRAN'S STRATEGIC RELATIONS WITH OMAN

To complete her scheme for effective control over the Strait of Hormuz in the 1970s, Iran regarded it as essential to establish close cooperation with Oman whose the northern territory borders this Strait. Since the narrow, deep-water channel of the Strait of Hormuz passes near to Omani shores, Iran viewed Oman's Musandam Peninsula and its islands as strategically of much significance in controlling these shipping lanes. Tehran announced Iran's readiness to assist littoral states with their security problems if invited to do so by their governments. This concern had impelled Iran to respond quickly to a request made by the government of Oman for assistance. Iran's assistance included ground, air and logistic support against the Dhufar rebels.

The interest appeared as early as Qabus's accession in 1970 when the Shah sent a congratulatory cable to the new Sultan. The establishment of diplomatic relations in August 1971 was followed by several meetings between the two rulers, and by early 1973, Iran had sent a half-dozen helicopters and crews to help in Dhufar. In April, the Iranian Prime Minister Amir Abbas Hoveida, admitted that Iran was responding to the Sultanate's request for aid.[17]

By the end of 1974, the total of Iranian forces in Dhufar had reportedly grown to between 1500 and 3500 troops, but Iran's role was even more pronounced in 1975 when the total reached a level of between 3500 and 5000 troops.[18] Iranian Phantom F5's patrolled the South Yemeni borders from their base at Thamarit, and Iranian destroyers shelled the part of the Dhufar Coast still under rebel control.

Iran's presence in Oman was obliquely criticised by almost all Arab countries, who saw this presence as a living proof of Iran's expansionism. Conservative governments in the Arab world introduced several schemes to reduce Iranian forces and Iranian involvement in Oman. One of these schemes was – as Oman's deputy Foreign Minister at the time, told this author – the unsuccessful Arab League mission in mid-1974. Subsequently, concurrent reports emerged that Egypt and Saudi Arabia sought to replace Iranian troops by Arab forces.

> Pressure on the Sultanate led to the statement by al-Zawawi (Oman's Foreign Minister of the time) on 10 October 1974, that the Iranian troops were being withdrawn from Oman – what he neglected to add was that they were being replaced by other units.[19]

A principal factor which allowed Iran to expand its involvement in Oman was Arab reluctance to become involved in response to Sultan Qabus of Oman's plea for help. The one exception was Oman's fellow monarchy of Jordan. The Jordanian support included the loan of combat troops to Oman in mid-1975 to hold the Thamarit Road, already recaptured from the rebel forces by the Iranians. Additionally Jordanian army personnel were assigned to training duty and to the engineering units in Oman. Some help also came from Saudi Arabia in the form of some financial aid and the use of its training camps by the Sultan's troops.

This assistance and the moral support provided by moderate Arab states was countered by help given by the radical Arab states to the rebels, the Popular Front for the Liberation of Oman (PFLO), and its predecessor groups. Chief among them was the former People's Democratic Republic of Yemen (former South Yemen) which had stood firmly behind the PFLO in matters of ideology and logistics since it gained independence in 1967. Former South Yemen also served as the main bridge between PFLO and the Communist world.[20] At various times, both the former Soviet Union and the People's Republic of China provided moral support and material to PFLO and the rebel soldiers received training in both countries. Iraq also was reportedly supporting PFLO on a considerable scale.

Once Iran became involved heavily, this situation changed largely in favour of the government forces.[21] The Chinese support to PFLO declined following the Sino–Iranian *rapprochement* of early 1973 and although Soviet aid was substantially increased, the gap was never adequately filled.[22] The Irano–Iraqi *rapprochement* of March 1975 was followed by the establishment of diplomatic links between Baghdad and Muscat and, thus, PFLO lost much of its foreign support. This altered situation paved the way for its ultimate defeat in late 1975.

In January 1975, however, Iranian troops successfully captured the port of Rakhyut in Dhufar which had previously been used by PFLO as its headquarters. In February the Iranians started to build a new fortified line, the Damavand Line, running northwards from Rakhyut, some 30 miles west of the old Hornbeam Line[23] which had been successfully built in early 1974. This line limited infiltration from South Yemen. In October 1975, Iranian troops were reported to have captured the hills at Shabut. This strategic point, some 5.5 miles west of Rakhyut, had linked the PFLO's logistic centre at Kharfat and the Sharshiti caves on the coast, an important stronghold of the PFLO. During the months of November and December 1975, some 194 guerrillas gave themselves up to the Sultan's forces.[24] Finally on 11 December 1975, Sultan Qabus announced before thousands of Omanis the end of the Dhufar battle.[25]

It might have been expected, with the apparent success of the anti-guerrilla warfare operation in Dhufar by the end of 1975, that Iran would pull out of Oman. But the Shah proved to be reluctant:

> As soon as Sultan Qabus desires the withdrawal of Iranian troops, we will leave. But the Sultan must himself say he no longer needs Iranian troops.[26]

Iranian troops remained in Dhufar albeit in a much reduced number, until they were pulled out by the provisional government of the Islamic Republic in 1979. Iran's determination to preserve the security of the Strait of Hormuz, which was demonstrated practically and

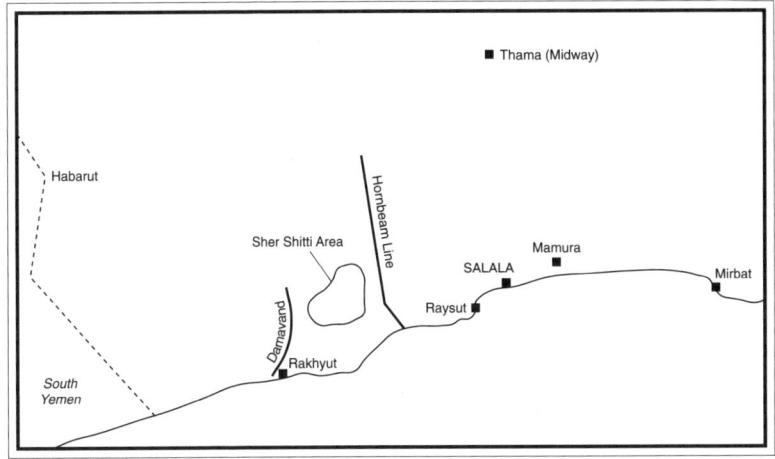

Figure 2.8 Dhufar Province

expensively during the Dhufar battles, led Iran to consider Oman's location at the Strait of Hormuz as of considerable significance. It was reported in 1973 that Iran asked Oman to inspect jointly all ships passing through the Strait of Hormuz.[27] The same reports indicated that the scheme would involve the establishment of a pollution control station on an island in or near the Strait.[28] The island concerned here could possibly be the island of Al-Qanam at the tip of the Musandam Peninsula. PFLO claimed at that time that the Sultan had allowed Iran to build a naval base on this island.[29] The radical Arab states launched a massive propaganda campaign against this suspected arrangement but Omani officials denied the entire matter.

However, in early 1975, an arrangement between Iran and Oman for joint naval operations to keep both coastal lines 'secure and free' was announced by the Omani Minister of Foreign Affairs.[30] During his flight over the Musandam Peninsula and the Strait of Hormuz in December 1977, this author spotted the site of a jetty partly constructed on the eastern side of Al-Qanam Island.

Questioned, about whether the construction of this jetty, apparently for naval purposes had anything to do with Iran's alleged desire of having a naval base at Al-Qanam, the accompanying Omani Officer told this author that it was for military purposes and friendly countries would be able to use it. This comment was confirmed by the British general then commanding Omani naval forces during this author's meeting with him in Muscat on 19 December 1977. The Al-Qanam base would include advanced radar system which covered the entire Strait of Hormuz, he added. Some Iranian and Omani officials, who preferred their names, ranks and positions to remain unmentioned, confirmed that the project was part of a joint naval operation by the Iranian and Omani navies.[31] Considering the fact that Oman did not at the time possess a naval force capable of participating significantly in the task of controlling the Strait of Hormuz, Iran thus achieved its goal of bringing the Strait of Hormuz under its complete control.

Following the 1979 Islamic revolution, Iran's involvement in the task of controlling the Strait of Hormuz was initially dropped. As the war with Iraq broke out and the strategic sensitivity of this Strait became better known to the new regime, control of the Strait of Hormuz gained new urgency. Armed units were again deployed at the strategic ports and islands alongside the gateway to and from the Persian Gulf.

A partly constructed jetty on the eastern side of Al-Qananm Island spotted and photographed by the author

The Omani Navy had a handful of patrol boats responsible for patrolling Oman's long coastline. In 1984, Sultan Qabus asked the other GCC countries for financial assistance to purchase helicopters, minesweepers and other equipment as well as to construct a naval base on Goat Island for the purpose of controlling the Strait of Hormuz. The Sultan's appeal received no favourable response. Some observers claimed in the 1980s that the Islamic Republic's initial lack of commitment to the control of the Strait of Hormuz has made Oman the sole policeman of that waterway.

> The Iranian revolution highlighted Oman's role as *de facto* sentinel of the Strait of Hormuz. One need only examine the Sultanate's pivotal location to understand why it is caught in the vortex of superpower rivalries. The United States has acquired rights to use the ports of Muscat and Salalah and a former British airfield on the island of Masirah, some 500 miles (800 kilometres) from Hormuz. These facilities will be part of a network of American bases ringing the Indian Ocean designed to guard the main tanker routes.[32]

Oman's pivotal location's strategic value is as undeniable as it is true that the United States, or any other superpower, would explore every possibility for improving their strategic position there as well. Nevertheless, the fact that matters at the Strait of Hormuz is that it is Iran that stops ships and searches them. This in itself is enough of an indication that Iran is still in control of this narrow Strait, enjoying a superior geostrategic position there.

When, early in the Iran–Iraq war, France announced that it was supplying Iraq with super-standard fighter planes equipped with Exocet missiles, the Islamic Republic threatened to close the Strait of Hormuz should French weapons be delivered to Iraq and used in the war against Iran. The weapons were delivered and the threat was not carried out. Closing the Strait by sinking tankers is not at all easy. The main channels of shipping are about one mile wide each and the water depth varies between 250 and 300 feet, while a fully laden supertanker draws only about 100 feet. Blocking the Strait by mine-laying would take only a few hours using modern ships, and an aircraft could do the job in less than one hour. But with the existing mine-detecting and minesweeping equipment in the Persian Gulf, the task of unblocking the Strait of Hormuz would take only a short time.

However, in spite of significant difficulties, Iran's cooperation with Oman in the Strait of Hormuz has grown closer and stronger since the 1979 Iranian revolution.

STRAIT OF HORMUZ AND IRAN'S RELATIONS WITH SAUDI ARABIA: THE GEOPOLITICS OF OIL PIPELINES

During the first half of the 1970s, Saudi Arabia was not clearly regarded by Tehran as the main rival for power in the Persian Gulf, rather, Iran in that period considered Iraq as the main rival and a potential danger to her interests and her role in the region. It was accepted by consent during this period that Iran and Saudi Arabia, partners in the regional and Western interests in the area, had similar basic aims: to prevent the spread of former Soviet influence and to check the growth of radical movements in the Persian Gulf and adjacent areas. But these mutual interests were partly in conflict with other interests of the two countries. Saudi Arabia then saw its main task of assuring the survival of the regime through promoting the spread of Islamic values. Whereas Iran at the time saw the long-term means for assuring the survival of its regime in the building of an independent industrial nation. Despite the coincidence of the two countries' overall political and strategic aims at this time which were closely related to those of the United States, ie curtailing Soviet influence in the area and promoting stability and moderation, real cooperation was prevented by element of increasing rivalry towards the end of 1974, and growing Saudi apprehension of Iran's ambition in the region. Saudi Arabia's suspicions of the Shah's ambitions were reflected especially in the following contexts:

1 *In response to Iran's growing military build up*
Although it has been suggested that Saudi Arabia's rapid military expansion which began in 1973, partly stemmed from the massive wealth it amassed from the quadrupling of oil prices in 1973,[33] it was in reality motivated largely by Western propaganda against Iran's massive military build-up. The Shah's early 1970s plan for creating the strongest army in the region, was regarded by many observers in the West, as well as in the region, as far too great for Iran's security needs. Much apprehension had been expressed both in the West and in the Arab world about the Shah's ambition to create the old Persian empire through territorial expansion and advancing control over the Arab oil fields of the Persian Gulf,[34] a perception that was given impetus by the Iranian seizure of the Gulf islands of Abu Musa and the two Tunbs in November 1971. The role of the Iranian Navy as a guarantor of security for the Persian Gulf from outside interference was alleged to have been another source of distrust in the region.[35]

It seems it was for these reasons that Saudi Arabia wanted more US involvement in the area to counter the weight posed by Iran and to some extent, by Iraq which was busy constructing the Umm al-Qasr naval base in association with the Soviets.

> Where Iran may genuinely want to exclude both superpowers from the Gulf, the Saudis may see themselves as being at the mercy of Iraq and Iran if the United States is not involved. Saudi Arabia requires US involvement as a counterweight to these regional powers.[36]

To create its own counterbalance *vis-à-vis* both Iran and Iraq in the region, Saudi Arabia launched a massive plan for military build up. Military expenditure increased to 6.771 billion dollars in 1975.[37] The arms purchases included various types of modern equipment from the West, mainly from the United States, who undertook to supply Saudi Arabia with the latest technology, especially in improving her air defence system by supplies of F15s and AWAKS aircraft radar.

2 *In response to Iran's presence in Oman, and the tightening of Iran's control over the Strait of Hormuz*

The presence of Iranian troops in Oman, in combat against the Communist-backed guerrilla movement in Dhufar was, in fact, privately welcomed by the moderate Arab states of the Persian Gulf, including Saudi Arabia. Arab ambivalence was manifested by the desire to have their security assured without making any effort on their own behalf, but, at the same time, fearing that such protection would lead to subordination.[38] It was this consideration of fear that led them to condemn Iran's military undertakings in Oman publicly. Prince (now King) Fahad of Saudi Arabia, for example criticised the presence of Iranian troops in Oman which was broadcast by Kuwait Home Service (10.00 mgt, 20 November 1975).[39]

> Abu Dhabi and Saudi Arabia's financial inducement to PDRY (former South Yemen) in 1974 and 1975 undoubtedly persuaded Aden to reconsider its position *vis-à-vis* PFLD. These states also served as intermediaries between PDRY and the Sultanate, as indicated by the visit of Aden's Foreign Minister, Mohammad Salih Muti, to al-Riyadh in July 1975, followed by his tour of the Gulf in November. Despite the seeming hesitance of al-Riyadh, Abu Dhabi, Kuwait and others to become involved, their interests clearly lay in strong opposition to the leftist threat presented by the Dhufar rebels. But their actions regarding the southern parts of the peninsula were equally motivated by resentment over Iranian soldiers on Arab soil.[40]

Saudi Arabia, therefore, apprehensive of Iran's ambitions in the region, adopted some precautionary measures. One such measure was the idea of forming a defence pact in partnership with all states of the Persian Gulf, except Iran and Iraq. This was about the strongest response to the Shah's earlier proposal of forming a collective pact for the defence of the Persian Gulf with the participation of all littoral states. To pave the way for the formation of such a pact, Saudi Arabia found it necessary to solve its age-old border differences with neighbouring states in the Gulf. The most famous undertaking of this kind at the time was the hasty boundary settlement with Abu-Dhabi in Buraimi and Liwa regions in 1974, whereby Saudi Arabia was given a corridor of access to the Gulf, in return for modifying her other boundary lines in the same district in favour of Abu-Dhabi.

Subsequently, in 1975, Saudi Arabia arranged with Kuwait to divide the two countries' neutral zone, without even sorting out such important issues as the question of sovereignty over the islands of Kubbor, Qaruh and Umm al-Maradim, and the question of actually dividing the oilfields of the former neutral zone. Though these moves proved to be valuable in settling part of geographical disputes in the Persian Gulf, they did not help Saudi Arabia's call for the formation of a security pact in the region without the presence of Iran and Iraq. This scheme suffered a severe blow at the time by strong opposition to it forcefully expressed by Iran. The scheme had to wait until May 1981 to materialise.

Other measures included the policy of strengthening the kingdom's armed forces and trying to find alternative routes for its oil exportation to bypass the Iranian controlled Strait of Hormuz. In the first instance, Saudi Arabia launched a project of industrial development at al-Jubail, northwest of Dhahran on the Gulf coast,[41] an important part of which was also concerned with the construction of a naval base there,[42] a move apparently in response to the construction of the Iranian naval bases at Bandar Abbas and Chah-Bahar, and Iraq's construction of a naval base at Umm al-Qasr. Saudi Arabia was also suspected of building a military base in the Bahrain islands.[43]

On the other hand, the Saudis, while increasing their military involvement in the Persian Gulf, launched a project to divert part of their oil exports from the Gulf routes to the Arab Sea and Red Sea through a network of pipelines built between the al-Hasa oilfields and the other coasts of Arabia, apparently in order to reduce their dependence on the oil routes through the Strait of Hormuz.[44] The idea of constructing these pipelines emerged in 1975[45] when Iran's control over the Strait of Hormuz was effectively established. The project, however, included three major lines to pipe parts of Saudi Arabia's oil output of the Eastern Provinces to the Red Sea and the Indian Ocean. These were:[46]

1 A 1,287 kilometres-long pipeline from the oilfields of Ghawar and Abqaiq to the new industrial centre of Yanbu on the Red Sea coast through Buraydah and Medinah, at an estimated cost of 1.500 billion dollars (1975 prices). Yanbu had been chosen as the site for a large industrial complex based on petrochemical and oil refining. The pipeline would provide the raw material for the new industries.[47] The work on this project began in 1977 and was completed in 1983.

2 A new pipeline was planned to link the oilfields of Hasa with Mukalla on the Indian Ocean with a line across the Empty Quarter and through the Democratic Republic of Yemen (former South Yemen). This project was perhaps the most ambitious of all. It was planned to cross the entire length of the Empty Quarter.[48] With regard to the fact that construction of Trans-Alaskan pipeline had proved that provided the money is available, almost any geographical hazard can be surmounted, construction of this pipeline might not face impossible technical and geographical obstacles. Money seemed not to be a problem in Saudi Arabia at the time, but it is significant to point out the obstacle which prevailed here was political. Most certainly, as long as the present regimes in Saudi Arabia and Yemen continue their political and ideological confrontations, implementation of such projects is bound to face major complications.

3 A shorter line was also suggested. It was planned to pipe oil, produced from the newly discovered Shaybah fields – south of the border with the United Arab Emirates – again to the Arab Sea, but via Dhufar Province of Oman.[49] This project was proposed in 1975, but was delayed, firstly because of fighting still going on in Dhurar, and secondly because the Saudis insisted on having complete sovereignty over the line in the Omani territories for security reasons.[50]

The Saudis and Omanis described the plan in terms of economic and environmental considerations. Mr Yusof Al-Alawi, then Oman's Deputy Foreign Minister (now Minister of Foreign Affairs) told this author in Muscat on 19 December 1977:

It is economically advantageous to build this pipeline (Shaybah–Dhufar). It is a shorter distance. The oil produced from the fields near the border with Oman is difficult to be piped to the north coasts . . . Now they are working on the line from Hasa to Yanb'u, and one of the aims in that project is to extend it to Alexandria in Egypt, where they can make use of the refining facilities already constructed there. So it is again very economic to build the Ghawar–Yanb'u pipeline.

The Shah's regime in Iran expressed an entirely different view on the issue. It regarded Saudi Arabia's policy of piping oil from their Gulf coast oilfields to the other sides of the Arabian peninsula as entirely based on strategic considerations. A senior official at the time – who wished to remain anonymous – told this author in Tehran, in early 1978, that:

> The move by the Saudis to construct new pipelines from their Persian Gulf coasts to the Red Sea and the Indian Ocean cannot be economically advantageous to them at all. This project is based on strategic considerations. The Saudis, not only believe that the Strait of Hormuz is a notoriously unstable area, and, therefore, they are unhappy with Iran's complete control over this Strait, but also they are thinking of reducing the significance of Iran's position at this narrow Strait, by reducing the Strait's role as the sole access route to and from the Persian Gulf.

The fact that the Hasa–Yanb'u pipeline (petroline) has a maximum capacity of 3 million barrels per day, and the planned Mukalla and Dhufar pipelines were projected for a daily capacity of 2 million combined, and the fact that Iraq's trans-Arabian pipeline – completed in 1985 – has a capacity of half a million barrels a day, together with Iraq's trans-Turkey pipelines of a combined capacity of 2 million barrels per day, a total of 7.5 million barrels of oil per day piped away from the Strait of Hormuz, could seriously undermine Hormuz's strategic significance. But not all of these projected capacity of pipelines materialised. Now only 4 million barrels of the region's 13 million barrels per day of exported oil – the lowest quantity since early 1970s – is piped away from the Strait of Hormuz. Since the exported oil is rising in terms of volume, exportation of 4 million barrels per day of the Gulf oil through pipelines cannot seriously affect Hormuz's strategic significance.[51]

It is noteworthy that at least 1.500 billion dollars was not the only expenditure that the construction of Petroline absorbed. Maintenance of this pipeline across Arabia is very costly. What is more important, the Saudis are bound to be closely concerned with the security of the Red Sea and its two highly vulnerable outlets, a task which will be extremely expensive. Therefore, and with regard to these factors, the idea that trans-Arabian pipelines would be economically advantageous attracts little sympathy. Even the Saudis themselves, while arguing that the projects were considered for economic and environmental reasons, made no secret of the fact that:

> Tanker terminals in the Red Sea and the Indian Ocean would provide not only new outlets *in case of war in the Gulf*, but also give some alternative means of exporting oil during bad weather that curtail or completely shut down tanker loading operations . . .[52]

Iran's argument on this issue, however, indicated its reaction to Saudi Arabia's decision to divert part of its exported oil from the Strait of Hormuz. Iran's official reaction came in the form of a warning that it would consider the construction of either pipelines as an unfriendly act.[53]

The rise to power of the Islamic Republic in Iran, in February 1979, made the Saudis – as well as other Gulf states – apprehensive of the Iranian would-be strategy of exporting revolution. Mutual suspicion between Iran and the Arabs of the region, exaggerated by certain Western sources did not help the situation at all. In the 1980s the Islamic Republic's initial expression of ideological charges – against the Arab regimes of the region – for 'not upholding their Islamic dignity by becoming the puppets of the super-powers', elevated the element of distrust amongst the Saudi leadership of Iranian intentions.

In 1981, Saudi Arabia used the opportunity – created by the Iran-Iraq war – and fulfilled its old desire for a pact in the Persian Gulf, without the participation of Iran and Iraq. In May that year, the Gulf Cooperation Council (GCC) was formed with the membership of Saudi Arabia, Oman, Kuwait, Bahrain, Qatar, and the United Arab Emirates, an arrangement which was strongly opposed by Iran in the 1970s. Moreover, throughout the 8 years of the Iran–Iraq war Saudi Arabia supported the Iraqi regime. This action caused relations to deteriorate further between the two countries, and the Mecca clashes of 1987, in which scores or Iranian Haj pilgrims were killed and wounded by the Saudi police, resulted in the two countries' relations being suspended.

Fresh efforts for the resumption of relations between the two countries began in late 1990. The formation of a new alliance between the GCC, Syria and Egypt, in the wake of the Kuwait crisis (6 March 1991) excluded Iran from security arrangements made for the Persian Gulf. This move has been viewed, by the Iranians, as yet another example of the Saudi policy of alienating Iran in the Persian Gulf.

Alienating Iran in the US-backed security arrangement between the GCC and Syria and Egypt is blamed on the Islamic Republic of Iran's policy of exporting revolution. Considering the fact that 'the policy of exporting revolution' has never been anything more than a myth and the fact that the government of the Islamic Republic of Iran has been continuously playing down the idea of exporting revolution, the reason argued for alienating Iran in the new security system in the Persian Gulf is not convincing.

Saudi Arabia's dislike of the participation of Iran and Iraq in a security system in the Persian Gulf is an old one. Its reaction to Iran's call in early 1970s for the formation of a collective security pact with the participation of all littoral states and no others, was negative. In 1973 Saudi Arabia proposed a security system in the Persian Gulf that would exclude Iran and Iraq, but would cooperate with them. Tehran, then, reacted strongly against it, and it was eight years later (1981) during the Iran–Iraq war that Saudi Arabia created the GCC. Saudi Arabia's main concern is that the fall of tribal systems of the Emirates would pave the way for the fall of its own regime. To prevent such an eventuality, the Saudis find it necessary to keep these traditional regimes in a tightly arranged system that would prevent any direct influence from Iran and Iraq, the other two permanent features of the Persian Gulf geopolitics, or from any other source for that matter.

Saudi-Iranian relations began to improve from 1996 when the Israeli coalition government of the mid-1990s began to negate the so-called Arab–Israeli peace process. Nevertheless, when Iran was hard at work to prevent the success in Afghanistan of the Taliban militia forces, Saudi Arabia supported and officially recognised this group as Afghanistan's legitimate government. Considering Saudi Arabia's unfriendly attitude towards the Islamic fundamentalist regime in Iran, her support for and recognition of Taliban Islamic fanaticism in Afghanistan only proves that Saudi Arabia's rivalry with Iran is still at work.

STRAIT OF HORMUZ AND IRAN'S RELATIONS WITH IRAQ: THE GEOSTRATEGIC FACTORS

Iraq is a Gulf state heavily dependent on the Strait of Hormuz for the overwhelming bulk of its trade with the outside world. Relations between Iran and Iraq have, since the state of Iraq came into existence, been overshadowed by the two countries' border disputes, especially in the Shatt al-Arab. In other words, geography is perhaps the most dominant factor in shaping relations between Iran and Iraq. The dual nature of Iraq's concerns *vis-à-vis* Iran stems from the country's geographical location on the northwesternmost part of the Persian Gulf with a narrow access to the international shipping lanes. On the one hand, Iraq enters open hostility with Iran over border disputes, and on the other, needs her cooperation for trading through the Persian Gulf and the Strait of Hormuz where Iran is in control. Border differences between Iran and Iraq date back to the time when the country, now known as Iraq, was part of the former Ottoman empire. The two countries' mutual boundaries – 120 miles[54] of which is formed by the Shatt al-Arab – were first defined by the treaty of Erzerum of 1847 concluded between Iran and the Ottoman empire. Although the Shatt was mentioned in the text of this treaty, there was no mention either of a definite ownership of it, or of delimitation of the boundaries there. In 1913 a major part of the mutual boundary was demarcated in accordance with the terms of the protocol signed that year. During the following year a major disagreement arose concerning mainly the Shatt, which, according to the 1913 protocol, was left under Ottoman sovereignty. Finally, towards the end of 1914, the two sides agreed on a settlement of the issue by placing the boundary in the middle of the river, from a point one mile below the mouth of the confluence of the river Karun to a point about four miles above it.[55] Iran still dissatisfied with the 1914 protocol, continued the dispute until December 1934, when the matter was taken to the League of Nations[56] by Iraq, an appeal which failed to produce a satisfactory result.

However, on July 4, 1937, the two governments reached an agreement and signed a new treaty, according to article 11 of which, the two countries' boundary line in the Shatt al-Arab followed the Iranian banks except that part of the river facing the port of Abadan where the Thalweg anchorage was defined as the boundary line.[57] This treaty also recognised the island of Mohallah as being under Iranian sovereignty.

Further renewal of the dispute occurred in December 1959, when the Iraqi military leader, General Qassem, dennounced the 1937 agreement and claimed Iraqi sovereignty over all the Shatt al-Arab. Qassem declared that Iraq was forced to sign the 1937 agreement under duress.[58] Since then the question of Shatt al-Arab has become an issue which has encouraged widespread political and ideological argument between the two countries.

On 15 April 1969, according to Iranian sources, the Iraqi Foreign Ministry informed the Iranian ambassador in Baghdad that ships flying Iranian colours should lower their flags, otherwise all ships bound for Iranian ports would be intercepted.[59] Amir-Khosro Afshar the Iranian deputy Foreign Minister made a statement before the Senate in which he enumerated instances of violation of the main provisions of the treaty of 1937 by Iraq, and declared that because of these violations, the treaty had been rendered null and void.[60]

Iran then sailed ships in the Shatt al-Arab, under the protection of armed forces, thus, unilaterally enforcing international regulations of Thalweg.[61] The danger of a serious conflict was imminent. Both Iran and Iraq were affected by the Shatt's strategic sensitivity. Both parties, thereafter, tried to reduce their strategic vulnerability by attempting to relocate their involvement in the Shatt's navigation facilities.

Iran's Action Under the Tarh-e Cham

Iran planned to replace Abadan's role, both in trade and communications by other ports on the Persian Gulf under a comprehensive project, generally known as the Tarh-e Cham (*tarh* means project, and *cham* stands for *chahar mantaqeh* which means four regions).[62]

Abadan (30° 20'N and 48° 16'E) lies on the east bank of the Shatt al-Arab on Abadan Island, about 27 miles above the estuary of the Shatt al-Arab. Until the disputes with Iraq over the navigation rights on this river escalated to an explosive scale, Abadan was Iran's most important port for the export of petroleum products. It is still important, but its disadvantageous strategic location of being within easy range of mortars emplaced on Iraqi territory – as it was proved to be during the wars of the 1980s – made Iran transfer its role to other ports on the Gulf. Having access to the Persian Gulf in approximately 1.050 miles,[63] Iran had the opportunity of implementing the project without much difficulty. A secondary reason that encouraged Iran to reduce dependence on the port of Abadan, was Shatt al-Arab's shallow depth – not more than 30 feet at its deepest – which was no longer suitable for the modern supertankers traffic. For both reasons, the ports of Bandar Bushehr, Bandar Shahpur (now known as Bandar Imam Khomeini), Bandar Mahshahr and Khark Island, were expanded by huge petrochemical, industrial and all electronic port facilities, within the said project which was completed in the early 1970s:

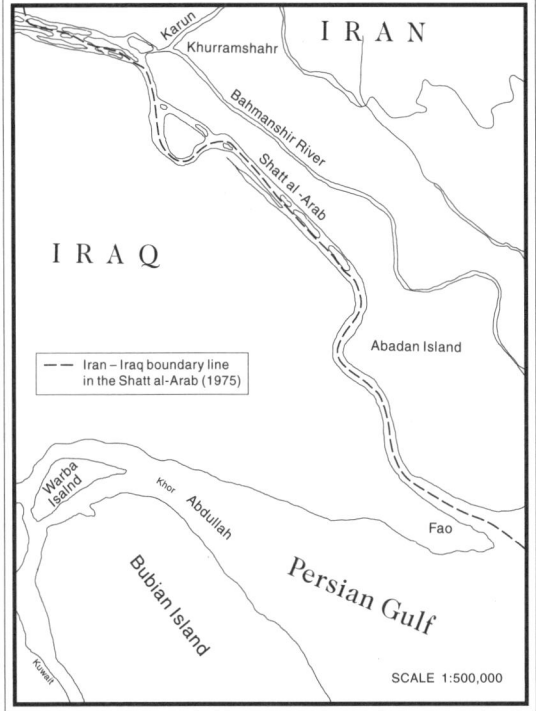

Figure 2.9 The Iran–Iraq river boundaries according to the 1975
Algiers agreement

1 Bandar Shahpur (now Bandar Imam Khomeini) – 30° 23'N and 49°
  07'E is built on a reclaimed area of the north side of the Khor-Musa
  about 45 miles from the open sea. The deep tidal inlet of Khor-
  Musa at the head of the Persian Gulf, can accommodate large ships
  at anchor.[64]

  During the implementation of the project, six jetties were
  constructed and the installation of three new jetties started in
  December 1974, bringing the total to nine. A new and ambitious
  plan set up in 1975 for the development of this port aimed at
  construction of an additional 28 new jetties.[65] Should these new
  development plans be completed, the port's capacity would increase
  fourfold from its 1975 average capacity of 12,000 tons per day.[66]

  This port is linked to the rest of the country by a major road
  system and by a railway via Ahvaz. Construction of a large

petrochemical complex began there by the Iranian National Petroleum Company in partnership with Allied Chemical Corporation[67] which was completed in 1971.

2 Bandar Mahshahr – formerly known as Bandar Mashur – located 55 miles east of Abadan on Khor Musa – was developed to handle parts of Abadan's role as an oil port. Khor Musa is deep enough, near Bandar Mahshahr for tankers to manoeuvre and berth at Bandar's six jetties.[68] This port, originally developed in the early 1940s to handle the crude oil exported from the Aghajari fields, 100 miles inland, was converted into the most modern oil-products port in the oil industry of its day. Through the expenditure of some 50 million dollars in the 1950s and the use of an electronic control system, installed in the 1960s and 1970s,[69] Bandar Mahshahr has for almost all practical purposes replaced the port of Abadan, as one of the leading ports exporting Iranian oil products. Some 38 oil-products of the Abadan refinery were transferred regularly through an elaborated system of pipelines to Bandar Mahshahr for export.[70]

3 Bandar Bushehr, is situated on a small peninsula 76 miles away from Khorramshahr, on the Persian Gulf. Bushehr too, underwent massive development projects. New jetties have been constructed and its road and communication network improved.

4 Khark, a small coral island, situated 25 miles off the mainland, in the Persian Gulf is the site of one of the world's largest oil terminals, a massive engineering feat, and a petroleum industry complex. In fact, many observers believe that the development of Khark Island is one of two major factors which intensified sharply Iran's involvement in the Persian Gulf during the 1960s[71] the other being the exploitation of offshore oil fields.

Iran's chief oil fields are connected to this island's terminals through four 30 inch diameter pipelines laid along the seabed. The land line, 40 inches in diameter, that starts at Aghajari oilfields and runs some 106 miles to the Persian Gulf – one of the world's largest crude oil delivery line at the time – has a capacity of over one million barrels per day. Khark Island receives the crude at a tank farm with 19 tanks and a capacity of 7,676 billion barrels. The huge storage capacity of the island is matched by its 6,000 feet-long jetty with 10 berths[72] that can accommodate the largest super-tankers which may be built in this century. The crude oil that arrives in the tankers can be loaded at the rate of over 10,000 tons per hour.[73] A large petrochemical complex was also built on Khark Island by the National Petroleum Company[74] in partnership with American Oil Company International (an affiliate of Standard Oil of Indiana).[75] Khark Island's industrial and port installations were heavily bombarded by Iraqi bombers during the latter years of the 1980s war but it managed to continue its oil exportation throughout the war. In the post-war period, reconstruction of this island was given high priority.

Apart from the transfer of the oil port from Abadan to the said four regions, the Iranian Navy too, moved its southern headquarters from Khorramshahr to Bandar Abbas on the Strait of Hormuz in 1972,[76] where a major naval base was constructed in the late 1960s.[77]

Iraq's Action

Iraq with its narrow and less suitable coastline on the Persian Gulf was less able to replace the port of Basra. In the 1960s, however, Basra continued to grow as Iraq's main port, albeit port Fao, near the estuary of the Shatt al-Arab had by then developed to the extent of being Iraq's main oil-exporting port. Fao's development started in 1950 and oil exports from it began in late 1951. A network of oil pipelines connected Fao with the oilfields of southern Iraq (Rumila and Zubair). The 1960s also witnessed completion of the Khor-Umaiyah oil terminal, south of Fao in the sea, which was later coupled-up by the construction of Mina Albakr (1970).[78]

However, apart from Fao's closeness to the Shatt al-Arab, the 25-mile unsuitable Iraqi coastline offered no other possibility for easing southern Iraq's vulnerability imposed by the Shatt al-Arab's strategic situation. Hence, Iraq found the idea of piping oil away from the Shatt al-Arab and the Persian Gulf a more favourable solution. Though exporting oil through other countries has more strategic disadvantages, as Iraq's existing trans-Syrian pipeline was closed in 1976 as a result of rising tensions with Syria. Yet Iraq found the pipeline projects more alluring than running the risk of Iranian fire-power stationed on the eastern side of the Shatt al-Arab and still having to face the Iranians at the Strait of Hormuz. In 1983 Iraq's trans-Turkey pipeline – with a daily capacity of 1.2 million barrels – was completed. The conclusion of another agreement with Saudi Arabia in 1985 provided her with the trans-Arabian pipeline with a capacity of one million barrels per day,[79] and a third pipeline (trans-Turkey II) with a maximum capacity of one million barrels per day. All these pipelines were closed during the Kuwait crisis of 1990–91. Iraq's limited access to the international waters of the Persian Gulf had at the same time tempted Baghdad to consider territorial gains in Kuwait and the two islands of Warba and Bubian. A number of Iraqi military activities against Kuwait which took place in the 1970s, together with Baghdad's tacit desire for sovereignty over Iran's southwestern province of Khuzestan, leave little doubt as to how misguidedly Iraq is trying to broaden its breathing space in the Persian Gulf.

Another strategic solution to the problem considered by both parties was the idea of diverting the course of the Shatt al-Arab. Following the 1969 Crisis in Iran–Iraq relations over the Shatt dispute, the Iranians started to talk of a feasibility study to divert the River Karun to the river Bahmanshir making it navigable and at the same time depriving the Shatt of a major source of water. This, they thought, would rid them of the Shatt al-Arab headache. Very soon the strategically disadvantageous nature of such a scheme was realised and the whole idea was abandoned. The Iraqis too, at one stage (after the 1988 ceasefire) while the peace talks with Iran were running into difficulties, began to discuss a similar idea to divert the course of the Shatt al-Arab to Khor-Zubair through Shatt al-Basra. They also realised that such a scheme would leave the entire area east of the Shatt in a disadvantageous situation.

However, during the period 1969–75 the two countries found themselves on the brink of an all-out military confrontation. Both parties tried hard to avoid direct armed conflict. Iran's action in November 1971 of seizing the islands of Abu-Musa and the two Tunbs near the Strait of Hormuz prompted Iraq to sever diplomatic relations with Tehran (1 December 1971),[80] and to step up pressure on Iranian citizens resident in Iraq by accelerating their expulsion.[81] Iran decided to make use of the potential advantages within Iraq. These were:

1 More than half the Iraqi population are Shiah Moslems. Since Iran is the only Shiah state in the world, the Shiahs of Iraq, who represent about 55 per cent of the total population of Iraq,[82] have a natural religious sympathy for Iran. Under the Shah, this phenomenon could not be exploited at all, mainly because the Shiah leaders in Iraq had little sympathy with the Tehran regime. During the wars of the 1980s, Iran tried to mobilise the Iraqi Shiahs by assisting an Islamic revolutionary movement led by

prominent Iraqi Shiah clergy (Hakim), but the effort produced little result.

2 A large colony of Iranian citizens lives in Iraq; their number has been put as high as one million.[83] But before this factor could be of any use to Iran, Iraq – in anticipation – accelerated the task of expelling them. The number of such Iranians expelled from Iraq between April 1968 and March 1972, according to Iranian sources, exceeded 60,000.[84] The number of the Iranians expelled from Iraq during the 1980s war exceeded this figure.

3 More important than the other advantages was the Kurdish movement of northern Iraq, whose population was then estimated at 15 to 25 per cent of the total population of Iraq.[85] Iran, according to all reliable sources had supported Kurdish forces in Iraq in the 1970s by supplying them with arms and ammunition. Iran's use of this movement eventually cornered Iraq and proved to be most successful.

Finally on 6 March 1975 the leaders of the two countries met during the Algiers OPEC summit and came out with a joint communiqué which declared:[86]

1 That they (Iran and Iraq) would define their frontiers on the basis of the protocol of Constantinople of 1913 and the verbal agreement of frontiers of 1914.

2 That they would define their river frontiers according to the Thalweg line, ie the middle of the deepest shipping channel.

3 That they would 're-establish security and natural confidence along their common frontiers' and undertake to exercise strict and effective control with the aim of putting an end to 'all infiltration of a subversive character from either side'.

4 That the parties would regard these provisions as indivisible elements of a comprehensive settlement, and in consequence any breach of any one of them as a violation of the spirit of the Algiers agreement.

Subsequent to this declaration, representatives of the two governments and committees of delineation and demarcation formed of experts from both countries, met from time to time in Tehran and Baghdad and worked out the draft of the comprehensive treaty of 1975, which was ratified by the two countries' parliaments and councils. Following the rise to power of the Islamic Republic in Iran and the disarray that had befallen Iranian armed forces in the early months of the revolution, Iraq revoked the 1975 treaty unilaterally and Iraqi troops crossed Iranian borders in pursuit of a quick victory. Though Iraq's initial advances were reversed, the war continued for eight years without either side coming out as the clear winner. Nevertheless during the Kuwait crisis of 1990–91 President Saddam Hussein of Iraq wrote to President Rafsanjani of Iran (14 August 1990) confirming Iraq's acceptance of a border settlement on the basis of the 1975 Algiers accord.

Strait of Hormuz and Iran's Geopolitical Relations with the GCC

With the success of the Islamic Revolution in Iran in February 1979, relations deteriorated initially with all Arab states of the Gulf. This was mainly because of the perception of an acute threat to their security, arising from either a direct undertaking by the revolutionary government of Iran in exporting the Islamic revolution to these countries, or as a result of an Islamic uprising in their own societies inspired by the Iranian revolution.

The impact of this perceived threat was felt more strongly in the countries of substantial Shiah populations: Iraq with 60 per cent; Bahrain with 70 per cent; Saudi Arabia and Kuwait with more than 10 per cent each of their population.

The Shiah communities of the said countries have had a history of protest against the ruling class of their countries, generally grieving of being treated as subservient and second class citizens. The success of the Islamic revolution in Iran inspired several demonstrations in Iraq, Bahrain and Saudi Arabia. These developments encouraged the Saudis to revive their old desire to create a security pact with the smaller states in the Gulf. Originally, this idea was put forward in 1973 in response to Iran's call in 1970–72 for a collective security pact in the Persian Gulf which was to include all countries littoral to the Gulf. Iran strongly opposed the idea put forward by the Saudis and declared that it would not tolerate an incomplete arrangement which could be a source of irritation in the region.

As the war broke out between Iran and Iraq in September 1980, the Saudis revived the old proposal. In a meeting of their Foreign Ministers in Riyadh, on 4–5 February 1981, the states of Saudi Arabia, Kuwait, Oman, the United Arab Emirates (UAE), Bahrain and Qatar agreed to establish a co-operation council of the Arab States of the Persian Gulf (GCC) which would provide a framework for the coordination of all government policies between the member states, with a view to safeguarding security and stability in the Gulf.[87]

Although this Co-operation Council is more divided than united in certain respects, it serves Saudi Arabia's desire of domination of the smaller states through closer cooperation. Other events have served this Saudi desire more effectively, especially in relation to Bahrain. From the beginning of its formation the GCC viewed Iran as the chief threat to the political status quo in the region. Shiah movements in the Arab states of the region were attributed to direct Iranian political activities.

On 13 December, 1981, Bahrain's security forces foiled an alleged coup with the arrest of a group of terrorists and the capture of a consignment of arms and radio equipment.[88] Those arrested (45 Bahrainis, 13 Saudi Arabians, one Kuwaiti and one Omani) were said to have been members of Tehran-based (Shiah) Islamic Front for the Liberation of Bahrain.

After interrogation of the detainees, Bahrain's Ministry of the Interior stated that the group had intended to launch attacks on government establishments on 16 December, Bahrain's national day.

The alleged coup attempt was attributed to Iran and the group was reported to have been trained in Iran, and its members were charged under section 122 of Bahrain's penal code for collaboration with a foreign power in activities hostile to the state,[89] which carried the death sentence.

The Foreign Ministry of Bahrain made an official protest to the Iranian chargé d'affaires on 13 December, and the Bahrain newspaper Akhbar al-Khalij named Hojatol-Eslam Hadi al-Mudaresi in Iran as the chief organiser of the plotted 'coup'. Mudaresi had fled to Bahrain from Iran under the Shah and returned to Iran after the Islamic revolution of 1979. The Iranian Ministry of Foreign Affairs quickly denied any complicity and Iranian media commentaries suggested that the accusation was part of a concerted campaign to tarnish the character of the Iranian revolution. Saudi Arabia was also prompt in accusing Iran of supporting and engineering the coup. Saudi Arabian Minister of the Interior, Prince Nayef ibn Abdul Aziz, visited Bahrain on 20 December 1981 where he declared that: 'The sabotage plot . . . was engineered by the Iranian Government and was directed against Saudi Arabia . . .'[90]

On the same day Saudi Arabia concluded a security agreement with Bahrain, and thus brought Bahrain another step closer to Saudi Arabian domination. Sheikh Mohammad bin Khalifa Al-Khalifah, Bahrain's Minister of the Interior, on the other hand, spoke of the need for a 'rapid deployment force in the Gulf that would be capable of quickly providing assistance when needed'.[91] A Peninsular Defence Shield was created subsequently in Saudi Arabia which is to be the military arm of the GCC.

The 73 detainees, accused of plotting to overthrow the rule of the Al-Khalifah in Bahrain, were tried in March and April 1982 and were convicted on May 23 that year of plotting a coup against the state, but were, surprisingly, given light sentences.[92] The attribution of the foiled coup attempt to Iran was universally accepted to be the truth mainly because of an earlier blunder by an Iranian cleric, Ayatollah Sadeq Ruhani. Ruhani had stated in September 1979 that he 'did not agree with the policies of the Shah's regime regarding Bahrain and that he would 'lead a revolutionary movement for the annexation of Bahrain unless its rulers adopted an Islamic form of government similar to the one established in Iran'.[93]

Although Ruhani was not an official of the Iranian government and his claims reflected his own personal opinion rather than the policy of the government of the Islamic Republic of Iran, and in spite of the fact that his claim of Islamic supremacy in Bahrain was qualitatively different from the ancient Iranian claims which were based on 'historical rights' of sovereignty over the island;[94] and also, despite the fact that the provisional government of the Islamic Republic of Iran had quickly denied any pretence to Bahrain and blamed Ruhani's 'unauthorised' statement on the revolutionary chaotic conditions of 'a thousand Chiefs' in Iran; the authorities in Bahrain, Saudi Arabia and other GCC countries would not budge and were not moved to consider the possibility of a second thought that the statement from the provisional government of the Islamic Republic of Iran might have truly reflected the actual situation in Iran and the claim of the extremist cleric might have truly been his own personal opinion aired in the chaotic situation in Iran.

However, Saudi Arabia, the GCC and Western sources did not give up the accusation of a 'Revival of Iran's claims to Bahrain'. John B. Allcock and co-editors, for example, claimed on pp. 365–6 of the third edition of their 'Border and Territorial Disputes', published in 1992, that 'the renewed Iranian claim to Bahrain was announced in September 1979 by Ayatollah Ruhani, a leading figure in the Iranian revolution; however, it was strongly rejected by the Bahrain government on 22 September'.

It was with the background of these events that the coup attempt of December 1981 in Bahrain and the revitalised Shiah movements throughout the Gulf, clearly inspired by the Iranian revolution, and the multiple Shiah bombings in Kuwait on 12 December 1983, again attributed to Iran, drew Bahrain and other GCC states much closer to Saudi Arabia. Neither the GCC nor their Western allies were ever prepared to doubt the nature of their own claims and fears *vis-à-vis* Iran, nor were they prepared to pay any attention to the explanations of the Iranian government.

It took much effort in the form of the publication of numerous articles in English, Persian and Arabic in the international journals (many by this author) explaining that the Shiah movements of Bahrain started in the late nineteenth century and continued throughout the twentieth century without a link of much consequence with Iran or any other countries of the region. These explanations led to a Syrian mediation which in turn led to the unfounded accusations against Iran being abandoned.

However, the new global and regional geopolitical circumstances have introduced new vulnerabilities to these old differences, as a result of increasing manipulation of regional geographical differences for the justification of new geopolitical orders. The balance of power in the Persian Gulf has, similarly, changed in the wake of the Kuwait crisis, introducing the United States as the single most powerful military presence in the region, closely associated with the Gulf Cooperation Council, with Iran trailing behind and Iraq still in a state of complete paralysis.

The Iranian frontiers in the Persian Gulf are in a state of partial flux. The majority of border agreements concerning division of the continental shelf have proved to be viable – notably those with Saudi Arabia, Oman, Qatar and Bahrain. Other areas of maritime division have not either been subject to existing treaties or are affected by the uncertainties related to the matters on the peripheries of the earlier agreements. An example of the former situation can be found in the northwestern corner of the Persian Gulf, where Iran, Iraq and Kuwait have failed to finalise division of the seabed and subsoil deposits, albeit Irano–Kuwaiti maritime boundary affairs are governed by a draft agreement which came into existence in 1962. What can be said of the latter is that acrimonious and capricious arguments have characterised a number of offshore settlements, none more so than those between Iran and Sharjah, the responsibility for the Arab side of which has, since 1992, been taken over by the United Arab Emirates. Here, three powerful undercurrents are discernible: one deriving from want of enhancing national identity (in the case of the United Arab

Emirates) within the principles of Jean Gottmann's 'iconography';[95] the other resulting from generic insecurity and suspicion between the respective governments which works within Jacques Ancel's postulation that 'there are no problems of boundaries, there are only problems of nations';[96] and third, arising from specific local matters of sovereignty and strategic control, as well as arising from political expediency of greater powers in the region, ie creating or maintaining disputes to justify military presence and big-power geopolitical considerations.

Meanwhile, considering that Iran is the largest country of the region, both in terms of population and coastline, together with her control of the most sensitive strategic waterways and islands in the Strait of Hormuz, and the fact that her dependence on secure trade via the Persian Gulf is vital, it is hard to envisage a circumstance in which Iran would cause complete destruction of possible Arab–Iranian co-operation in the region.

Finally, it is noteworthy that UAE claims of sovereignty over the islands of Tunbs and Abu Musa in late 1992 did not affect Iran's relations with other GCC members in large measure. This was in spite of much hope in Abu Dhabi that a strained Iran–GCC relation would put enough pressure on Tehran to make some concession regarding

Women carrying water to the villages at Qeshm Island

56

the said islands (the case will be studied at length in section IV of this book),

Increasing co-operation with Iran of such Arab states as Kuwait, Saudi Arabia, Qatar and Oman is, perhaps, a good indication of how these geographical factors work in favour of growing Arab-Iranian relationships in the Persian Gulf. Even political figures generally considered as belonging to the right wing of the Saudi regime, like Defence Minister Prince Sultan bin Abdel-Aziz, proposed only a week after Saudi Arabia and other members of GCC, and the so-called Damascus Declaration issued in January 1996 their statement of support for the UAE position relevant to the three islands, that 'Saudi Arabia wants the best possible relations with Iran'.[97]

Section II

Historical and Geographical Foundations of Territoriality in the Persian Gulf

Chapter 3

Historical Foundations of Territoriality in The Persian Gulf

IRANIANS AND ARABS IN THE GULF

There are myths dating the origin of the people of the Persian Gulf to the meeting of three branches of mankind on the shores of the Gulf in about 10,000 BC: the Dravidians of the Makran coasts absorbed by their Baluchi conquerors; the Semites of the Arabian highlands who displaced or absorbed the original Hamitic Euro-African aborigines; and the proto-Elamites of southwestern Iran.[1]

The political map of the Persian Gulf in the last centuries BC was simple. The Gulf first experienced something like a 'state' in the modern sense of the term in the mid-sixth century BC when the Achaemenians (559–330 BC) consolidated their federative empire, which included most of the civilised world of the time, stretching from India in the east to Egypt and Libya in the west. The southern flanks of the empire were formed by the entire southern coast of the Gulf, and the Achaemenians made use of the strategic location of the Strait of Hormuz, sending naval fleets to discover sea routes linking India to Egypt via Persia and the Gulf. They introduced the *qanat* (underground water channel) system to the four corners of the world ('the four countries of the federative empire').[2] The *qanat* system was introduced to Oman and the southern coasts of the Persian Gulf at the time of Darius the Great (521–485 BC), the Achaemenian. John Wilkinson, an authority in Omanology, states:

> Sulayman is the hypostasis of King Solomon whose connection with the Queen of the 'Sabaean Kingdom' is celebrated. Less well known, perhaps, is the fact that in Persia he tends to be partially identified with

61

the even more legendary Jamshid; thus in folklore it was this Jamshid-cum-Sulayman, and not the Achaemenids, who built Persepolis (Takht-i-Sulayman, Takht-i-Jamshid). This is significant in the Oman context because when Sulayman visited Oman and ordered the *qanat* to be built he was on his journey from Istakhr, that is the Achaemanid capital of Persepolis.[3]

It is entirely plausible that the legendary Jamshid was none other than the Achaemenian Darius the Great who had completed the building of 'Takht-e Jamshid', Persepolis. (There are several historical indications which convince the author of this theory but this book on the maritime boundaries is not the forum for discussing them.)

The original settlers of the lower coasts of the Persian Gulf must have been peoples of the Achaemenian federative empire (sixth century BC). Iranian settlement of the southern coastlands of the Gulf increased under the Parthians (270BC–224AD), who made great progress in seafaring in the Gulf.[4] Traces of their contribution are still to be found in the world of sea-faring, such as the terms *navi* (navy, naval), *navkhoda* (naval captain), *bar* (port, as in Zanzibar, Malabar).

Iranian domination of these coasts was consolidated under the Sassanians (224–651AD). There is little evidence of major Arab settlement on the southern coasts of the Gulf before the Islamic era,[5] but Arab migration to the coasts of the lower Gulf began at the time of Artaxerxes (Ardeshir Papakan, 224AD), founder of the Sassanian federative empire. He defeated their king Satiran and regained control of these coastal regions.[6] Territorial strife between the Persian and Roman empires settled Iran's western flanks in Mesopotamia, where the Sassanians created their frontier-keeping vassal kingdom of Hirah.[7] Nevertheless, Arab raids and encroachment on Iranian dominions of the southern coasts of the Gulf became more frequent. Shapur I made successful naval retaliations, but the raids continued until Shapur II (309–325AD) put an end to the problem for some time, as Sir Arnold Wilson notes in *The Persian Gulf*, quoting early Islamic historians and geographers:

> The reign of Shapur II (309–37AD) was marked by frequent raids upon the Persian coasts by the Arabs of Hajar, which then included Hasa, Qatif and Bahrain. Almost for the first time since the expedition of Sennacherib, we read of a naval expedition against these raiders in the Persian Gulf, commanded by the king himself, which was completely successful.[8]

This brought Arab migration to these coasts to a halt, albeit temporarily. The main Shanu'a groupings of Arab immigrants from the interior of Arabia were established in the mountains of Masandum and Oman proper in the early sixth century AD, when the Kawadh (Qobads) ruled those regions. It was probably in association with this migration into Oman that elements of the Kinda also came to settle in the mountain areas of Jabal Kinda near Buraimi Oasis. Other Arab migrants who settled in the desert and border areas of Oman formed the Azd Federation. Faced with this massive new tribal union of migrant Arabs, the Iranian rulers of the region had no alternative but to accord the newcomers a degree of autonomy under their own tribal leadership.[9]

The country of Oman was called 'Mazun' or 'Masun' in the period of Iranian rule and its threshold, from the direction of the interior of Iran, was called 'Mazundam' or 'Masundam' The term *dam* in old and modern Persian means 'threshold', in reference to both time and space, such as *Sobh-dam* which means dawn (the threshold of the morning), or *bagh-dam* or *dam-e-bagh* which means the threshold of the garden. The term 'Masundam' therefore, means 'threshold of Masun-Oman'. This name now refers to the Musandam Peninsula, which is indeed the 'threshold' of Oman from the direction of Iran. The term 'Oman' also existed at that period in the form of 'Umana', the name of port Sohar near Muscat.

The following verse is attributed to an Omani author, Sihan bin Sa'id:

The Kasra (Khosro Anushirvan) named Oman Maazun and
Maazun, oh friend; is a goodly land.
A land abounding in fields and groves
With pastures and unfailing spring.[10]

Referring to old historical geographies such as those by Tabari and Ya'qubi, concerning Iranian control of Masun (Oman) and the Musandam coasts of the Persian Gulf and Arab immigration to that region, Wilkinson points out that the Arabs enjoyed full autonomy in the desert borderlands and in much of northern Oman and the coast of the Gulf of Oman, where their capital was Tu'am and their main trading port Diba[11] or Daba on the Musandam Peninsula.[12] The Iranians, meanwhile, continued their direct rule in the interior of Masun (Oman) and the coastal regions of the Persian Gulf. Any Arabs living in these parts were treated in the same way as the rest of the inhabitants, generally referred to as *Shahrvand*, ie *Ahl al-Bilad* or citizens.

In order to consolidate Iranian control of the region, Khosro Anushirvan modified the old feudal organisation and established a military landed class (the Asvaran and Marzbanan) who were directly answerable to the Iranian governor installed in the interior of Masun at Rostaq, a locality which still bears the same name. Rostaq was chosen as a major fortified centre for three reasons: first, it had relatively easy access both to the major trading port of Umana (Sohar) where the main Iranian garrison was quartered at Dastgerd, and to the fort of Dama (near modern al-Sib) which controlled the southern end of the Batina coast; secondly, it lay in a region of major new land development; and thirdly, it was situated in the heart of the main Shanu'a settlement area.[13] The Iranian governor of Masun recognised the status of the Mawali Shaikh and appointed him as Julanda (*jelaudar*, leader) over the Arabs. He was accorded the right to collect taxes in Arab settlements, and was expected, in return, to maintain a discipline amongst the tribes.[14]

Arab and Islamic historians and geographers of the early Islamic era, such as Tabari, Mas'udi, Yaqubi, confirm that all areas of the Gulf belonged to Iran in the historical times. The 4th century AH Arab historian/geographer, Ibn Hauqal an-Nasibi al-Baghdadi, for example, states in his Surat al-Ardh:

> As has repeatedly been said: the Persian Sea is a gulf branching out of the ocean in the vicinity of China and Waqq country; and that is a sea which goeth forth from the vicinity of the countries of Sind and Kirman and Persia, and among all other countries it is named after Persia because there has been no other country around it more advanced than Persia; and, verily the kings of Persia had, from the ancient times, the strongest hold, and they have to this day, the strongest control of the places far and wide of this sea.[15]

Maqdasi, another Arab geographer/historian of the early Islamic centuries, states:

> most people call it [the gulf between Persia and Arabia] the Persian Sea as far as the Yemen and indeed are most of its shipbuilders and shipcaptains Persian . . . Most people in Aden and Jeddah are Persians . . . In Sohar they call each other by Persian names and speak Persian. Sohar is the centre of Oman . . . and most of its people are Persians.[16]

Confirmation of Iran's control of all areas of the Gulf in later periods can be found in European documents. Quoting documents of Portuguese-Safavid periods in his *Notes*, Captain Robert Taylor of British India, for instance, remarks:

. . . Since the Arabs have retaken Muskat (1620s), and the Portuguese have no strength in the Gulf, every man that goes a fishing pays to the king of Persia five Abbasees[17] only (the Portuguese used to extract 15), whether his success be good or bad. The merchant also pays some small trifle to the king, on every thousand oysters.[18]

The Aboriginal Iranians

Of the aboriginal Iranian inhabitants of the lower coasts of the Persian Gulf, at least two groups are identifiable: the Baharinahs of Bahrain (maritime and coastal); and the Komazerah of Shihuh of Musandam.

The Baharinahs of Bahrain

The aborigines of Bahrain (maritime and coastal), generally known as Baharinahs, are Shiah Muslims and their number in maritime Bahrain alone is estimated at more than 50,000. Their number in Qatar, Abu Dhabi and Saudi Arabia is not known. They have largely been absorbed by the local Arab population and thus considered by some as Arabs. Some others consider them as immigrants from Iran of the time immediately preceding the advent of Islam.

The Komazerah of Shihuh of Musandam

There are a number of theories on the origin of the Shihuh tribes. Colonel Wilson considers them as being 'a small negrito race, prior in origin to Semitic stock of Arabia.[19]

Oman a book of general information on the Sultanate of Oman, considers the people of Oman as of the same origin as the Persians and indicates that the present day Shihuh people are the descendants of the early people of the region who are darker than all other Arab tribes.[20]

In an article in the *Geographical Journal*, Walter Dastal asserts that Shihuh is composed of two original clans: an Arab clan and an Iranian clan. The Iranian clan of Shihuh, Komazerah is introduced as of Baluchi origin.[21]

Whereas the Iranian branch of the Shihuh confederation represents the original inhabitants of Musandam and northern Oman, the Arab branch is said to have arrived in southeast Arabia from Yemen in waves of immigration led by a certain Malek bin Fahm during the second century AD, and they are not of a single root. Islamic historical sources such as *Tarikh-e Tabari* and *Tarikh-e Masudi*, trace the origin of all Arab tribes of Arabia and beyond to Yemen.[22] Shihuh tribesmen speak in a particular language which is a combination of Arabic and Persian with some Indian words. Whereas some observers consider this language as an Arabic dialect[23] the aforesaid book from the Oman Ministry of Culture and Information indicates that the Shihuhs speak in two languages: Arabic and Persian.[24]

The two tribesmen from the Komazerah of the Shihuh who talked to this author in Khasab in December 1977, spoke in a Persian dialect much akin to the old Iranian languages spoken in the rural areas of Iran. Their Persian was barely comprehensible with vocabularies unknown in standard modern Persian.[25]

Politically, up until very recently, the Shihuh accepted no authority other than their own. Their attitude towards outside authorities had been hostile and it was not safe to enter their territories until recently. The Komazerah were in conflict with the Arab tribes of the region, and when British authority was established in support of the Qawasim (Qasemis) of Musandam in the first half of the nineteenth century, Komazerah and the Azd tribes of Musandam created the Shihuh confederation which remained independent until recent decades.

The Shihuh continued its independent attitude in spite of the political division of the region and the emergence of political boundaries in the 1950s and 1960s which allocated the Shihuh region to the Sultanate of Oman (former Muscat and Oman). It was only in 1976 when Sultan Qabus of Oman was welcomed during his visit of Shihuh district that Oman's jurisdiction over the Shihuh was openly acknowledged by the Shihuh themselves.[26]

THE MEDIEVAL SETTLERS

The main factors encouraging movements of population from the interior of Iran to the Gulf were those related to the development of the Gulf community.

With the advent of Islam, the process of conglomeration of a community particular to the Gulf began. Migration to the southern coasts continued from both Iran and the Arabian highland. Moreover, the Gulf very soon became a major centre of political movements against Arab caliphates of Damascus and Baghdad.

The Khawarej, the Qarmatian and the Zangis were of more noticeable movements in this period. Increased trade between the two shores, on the other hand, added to the impetus encouraging cultural mixture in the region. The new immigrants were gradually absorbed by the original settlers and by the immigrants of the earlier periods. Geographical location also brought the Gulf to the heart of the old world as great routes of trade had to pass through this region. These factors together with lucrative economic activities such as trade and pearl fishing strengthened the Gulf community. The most noticeable characteristics of this unique community are its racial and religious tolerance and mixture; and its unique language[27] and traditions, clearly different from those of both Persian and Arabic.

By the mid-eighteenth century, the Ottomans had succeeded in expanding their realm southward to include Basrah; the Otubi tribes – the Al-Sabah and Al-Khalifah – who had migrated from Najd to the northwestern corner of the Gulf in about 1710, established their control over Kuwait and Bahrain respectively in the mid-eighteenth century; the Qasemis of Musandam coasts and the Muscatis and Omanis expanded their authority in the northern areas of the Greater Musandam Peninsula and in the southeastern corner of the Gulf; the British gradually brought the southern half of the Persian Gulf under their control and by the mid-nineteenth century began implementation of their policy of 'depersianisation of the Persian Gulf'.

The most noticeable Iranian immigrants of this period to the southern coasts of the Gulf were Khamarah, Al-Bu Maher, Al-Ali, and the Bani Hawalah including Qasemi families of Sharjah and Ras al-Kheimah. Most of these immigrants became tribally organised in their new environment and now, on the whole, are known as Arabs.

THE GULF FROM THE ADVENT OF ISLAM TO THE SAFAVID ERA

The southern half of the Persian Gulf was known in the immediate post-Islamic centuries as 'Oman' to the east and 'Bahrain' to the west.

The first Arab conquest in the Gulf took place at the time of Omar, second Rashidin Caliph. Harrirah, a companion of the prophet of Islam, was assigned to conquer the Gulf region. First he conquered Bahrain, whence he extended his authority to the rest of the Gulf. At the time of 'Ali ibn Abi-Talib, the fourth Rashedin Caliph and the first Shiah Imam, an Azd Shaikh was assigned as governor of Oman. This governorate was overthrown shortly afterwards by the Khawarij, who had rebelled against both Ali and his adversary, Mu'awiya, founder of the Umayyad Caliphate of Damascus.

The Abbasid Caliph Mansur sent the Marvrudi Khazim bin Khuzaimeh, the fourth ruler of the Khuzaimeh dynasty in Khorasan, to put down the Khawarij movement in the Gulf. He was the first Iranian to subdue the Gulf in the post-Islamic era. The Khawarij movement was followed by another rebellion against the Caliphate by the followers of Sahib az-Zang. They gave way in turn to the Qarmatians, who extended their power over the entire Gulf region as far southwest as the Hijaz and Mecca.[28]

The Qarmatian movement was put down by another Iranian leader, the Buyid Amir Mo'ez ad-Dauleh Dailami (334–356/936–938). Although the Iranians began a revival of their identity and independence almost from the beginning of the emergence of the Arab Caliphate, and the Samanids and Saffarids ruled Iranian states (in 204/819–20 and 253/857–8 respectively), the Buyids were the first dynasty in the post-Islamic era to restore Iranian sovereignty in the Persian Gulf. Mo'ez ad-Dauleh and his nephew Amir Azod ad-Dauleh Dailami (356–367/967–977/8), the most significant ruler of the first post-Islamic Iranian dynasty, not only added Mesopotamia to their dominions, but recovered control of the southern Gulf in 367/977–8.[29]

In 456/1063 Emad ad-Dauleh captured Oman on behalf of the Seljuqs of Kerman from other local Persian authorities such as the Seljuqs of Fars. In the late twelfth century, Abu Bakr Sa'd-e Zangi, of the Atabegs of Fars, brought Oman, Bahrain and other parts of the southern coasts of the Gulf under his rule. Islands in the Gulf, including Greater Tunb, Lesser Tunb and Abu Musa, were dependencies of the Atabegs. Iranian domination of the lower Gulf continued until the arrival of the Portuguese in the region, and was revived by the Safavids.

Whereas the southern coastal regions of the Persian Gulf formed the southern flanks of the pre-Islamic Persian empires, under the post-Islamic Iranian authorities they became more of a contact zone between Iran and the Arabs of Arabia proper. In those time, of course, frontiers in the region were broad, undefined zones of contact between differing political entities; modern European concepts of territoriality and boundary were not introduced into the Gulf until the arrival of the British. Individual socio-political units, such as tribes or small independent local authorities living in these zones of contact, paid tribute and declared loyalty as they deemed expedient to either power situated at the two extremes of the frontier zone of the southern Gulf.

FROM THE SAFAVIDS TO MODERN TIMES

Starting in 1501, the Safavid Shahs restored Iran's full cultural independence and national identity. They recovered and consolidated Iran's traditional territorial dominions south of the Gulf, holding them undisturbed until the fall of the empire in the 1720s. The Safavids revived Sassanian traditions of political and administrative organisation and created 29 *ayalat* (autonomous provinces) and *beglerbegi* (semi-autonomous governorate-generals) in the country. One of these was the *ayalat* of Fars in southern Iran, which included all ports and islands of the Persian Gulf. Shiraz, capital of Fars, administered the affairs of the districts and islands of this *ayalat*, and received their taxes.[30] A Safavid prince was in charge of the *ayalat*, which effectively made it an autonomous principality.

This form of political and administrative organisation, vague as it was, remained in force until the late nineteenth century. Relations between the political centre of the country and the outer principalities and dependencies were not clearly defined; this was a distinct handicap, which began to be felt especially with the introduction to the region of new, more precise European systems of legal and political relations between the centre and peripheries.

Traditional ties between Iran and Muscat and Oman were loose. Not surprisingly, the movement of population between the two shores of the Gulf continued freely. The Qasemis of northern Oman were active in the 1720s on the northern shores and on Qeshm Island, giving no indication that they were operating within the jurisdiction of any state other than Iran.

After the chaos following the downfall of the Safavid empire, Nader Shah Afshar (1736–47) restored control throughout Iran. In the Gulf he brought stability, reasserting Iran's control of the northern sections of ancient Masun (Oman) in the 1730s. When war broke out in the 1740s between Sa'id bin Ahmad of Muscat and the Imam of Oman, and the Omanis asked for Iranian support, Nader Shah despatched troops stationed in the Musandam area to their aid.

> The Persians, after a number of setbacks, took both Muscat and Sohar, but Nadir's military commitments elsewhere prevented him from sending enough reinforcements for the 'invaders' to be able to retain their hold over the country. . . . The only tangible and lasting result of this expedition was the replacement of the decadent Ya'riba dynasty (of Oman) by the virile one of Al-Bu-Saids (of Muscat).[31]

The Muscat authority soon reactivated traditional ties with Iran without actually considering the northern sections of old Oman, the Musandam Peninsula, and other parts of the southern coasts as being anything but under a mixed Irano–Omani control. Iran's traditional position in those areas, albeit vaguely defined, enjoyed an ongoing *de facto* recognition.

After Nader Shah's assassination in 1747, Oman, Bahrain and the rest of the southern coasts of the Gulf began a life of their own, and Iran's control of its ports and islands in the Gulf fell once again into jeopardy. Meanwhile, the Ottomans succeeded in expanding their realm southward to include Basrah. The Utoobi tribes established control over Kuwait and Bahrain. The tribes of the Musandam Peninsula and other coasts of the lower Gulf, who had stayed peaceful during Nader's reign, resumed their old activities outside the Peninsula.[32] The Qasemis of the Musandam coasts and the Muscatis and Omanis extended their authority in the northern areas of the Greater Musandam Peninsula and in the southeastern corner of the Persian Gulf.

Disorder continued until Karim Khan Zand's rise to prominence in central and southern Iran in 1757. Unlike Nader Shah, the Zand leader, in his struggle for power in Iran, sought Arab friendship and co-operation on both shores. His leniency towards the Arab tribes proved advantageous for the Qasemis on their way to supremacy in the subsequent period. They began, as the British alleged to organise effective interference in maritime trade and commerce, and by the turn of the nineteenth century, their sea power had grown substantially.

Tribes such as the Qasemis roamed freely on land and at sea, benefiting from the vague and often confused state of sovereignty in their region between Iran and Oman. When there were outside threats to the region, however, Iranians and Omanis joined forces and defended their interrelated domains. The best example of this was at the turn of the nineteenth century, when the Wahhabis established control in parts of Musandam in 1803 and turned their attention towards Oman; an Irano–Muscati and Omani military alliance overthrew their authority and removed the threat.[33] This event further strengthened the mixture of Iranian, Muscati and Omani control in the coastal regions of the Lower Gulf. In due course, as we shall see, the rulers of Muscat and Oman entered a series of agreements with the Iranian government whereby the former ruled parts of the southern coasts of Iran and imposed their power on Bahrain and other coasts of the lower Gulf.

The rise to prominence of Russian and British powers in the eighteenth and nineteenth centuries, and Iran's location to the south of the former and west of the latter (the British Indian Empire), had an immense impact on Iranian political geography. The two wars fought with the Russians, concluding with the Treaties of Golestan (1813) and Turkmanchay (1828), together with the Anglo–Persian peace treaty of Paris (1857), signalled Iran's territorial disintegration.

The arrival of the British in the Persian Gulf, and the expansion of their imperial activities in the region, introduced a new and powerful challenge to Iranian authority and influence, and was instrumental in introducing European concepts of territoriality and boundaries, with which Iran was totally unfamiliar. Traditionally, rights to territory had been intermingled in the southern parts of the Gulf and northern Oman, where Iranians and Omanis had lived side by side for centuries without any dividing line between them. The whole area was the frontier or the zone of contact between Iran and Oman. The offshore islands were considered by common consent to be under direct Iranian sovereignty, yet nothing prevented the tribes of the southern Gulf territories, under common ownership, from living and working in the islands or in the northern coasts of the Gulf. People from the southern coasts could travel freely to Iran and live there indefinitely even as recently as 1945.[34] It was only in the 1950s that the Iranian authorities introduced official restrictions on border-crossings in the Gulf, at the time when British arbitrator Julian Walker began defining territories and boundaries within the emirates, giving them territorial statehood. When considering this whole situation, it is not surprising that ownership of the territories of the southern coasts of the Gulf were traditional, ill-defined (from a modern legal point of view) and unsupported by legally binding written descriptions, whereas Iran's ownership of the Gulf islands was undisputed.

Having established themselves as the masters of the eastern waters, the British considered control of the Persian Gulf and the Strait of Hormuz to be essential for the security of India. Expansion of their influence in the region inevitably challenged Iran's actual possessions and political posture.[35] They began implementing a policy of severing the traditional ties in the region. This policy involved curbing Iranian influence by separating as many islands and coastal districts from Iran as was possible. With this priority they moved forces into the Gulf on the pretext of eradicating acts of alleged piracy by the tribes of the lower Gulf. British naval units, commanded by General Sir William Grant Keir, attacked Jolfar (now Ras al-Khaimah) and defeated

Qasemi forces in 1819. A treaty was signed in February 1820 with five shaikhs of the Musandam Peninsula, whereby they brought their tribes under British control. Articles 3, 6 and 10 of this treaty provided some hints of British recognition of these tribal units, for the first time, as political entities independent of each other and of neighbouring states. Article 3, for instance, allowed the tribal chiefs

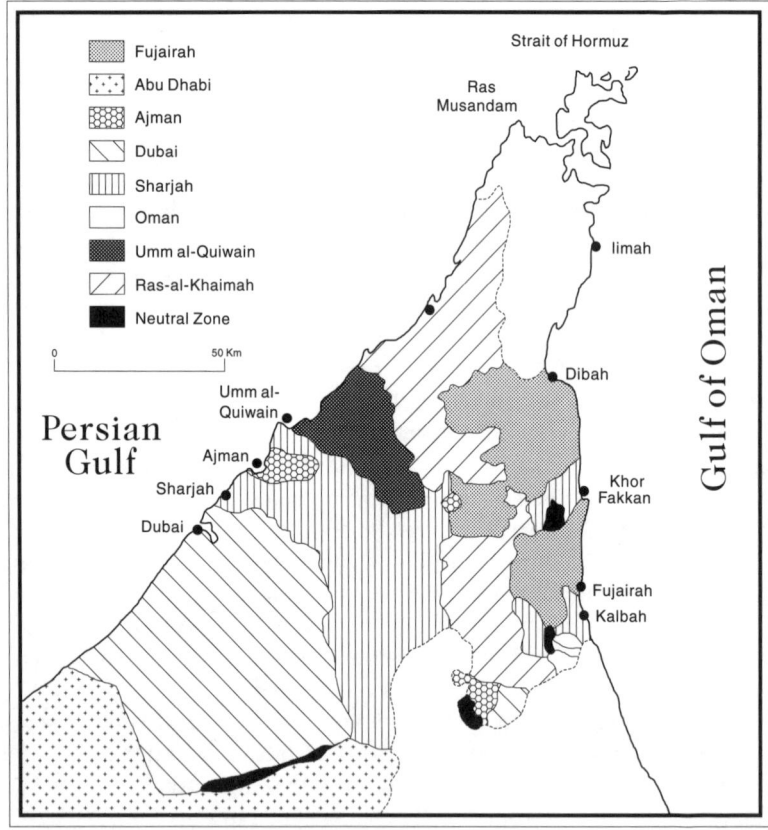

Figure 3.1 Territorial division amongst the seven emirates forming the United Arab Emirates

(The Emirates of the Musandam Peninsula (Members of the United Arab Emirates) were created after the signing of the treaty of 1820 with the British, and the territorial divisions of the late 1950s and early 1960s. Together they created the United Arab Emirates in 1971.)

signatory to the treaty to 'carry by land and sea a red flag, with or without letters on it'.[36] This was to become the independent tribes' flag of identity, while their transformation into territorial states had to wait for more than a century.

Chapter 4

Maritime Boundaries in the Persian Gulf

INTRODUCTION

As the government of Great Britain announced in January 1968 the decision of withdrawing Pax-Britannica from the Gulf, the states in the region developed a sense of urgency for closer co-operation that would enable them to fill the gap potentially emerging in the wake of the British withdrawal. To this end, settlement of outstanding territorial and boundary differences became a necessity, especially in the offshore areas of the Gulf where exploration and exploitation of new oilfields was expanding rapidly.

This expansion in offshore oil exploitation underlined the urgency of defining various states' boundaries before the matter developed into an issue of conflict.[1] Iran had in 1965 started negotiations with the British for offshore boundaries settlements in the Gulf, but successful negotiations had to wait until the late 1960 and 1970s.

The Anglo–Iranian negotiations, however, established the median line of the Persian Gulf as a principle upon which the continental shelf between Iran and her Arab neighbours was to be divided in that sea. It was on the basis of this principle that the subsequent continental shelf delimitation agreements in the Persian Gulf were achieved.[2]

On 11 February 1966 Mohammad Reza Amir Teimur of the Iranian Ministry of Foreign Affairs and Sir Roger Allen of British Foreign Office initialled an agreed minute in which Iran on the one side, and Great Britain on behalf of its protectorate Arab states of the Persian Gulf, on the other, reaffirmed the principle of the median line of the Persian Gulf as the basis for dividing the continental shelf of that sea, and divided the Iran–Qatar continental shelf.[3]

The issue of defining the baseline for determining the width of territorial sea has been considered since the 1930 conference at The Hague. The 1958 Geneva Convention determined methods of defining the baseline which have largely been adopted by the 1982 UN Convention of the Law of the Sea. Articles 4 to 14 and 16 deal with seven possible geographical shapes of coastal lines, most of which apply to the coastal lines of the Persian Gulf.

With an area of 60,000 square miles and an average depth of about 165 feet, the whole of the Gulf is an extended continental shelf, and its geographical shape – a curved rectangle – put Iranian territories on the one hand, and territories of most Arab states of the lower Gulf on the other, on opposite sides to each other. Such a geographical situation necessitated the consideration of a median line down the Gulf. But the problem was that different states claimed different base lines. The location of different islands – claimed by some governments to be the base line – added further complications to the matter. Solving this whole area of disagreement needed real co-operation and understanding which was, at the time, elevated by the announcement of the said British decision.

Iran had announced on 15 July 1934 her territorial waters in the Persian Gulf, Strait of Hormuz and Gulf of Oman to be six miles from the low-water marks of her coastline. On March 19, 1949 Iran announced her rights to continental shelf oil exploration. Thereafter the littoral Arab states of the lower Gulf followed Iran's example and each issued a similar declaration: Saudi Arabia on 29 May 1949; Qatar on 8 June 1949; Abu Dhabi on 10 June 1949; Kuwait on 12 June 1949; Dubai on 14 June 1949; Sharjah on 16 June 1949; and Umm al-Quwain and Ajman on 20 June 1949.[4]

On 18 May 1955 Iran claimed the seabed resources of its continental shelf in the Persian Gulf, Strait of Hormuz and the Gulf of Oman. On 22 April 1959 Iran changed the limits of her territorial sea from six to 12 nautical miles in the Persian Gulf and the Gulf of Oman[5] and later claimed an area adjacent to her territorial sea, as her contiguous zone, the outer limit of which is 24 nautical miles from the baseline.

Iran and the Arab states of the region have claimed exclusive fisheries zones of their own and continental shelf claims extended to continental shelf boundaries to be established at the equidistant lines. In the Gulf of Oman, Iran has claimed an exclusive fisheries zone extending to the equidistant line with the United Arab Emirates and Oman.

Anticipating the existence of oil or gas structures across future boundaries in the maritime areas of the Persian Gulf, Iran decided to enforce a provision in her continental shelf agreements with the states on the opposite side of the sea preventing inappropriate exploitation of such structures.

According to this provision, which appeared in all Iran's continental shelf boundary agreements in the region, if a petroleum structure extends across the boundary and could be exploited from the other side of the boundary, then (i) there shall be no sub-surface well completion within 410 feet of the boundary (1640 feet in the case of maritime boundary with Saudi Arabia) without the mutual agreement of the two parties; and (ii) the two parties shall attempt to agree on co-ordination or unitisation of operations with respect to such structures.

In the Persian Gulf, like elsewhere in the world, the laws concerning maritime areas of littoral states have developed gradually. Among others in this region the government of Iran compiled all its laws of maritime areas of the Persian Gulf and Oman Sea in one single comprehensive text in 1993. This single act was protested against by the government of the United States in January 1994 and the US protest was replied to by the government of the Islamic Republic of Iran in the same year. Both texts and the act itself contain many important legal aspects of maritime delimitations which go beyond the scope of the main discussion of this book on maritime political geography. These texts are, therefore, reproduced at the end of this chapter in the form of an appendix as an example of the legal aspects of maritime delimitations of the world in general, and of the Persian Gulf in particular.[6]

However, in 1960 Oman and the Yemen had granted fishing concessions to Japan, the Soviet Union and South Korea in their Exclusive Fishing Zone in the Gulf of Oman and the Arab Sea. To clarify the inherent obscurity of this undertaking, Oman declared in 1981, an Exclusive Economic Zone in its adjacent waters. The limits of these zones were still uncertain until the United Nations declared in 1982, that all coastal states are entitled to a 200 nautical mile Exclusive Economic Zone. This UN law of sea convention not only standardised the 200 nautical miles of the body of sea as the EEZ entitlement of the coastal states, but also standardised the territorial waters of the coastal states to 12 nautical miles offshore.[7] Nevertheless, by reason of their on-going territorial disputes with Bahrain and Iran, the governments of Qatar and the United Arab Emirates officially declared their belts of territorial waters at 12 nautical miles as late as 1992 and 1993 respectively.

The eight states littoral to the Persian Gulf need, at least, 16 continental shelf boundaries among them (for the purpose of this study, internal United Arab Emirates' boundaries are not considered). Of these 16 continental shelf boundaries, seven have been negotiated of which the following six have entered into force: Bahrain–Saudi Arabia, Iran–Saudi Arabia, Iran–Bahrain, Qatar–Iran, Qatar–United Arab Emirates (Abu Dhabi), Iran–Oman. There are at least ten other continental shelf boundaries to be settled in the region. These are: Iran–United Arab Emirates; Oman–United Arab Emirates (one undefined boundary in the Persian Gulf and two boundary lines in the Gulf of Oman and Arab sea); Qatar–Saudi Arabia (the case of Dohat al-Salwa); Saudi Arabia–Qatar (the case of Khor al-Adid; Saudi Arabia–Abu Dhabi (the case of Khor al-Adid); Kuwait–Iran (the case of Golden Triangle) which has been negotiated; Kuwait–Iraq (the case of Golden Triangle); Kuwait–Saudi Arabia; Iran–Iraq (the case of Golden Triangle); Bahrain–Qatar (the case of Hawar Islands).

Of these the Iran–United Arab Emirates continental shelf boundaries appear to be the most complicated of the kind in the Gulf, not only because there are seven emirates of the UAE each claiming its own continental shelf limits, but also because of the joint Iranian–Sharjah sovereignty exercised in Abu Musa island.

The Oman–United Arab Emirates continental shelf boundaries are not defined owing to the age-old inland boundary disputes in the Musandam Peninsula between Oman and the emirates of Sharjah in the Gulf of Oman and Ras al-Kheimah in the Persian Gulf.

The Saudi Arabia–Qatar and UAE continental shelf is not divided mainly owing to the Qatar–Bahrain dispute over the Hawar Archipelago in the al-Salwa Bay on the one side of the Qatar Peninsula, and the complication that the 1974 Saudi Arabia–Abu Dhabi boundary agreement has caused in the Khor al-Udayd Bay on the other. It was announced in October 1996 that Saudi Arabia and Qatar jointly commissioned a French company to demarcate their mutual inland boundaries.

The Iraq–Kuwait maritime boundaries are not negotiated because of the two states' inland territorial and boundary disputes which automatically include the offshore areas of the two countries.

Kuwait, on the other hand, has not been able to define her continental shelf limits with Saudi Arabia owing to their disagreements on the question of sovereignty over the islands of Kubbor, Qaruh and Umm al-Maradim.

Defining the Iran–Iraq continental shelf boundaries in the so-called Golden Triangle will depend, on the one hand, on the settlement of Iraq–Kuwait territorial and boundary disputes, and on the other, it will depend on the final settlement of Iran–Iraq boundary dispute in the Shatt al-Arab.

Official delimitation of the continental shelf boundaries between Iran and Kuwait is similarly prevented by territorial and boundary disputes between Iraq and Kuwait albeit the two signed a draft agreement in 1962 governing their mutual maritime areas. Here also Iran believes that its baseline must start from Kark Island as it did in the case of maritime boundary delimitation with Saudi Arabia. Kuwait, in response, claims that its baseline must start from its Failakah Island which is situated in the middle of the sea and this is not acceptable to Iran.

Bahrain and Qatar have not been able to negotiate delimitation of their continental shelf boundaries owing to their conflicting claims of sovereignty over the Hawar Archipelago which will be discussed in the third section of this book.

The six continental shelf boundaries, defined and delimited in the Gulf, are between the following countries: Bahrain–Saudi Arabia, Iran–Saudi Arabia, Qatar–Iran, Iran–Bahrain, Qatar–UAE, Iran–Oman.

BAHRAIN–SAUDI ARABIA

Bahrain and Saudi Arabia were the first states to define their maritime boundaries in the Gulf. This boundary agreement was signed on 22 February 1958 and came into effect on 26 February of that year.

Defiance of Iran's claims of sovereignty over Bahrain Archipelago – vigorously pursued in the 1950s and 1960s – were thought in Tehran to have been the motivation for the signing of this agreement. This is why Iran protested to Saudi Arabia against the signing of this agreement with Bahrain.

The agreed boundary between Saudi Arabia and Bahrain represents a negotiated settlement and should not be characterised as an equidistant line, albeit the first article of the agreement states that the boundary is based on 'the median line'. The boundary is determined as a line of 14 midpoints between preselected and agreed coastal points. Low tide elevations and location of small islands were ignored in this selection process.

Geographical landmarks of both states are cited in Article 1 of the agreement, but precise co-ordinate values are not given for the turning or terminal points. While the turning or terminal points are equidistant between the two selected coastal points, other coastal features may be closer to the boundary (see Figure 4.1). A hexagon has been delimited north of Bahrain, virtually within which Saudi Arabian jurisdiction is identified where revenue

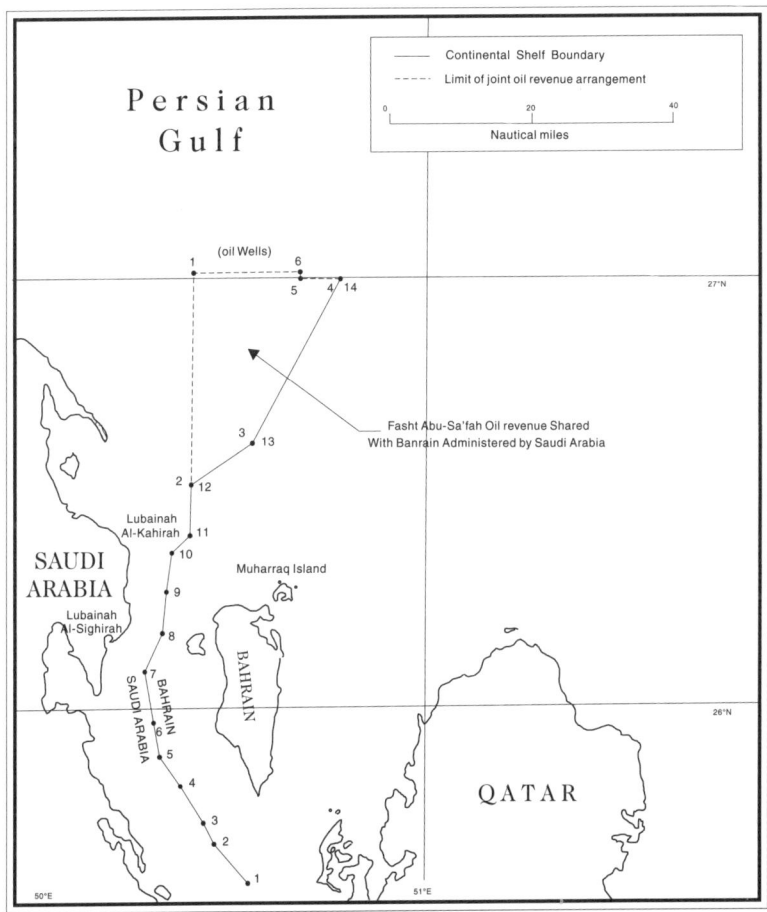

Figure 4.1 Saudi Arabia–Bahrain Continental Shelf Boundaries (based on the map appearing in *Limits in the Sea* No. 94)

gained from hydro-carbon exploitation is to be shared with Bahrain.[8]

The Bahrain–Saudi Arabian maritime boundary delimitation of 1958 was not only the first of its kind to be agreed in the Gulf region, but also was the first of its kind to incorporate the sharing of revenues from seabed resources.[9] Bahrain had long claimed this maritime area and the islands of Greater and Lesser Lubianah. The Bahrain Petroleum Company (BAPCO) began operating in the region of these islands in 1941.

These operations were suspended in 1941 after objections from Saudi Arabia. A few years later it appeared that the two sides were about to agree on the division of the Bu Saafah seabed area, but the Anglo–Saudi frontier complications deadlocked these negotiations. It was perceived by the British in 1957 that the Saudis were considering the Bu Saafah hexagon to be divided equally between the two sides.[10] A year later (1958) during his state visit to Saudi Arabia, the Ruler of Bahrain conceded Bu Saafah to a shared Saudi–Bahrain zone in return for a permanent half share of the oil revenues of that area's oilfield. In effect, the Ruler of Bahrain obligingly more or less gave away Fasht Bu Saafah to Saudi Arabia.[11]

In a report to the Ministry of Foreign Affairs, Iran's ambassador in India reported in March 1958:

> As has been learnt from reliable sources, a highly placed official of the government of Bahrain, by the name of Yusof Shiravi departed for Riyadh on Wednesday carrying with him the text of an agreement signed by Shaikh Salman bin Hamid Al-Khalifa, for the signature of the King of Saudi Arabia. According to this agreement, the ruler of Bahrain undertakes to transfer oil resources situated in the Bahraini territorial waters to the government of Saudi Arabia in return for receiving 50 per cent of the oil income from the wells dug by Saudi Arabia.
>
> Meanwhile, the British political representative residing in Bahrain has also accepted this agreement on behalf of his government and a memorandum concerning this is due to be issued within the next one day or two . . .[12]

Whether or not the ruler of Bahrain gave away Bu Saafah maritime areas or transferred them to the Saudis, this agreement left the technical management of Bu Saafah entirely in the hands of Saudi Arabia. Production from this field began in 1966 and Saudi Arabia began to share the revenue from it with Bahrain in 1974.

Income from this source has for many years equalled half of Bahrain's oil income. Saudi Arabia decided in late December 1992 to allow Bahrain to receive 70 per cent of all revenue from the field for a period of two years.

IRAN–SAUDI ARABIA

The continental shelf boundary agreement between Iran and Saudi Arabia was signed in 1968. Continental shelf legal experts consider this boundary agreement as a unique example of a new maritime boundary settlement.[13]

The part of the Persian Gulf where this boundary line is defined is 138.7 nautical miles wide. Nevertheless, coastlines considered in the negotiations for this agreement are between 95 to 135 nautical miles with the deepest point being 246 feet.

For years the two countries had experienced a complex dispute in the areas of their mutual offshore boundaries. The dispute included the question of ownership of the two Farsi and Al-Arabyah islands and the overlapping oilfields of their claims. Both Iran and Saudi Arabia had granted concessions to different oil companies. When the overlapping areas of the two concessions were realised, the two countries decided to settle the problem on the basis of the international principle of median line. The problem which slowed down the progress of negotiations was that Iran insisted on the low water mark of Khark Island be considered as the base line. But Saudi Arabia insisted on a shore-to-shore median line with no regard to Khark or any other island.

Interviewed by this author on Thursday 4 April 1996, Dr Parviz Mina, Iran's chief technical negotiator in the continental shelf delimitation negotiations of 1968 with Saudi Arabia, disclosed that:

> Initially, the uncompromising Saudi posture led to the continental shelf delimitation between Iran and Saudi Arabia being negotiated on the basis of no effect for Khark Island. Such an arrangement would naturally shift the boundary line closer to the Iranian coasts in an area of the sea with substantial oil deposits and highly valuable seabed resources.
>
> Learning of the particulars of this method of maritime settlement, the Shah was not accommodating; he asked us to find ways of giving full effect to the geographical situation of Khark Island in the delimitation calculations. Fortunately King Faisal had enough goodwill to accept a proposal for solution based on giving half effect to Khark Island.
>
> Not only did this adjustment shift the boundary line to the proper median line of the Persian Gulf, but gave Iran her rightful share of the huge oil resources of the border area.

Negotiations continued however, until 24 October 1968 when Iran and Saudi Arabia successfully delimited their mutual continental shelf boundary on the basis of:[14]

1 recognising Iran's sovereignty of Farsi Island and Saudi Arabian ownership of Al-Arabyah Island;
2 territorial waters of 12 nautical miles from the low water mark of the two islands of Farsi and Al-Arabyah; to be respected for both islands, but where they overlap, the median line would run half-way between them (see Figure 4.2);
3 recognition of Khark Island's low water mark as part of Iran's mainland coast line, and delimitation of the median line on that basis;
4 a 1640 feet oil exploration restriction area to be applied to either side of the entire length of the median line which would prevent the two parties from drilling diagonally for oil from the other side.[15]

This agreement was signed on 24 October 1968 and enacted on 29 January 1969.

Article 3 cites the co-ordinates of the turning and terminal points:

(a) Except in the vicinity of Al-Arabiyah and Farsi, the boundary line is determined by straight lines between the following points whose latitude and longitude are as specified below:

Point	Northing	Easting
1	27° 10.0'	50° 54.0'
2	27° 18.5'	50° 45.5'
3	27° 26.5'	50° 37.0'
4	27° 56.5'	50° 17.5'
5	28° 08.5'	50° 06.5'
6	28° 17.6'	49° 56.2'
7	28° 21.0'	49° 50.9'
8	28° 24.7'	49° 47.8'
9	28° 24.4'	49° 47.4'
10	28° 27.9'	49° 42.0'
11	28° 34.8'	49° 39.7'
12	28° 37.2'	49° 36.2'
13	28° 40.9'	49° 33.5'
14	28° 41.3'	49° 34.3'

(b) In the vicinity of Al-Arabiyah and Farsi, a line laid down as follows:

At the point where the line described in paragraph (a) intersects the limit of the belt of Farsi, the boundary shall follow the limit of the belt on the side facing Saudi Arabia until it meets the boundary line set forth in Article 1 which divides the territorial seas of Farsi and Al-Arabiyah; thence it shall follow that line easterly until it meets the limit of the belt of territorial sea around Al-Arabiyah; thence it shall follow the limit of that belt on the side facing Iran until it intersects again the line described in paragraph (a)'[16]

Figure 4.2 Iran–Saudi Arabian Continental Shelf Boundaries

The boundary is 138.7 nautical miles in length and has 16 turning and terminal points of above description. In the south this boundary joins the Iran–Bahrain continental shelf boundary. Small Saudi Arabian islands have not been given effect in the calculation of the equidistant line. For the northern 25 percent of the boundary, the Iranian island of Khark has been given half-effect on the determination of the equidistant line. Khark is situated approximately 17 nautical miles from the Iranian mainland and has an area of about 12 square nautical miles. In principle, this segment of the boundary generally has been determined by calculating equidistant lines giving full weight to Khark base points and then disregarding completely the effect of the island and then splitting the areal difference. From the agreement it is not known for certain if this was the exact method utilised.[17]

Considering enormous complications caused by various claims from both Iran and Saudi Arabia, it is not impossible to imagine that this boundary would not have been settled in an ordinary circumstance in the region for many years. Settlement of these boundaries with all their complications needed expediency, goodwill and indulgence from both governments. These were exercised owing to the political urgency that had emerged as a result of the announcement in January 1968 by the British government of withdrawing their presence from the Gulf by December 1971. There were a number of coincidences in Iranian and Saudi Arabian political considerations at the time which assisted a speedy settlement of this boundary dispute: both governments had special relations with the United States which encouraged co-operation between the two for the preservation of status quo and stability in the region in the wake of British withdrawal from the Gulf; both governments were determined to keep the Soviet Union's geopolitical ambitions in the Persian Gulf at bay; and both governments were determined to counter strategic threats posed by the Baathist regime of Iraq in the region. This coincidence of political considerations, further strengthened by the British announcement, created the political urgency which encouraged the two governments to employ their top experts to settle their mutual boundary complications.

QATAR–IRAN

Following its continental shelf boundary agreement with Saudi Arabia in 1968, Iran moved to delimit similar boundaries with other states on the opposite side of the Persian Gulf. Qatar was, at the time, the only Arab state of the region, other than Saudi Arabia, ready and able to enter such agreements with her neighbours.

Iran and Qatar are situated opposite each other on the Persian Gulf. Their continental shelf boundary, which was delimited on the equidistance, is approximately 131 nautical miles in length and involves six turning and terminal points. It runs in a northwesterly-southeasterly direction in the central part of the Persian Gulf (see Figure 4.3). The precise location of the terminal point in the northwest will not be known until a Bahrain–Qatar boundary is calculated. In the southeast, the terminal point coincides with the northern terminal point of the Qatar–Abu Dhabi maritime boundary. Here, Qatar had in the same year (1969) delimited a continental shelf boundary with Abu Dhabi. The northward terminus of this boundary was defined in the two states' agreement by specific geographic co-ordinates. Iran and Qatar used this same point, which is approximately equidistant from Iran, Qatar and Abu Dhabi, as the southern terminus of their boundary. The course of the boundary is described in Article 1 of the treaty as:

> The demarcation line separating the territory of Iran on the one hand and that of Qatar on the other merges with the geodesic line linking following points:
> **Point (1)** is the one located at the extreme western part of the most western zone of the demarcation line north of the continental shelf belonging to Qatar and which is linked to **point (2)** below at an angle of 27.8°, 14', 27" by a geodesic demarcation line.

Latitude	Longitude
Point (2) 27° 0' 35"	51° 23' 00"
" (3) 26° 56' 20"	51° 44' 50"
" (4) 26° 33' 25"	52° 12' 10"
" (5) 26° 06' 20"	52° 42' 30"
" (6) 25° 31' 50"	53° 02' 05"[18]

These boundaries were negotiated on the basis of the two mainlands' actual coastlines according to the negotiations and agreements of Iran and Britain in 1966. This meant that Iran had ignored the pertinancy of the geographical situation of its islands of Kish, Lavan and Hendorabi in this agreement. This was done on the understanding that Iran's undisputed sovereignty over these islands was acknowledged.[19]

Since Iran was still claiming sovereignty over Bahrain at the time of the negotiations with Qatar, together with the fact that Qatar and Bahrain had no continental shelf boundary between them for reasons of their own territorial disputes, locating a northwestern terminus of the Iran-Qatar boundary became a major difficulty. This forced the Iranians make a decision particularly on specifying the northwestern point of the start of their continental shelf boundary with Qatar. In a report to the Minister of Foreign Affairs, the Legal Department of that ministry stated in 1968 that:

> It has been commented in that context that Bahrain islands, situated on the west of Qatar peninsula, are indivisible parts of Iran – in any event they have separate continental shelf and the spot where borders of Iran's mainland's continental shelf and these islands and Qatar peninsula come together can be accepted as the western point of the start of Iran–Qatar continental shelf boundaries.'[20]

The northwestern terminal point on the Iran–Qatar boundary was, thus, described as lying on a specified azimuth.

Economic considerations motivated the parties to delimit the boundary but did not affect its location. Qatar had issued offshore concessions to the Continental Oil Company, the Shell Company of Qatar Petroleum Company Limited, and Iran had granted offshore concessions to Iranian Offshore Petroleum Company and Lavan Petroleum Company.

Anticipating the existence of a trans-boundary petroleum structure, which later materialised in the form of a huge natural gas field, the agreement contains a provision that would appear in all Iran's subsequent continental shelf boundary agreements, providing that, a petroleum structure extends across the boundary and could be exploited by directional drilling from the other side of the boundary, then:

(i) there shall be no sub-surface well completion within 410 feet of the boundary without the mutual agreement of the parties; and

(ii) the parties shall attempt to agree on co-ordination or unitization of operations with respect to such structures.

Environmental considerations were not taken into account in the delimitation. From the point of view of legal regime, the agreement deals exclusively with continental shelf jurisdiction. It expressly states that it does not affect the status of the superjacent waters or airspace.

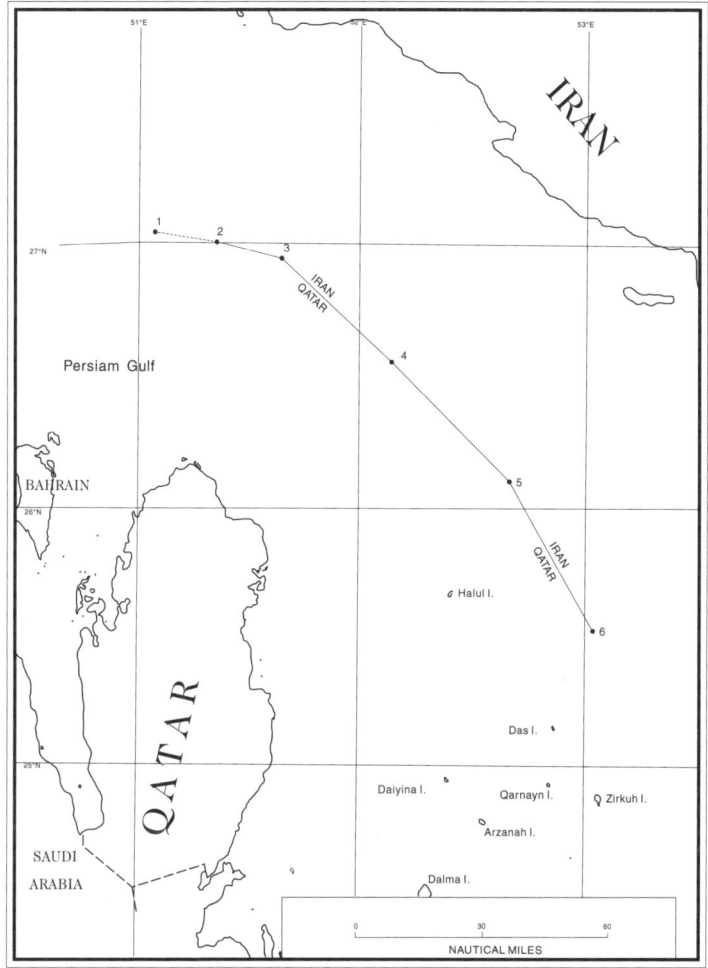

Figure 4.3 Iran–Qatar Continental Shelf Boundaries
Based on the map appearing in Limits in the Sea No. 94

Geographically, the opposite relationship of the parties' coasts was
the predominant factor affecting the location of the boundary, which
was delimited by use of the equidistance method, whereas geology
and geomorphology did not affect the delimitation. The seabed in the
vicinity of the boundary averages only 100–265 feet in depth and
contains no significant relief features.

The delimitation was part of an effort by Iran to establish her continental shelf boundaries in the Persian Gulf for economic reasons and for reasons of political geography. Iran had declared a system of straight baselines at the time of the agreement. This claim did not affect the delimitation, however. The boundary was delimited using the equidistance method, disregarding islands, rocks, reefs and low-tide elevations. The boundary was delimited so as to be equidistant from the nearest points on the coast of the opposite's mainland territories. It consists of geodetic lines connecting the turning and terminal points, illustrated on British Admiralty Chart No. 2837, copies of which were signed by representatives of both governments.[21] This agreement was executed in Persian, Arabic and English languages, all text being equally authoritative.

This maritime boundary agreement was signed on 20 September 1969, and entered into force upon the exchange of instrument of ratification on 10 May 1970.[22]

IRAN–BAHRAIN

In 1971, shortly after Iran's claims of sovereignty to the Bahrain archipelago were withdrawn, the two states entered negotiations aimed at defining their mutual boundaries.

The actual task of delimitation of the Iran–Bahrain continental shelf areas was not complicated at all. But, Bahrain's disputes with Qatar over the Hawar archipelago, which has prevented delimitation of continental shelf boundaries between them, was a matter of some concern. Nevertheless, since the northern tip of the two states' continental shelf boundary could not differ much from whichever way the Bahrain–Qatar continental shelf boundaries went, conclusion of the Iran-Bahrain treaty of 17 June 1971 met little difficulty.[23]

Article 1 of the treaty specifies the course of the boundary line as follows:

The line dividing the continental shelf lying between the territory of Iran on the one side and the territory of Bahrain on the other side shall consist of geodetic lines between the following points in the sequence hereinafter set out:

Point (1) is the easternmost point on the easternmost part of the northern boundary line of the continental shelf appertaining to Bahrain as formed by the intersection of a line starting from the point having the latitude of 27° 00' 35" N longitude

88

51° 23' 00" E, and having a geodetic azimuth of 278° 14' 27", with a boundary line dividing the continental shelf appertaining to Bahrain and Qatar, thence:

	Northing	Easting
Point (2)	27° 02' 46"	51° 05' 54"
Point (3)	27° 06' 30"	50° 57' 00"
Point (4)	27° 10' 00"	50° 54' 00".[24]

The Iran–Bahrain agreement delimits the continental shelf boundary of the maritime area of the two countries in the central part of the Persian Gulf.

This boundary extends for a distance of 28.28 nautical miles, and connects four points by straight lines. The terminal points of the agreed boundary were determined by Iran's existing boundary with Qatar and Saudi Arabia. Point 1 of the boundary is undermined and is to coincide with point 2 of the Iran–Qatar boundary of 1969, and point 4 coincides with point 1 of the Iran–Saudi Arabian boundary of 1968.

These points are not equidistant from the nearest points on the two countries' land territories. Terminal point 1 (eastern) of this boundary is approximately 10 nautical miles closer to the Iranian coasts than those of Bahrain, and terminal point 4 (western) is approximately 5 nautical miles closer to Iran than to Bahrain. This occurred probably because of Bahrain's location in the sea which makes the Iran–Bahrain median line at point 4 of this boundary fall about 5 nautical miles south of the general Arab–Iranian median line in the Persian Gulf. The Iranians must have agreed on bringing the two countries' median line at point 4 to the said general median line in the Persian Gulf. These two terminal points, nevertheless, appear to have been established by use of the equidistance method. This can be attributed to the scale of the particular hydrographic chart used to plot these points.

The agreement which was signed on 17 June 1971, entered into force upon the exchange of instruments of ratification on 14 May 1972.[25]

Geographically, the equidistance method was used to establish the turning and terminal points on this boundary reflecting the opposite relationship of the two countries' coasts, while neither geology nor geomorphology played a role in the delimitation of this boundary. The waters in the vicinity of this boundary are quite shallow, but on the deep scale of the Persian Gulf average, ranging from approximately

200 to 250 feet. The sea bed is relatively flat and devoid of any distinguishing geomorphological features.

Delimitation of this boundary was primarily motivated by economic considerations. Both Iran and Bahrain had granted offshore concessions prior to the delimitation to various companies.

The preamble to the agreement states that the parties are 'desirous of establishing in a just, equitable and precise manner', the boundary between their respective continental shelves. The boundary line has been illustrated on the British Admiralty Chart No. 2847 (scale 1:750,000) and consists of geodetic lines joining the co-ordinated points.

Although Iran has claimed a straight baseline system, this claim did not affect the location of the two equidistant turning points on the boundary. The Iranian islands of Nakhilu and Jabrin were, nevertheless, given full effect in the location of the two equidistant turning points because the islands were within Iran's straight baselines. These islands are situated slightly more than 3 miles off the Iranian mainland.

The Bahraini island of Al-Moharraq (which is that country's second most important island and is connected to Bahrain's main island, Manamah, by a causeway) was considered a part of the Bahrain's mainland for delimitation purposes.

With respect to trans-boundary deposits, the agreement provides that if a petroleum structure extends across the boundary and could be exploited by directional drilling from the other side of the boundary then:

(i) there shall be no sub-surface well completion within 410 feet of the boundary without the mutual consent of the parties; and
(ii) the parties shall attempt to agree on co-ordination or unitization of operations with respect to such structures.

As for the legal regime considerations, the agreement delimits the boundary 'between the respective areas of the continental shelf over which [the two countries] have sovereign rights in accordance with international law . . . ' It provides further that 'nothing in this Agreement shall affect the status of the superjacent waters or air-space above any part of the continental shelf'. Iran subsequently claimed exclusive fisheries jurisdiction in the Persian Gulf coextensive with its continental shelf jurisdiction.

This treaty provides for a 410 feet restricted zone on either sides of the line, within which the two governments are prohibited from

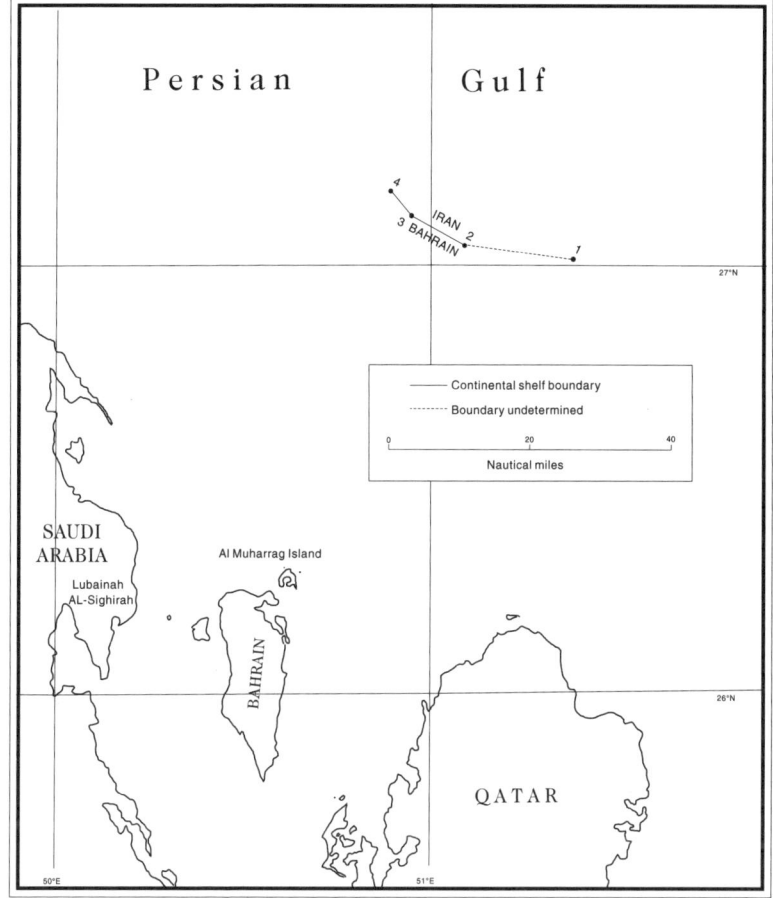

Figure 4.4 Iran–Bahrain Continental Shelf Boundary
based on the map appearing in Limits in the Sea No. 94 (1981)

drilling for oil.[26] The agreement was reached on the basis of the British Admiralty map No. 28447.[27]

The Iran–Qatar agreement, which was signed some 21 months earlier than the Bahrain–Iran agreement, appears to reflect an assumption that the Bahrain–Qatar boundary, when eventually determined, would intersect the common geodesic to the west of the eastern extreme point (as otherwise no point would exist which would satisfy the description of point 1 in the Iran–Qatar agreement).[28] The

Iran–Qatar agreement does not, however, impose a westward limit on the location of the intersection point. The point at 27°02' 46" N 51°05' 54" E (the *western extreme point*), which is point 2 of the Bahrain–Iran agreement, is not referred to in the Iran–Qatar Agreement. The Iran–Qatar agreement does not, therefore, *per se* prevent Qatar from claiming a boundary which will intersect the common geodesic at or west of the western extreme point.

The Bahrain–Iran agreement, for its part, appears to reflect an assumption that the Bahrain–Qatar boundary, when eventually determined, would intersect the common geodesic to the east of the western point (as otherwise no point would exist which would satisfy the description of point 1 in the Bahrain–Iran agreement).[29] The Bahrain–Iran agreement also appears to assume that this intersection would be located to the west of the eastern extreme point. Qatar may argue on the basis of this assumption that Bahrain, having signed the Bahrain–Iran agreement, may not today claim a boundary which will intersect the common geodesic at or east of the eastern extreme point.

It seems difficult to believe that Iran would have signed agreements with Qatar and Bahrain respectively which might give rise to conflicts between the two countries' respective claims, without protecting itself against the possibility of such conflicts. One is therefore tempted to speculate that Qatar may have assured Iran that it would not subsequently claim a boundary with Bahrain which would intersect the common geodesic at or west of the western extreme point, and that such an assurance may have been transmitted to Bahrain in the course of negotiating the Bahrain–Iran agreement.

The mere fact that Qatar or Bahrain may, during negotiations, have made a prediction as to the other state's probable negotiating posture, or a statement concerning its intentions *vis-à-vis* the other state, will naturally not bind the other state.

QATAR–UNITED ARAB EMIRATES (ABU DHABI)

Qatar and Abu Dhabi signed a continental shelf boundary agreement on 20 March 1969. This agreement entered into effect on the same date. The two states recognise in this agreement the United Arab Emirates' (Abu Dhabi's) sovereignty over Dayyanah island and Qatar's sovereignty over the Islands of Al Ashat and Sharaiwah (see Figure 4.5). The course of the boundary line is described in Articles 3 and 4 of the agreement as follows:

3. Neither country now has any territorial claim upon the other with respect to the islands or offshore areas falling outside its agreed offshore areas

4. The agreed offshore boundary referred to in paragraph (3) above shall be as follows

(i) A straight line from point 'A' with geographic coordinates latitude 25°31' 50" N, longitude 53°02' 05" E, to the point 'B' which coincides with the location of al-Bondaq well No. 1 with geographic co-ordinates latitude 25°05' 54.79" N, longitude 52°36' 50.98" E.

(ii) A straight line from point 'B', as defined above, to point 'C' with geographic coordinates latitude 24° 48' 40" N, longitude 52° 16' 20" E.

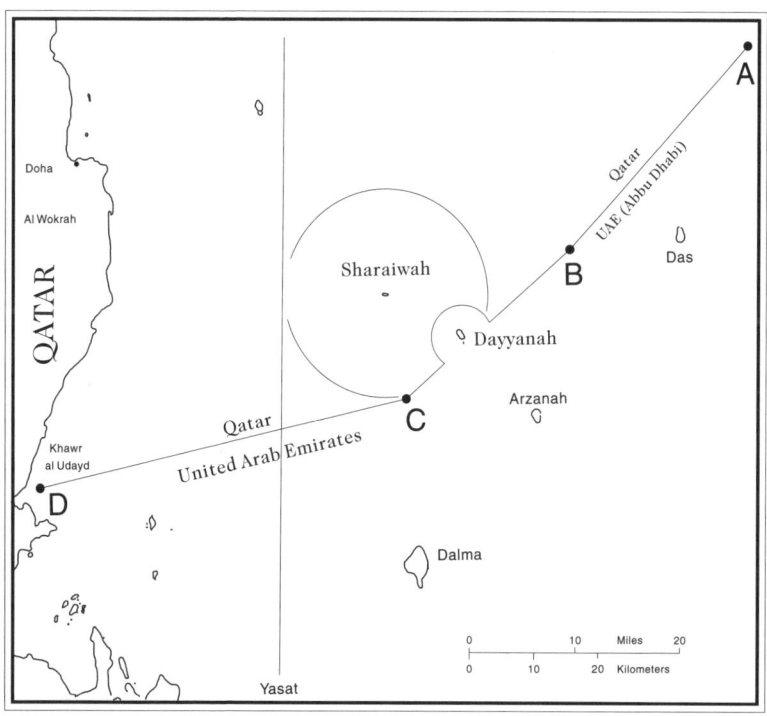

Figure 4.5 Qatar–UAE (Abu Dhabi) Continental Shelf Boundaries

(iii) A straight line from point 'C' as defined above, to point 'D' at the mouth of the Khaur al-'Adid on the territorial waters boundary, with geographic coordinates latitude 24° 38' 20" N, longitude 51° 28' 05" E.[30]

This boundary has four turning points and is 115 nautical miles in length. The northeastern terminus, point 'A' is a tripoint situated approximately equidistant from the Iran–Qatar–Abu Dhabi mainlands. Turning point 'B' coincides with the location of an Abu Dhabi oil well of Al -Bondaq, the profit from which, in accordance with the treaty, will be shared equally between the two states. Between points 'B' and 'C' the boundary most likely curves around Dayyanah Island, leaving it in Abu Dhabi's territory. The inference from Article 3 of the treaty is that this Abu Dhabi island would receive a 3-nautical mile territorial sea, albeit no specific reference is made to this in the treaty. The line as shown on Figure 4.5 should be viewed as one interpretation of the agreement. Point 'C' is purely a negotiated turning point with no apparent basis. The landward most point, point 'D' is situated at the intersection of their 3-nautical mile territorial waters in the Khor al-Udayd bay.[31]

IRAN–OMAN

Iran and the Sultanate of Oman defined and delimited their mutual continental shelf boundaries in the Strait of Hormuz. This agreement – signed on 15 July 1974 and entered into effect in January 1975 – also provides for a 410 feet oil exploration restriction on either side of the line.[32] The 12 mile territorial waters of the two countries at the Strait of Hormuz overlap in a stretch of 15 miles where the median line puts both territorial water limits and continental shelf boundaries on the same line.

The Iran–Oman boundary treaty of July 1974 defined the two countries' continental shelf boundaries on the basis of British Admiralty Chart No. 2888 of 1962. It coincided with another agreement between the two governments which allows both countries to patrol in each other's respective territorial seas for the maintenance of security in the Strait of Hormuz.[33]

Iran and Oman have opposing coasts in the Strait of Hormuz area. The northern Oman coast of Musandam, that part which constitutes the elbow of the Strait, consists largely of offshore islands. Iran's coastline is also fringed with islands.

The boundary agreement of 1974 does not specify any method of delimitation except that the boundary line is clearly calculated on equidistance between the coastlines of the two countries' islands. Article 1 of the agreement defines the turning and terminal points (22 in all) in the following manner:

The line dividing the continental shelf lying between the territory of Iran on the one side and the territory of Oman on the other shall consist of geodetic lines between the following points in the sequence hereinafter set out:

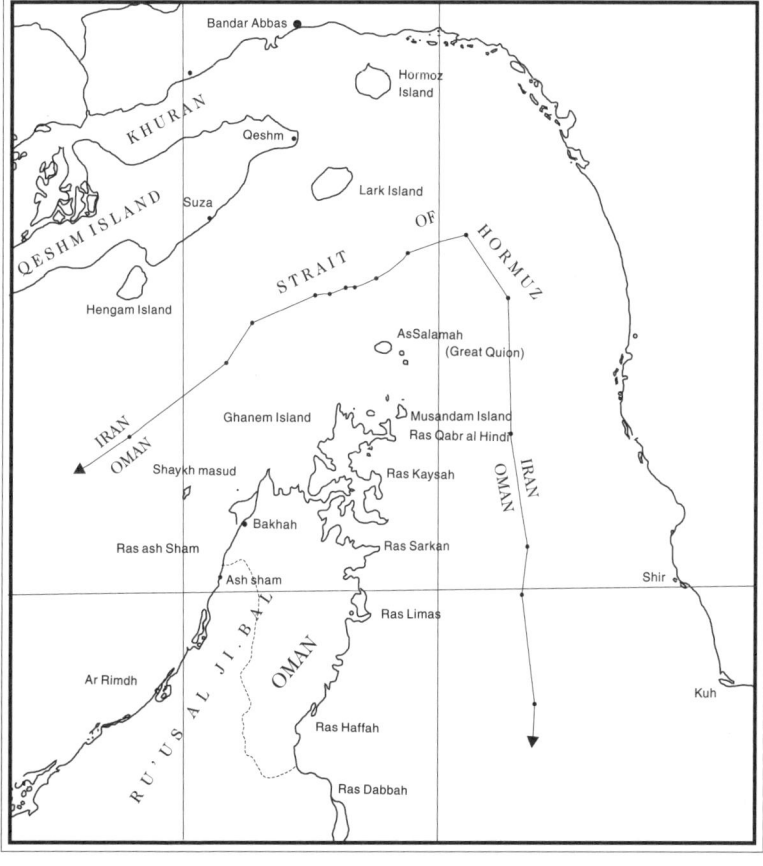

Figure 4.6 Iran–Oman Continental Shelf Boundaries and shipping lanes in the Strait of Hormuz

Point (1) is the most western point which is the intersection of the geodetic line drawn between point (0) having the co-ordinates of 26° 14' 45" N, 55° 42' 15" E, and point (2) having the co-ordinates of 26° 16' 35" N, 55° 47' 45" E, with the lateral offshore boundary line between Oman and Ras al-Khaimah.

	Northing	Easting
Point (2)	26° 16' 35"	55° 47' 45"
Point (3)	26° 28' 50"	55° 52' 15"
Point (4)	26° 28' 40"	56° 06' 45"
Point (5)	26° 31' 05"	56° 08' 35"
Point (6)	26° 32' 50"	56° 10' 25"
Point (7)	26° 35' 25"	56° 14' 30"
Point (8)	26° 35' 35"	56° 18' 30"
Point (9)	26° 37' 00" W. Intersect of Larak 12m	56° 19' 40"
Point (10)	26° 42' 15" E. Intersect of Larak 12m	56° 33' 00"
Point (11)	26° 44' 15"	56° 41' 00"
Point (12)	26° 41' 35"	56° 44' 00"
Point (13)	26° 39' 40"	56° 45' 15"
Point (14)	26° 35' 15"	56° 47' 45"
Point (15)	26° 25' 15"	56° 47' 30"
Point (17)	26° 16' 30"	56° 47' 50"
Point (18)	26° 11' 35"	56° 48' 00"
Point (19)	26° 03' 05"	56° 50' 15"
Point (20)	25° 58' 05"	56° 49' 50"
Point (21)	25° 45' 20"	56° 51' 30"

Point (22) is the most southerly point located at the intersection of the geodetic demarcation line drawn from point (21) (specified above) at an azimuth angle of 190° 00' 00" and of the lateral offshore boundary line between Oman and Sharjah.'[34]

This boundary runs for approximately 124.8 nautical miles and has 20 turning points. The terminal points, both in the Persian Gulf and in the Gulf of Oman, are not defined pending Oman's negotiations with the United Arab Emirates on their mutual continental shelf boundaries on both sides. This boundary in the Strait of Hormuz is essentially an equidistant line except for one area in which the boundary line follows the 12 nautical mile arcs drawn from the Iranian Island of Larak.

96

OTHER AGREEMENTS

In the other parts of the Gulf, though no official offshore agreements exist between Iran and the other states, median line, is in practice, the principle of their mutual boundaries. Such understandings exist between Iran and some Arab countries like Kuwait[35] and between Iran and some emirates of the UAE. With Sharjah, the 1971 memorandum of understanding on Abu Musa Island provides for the enforcement of the Iranian regulation of 12 miles of territorial waters, from the island's low water mark base line. Sharjah had granted a concession to the Butes Oil and Gas Company, prior to the 1971 agreement with Iran, for the exploration and exploitation of oil from Abu Musa's offshore oilfield of Meidan Mobarak. The 1971 agreement with Iran permitted the BOGC to continue oil exploration in that oilfield, but the profit from it was agreed to be equally shared by Iran and Sharjah. Abu Musa's 12 miles of territorial waters, on the other hand, overlapped that of Umm al-Quiwain's, where Oxidental Oil Company was given an exploration concession. The problem was subsequently settled by an informal agreement which granted Umm al-Quiwain 15 per cent share of the oil revenues from the area.[36]

An agreement was signed on 31 August 1974 between Iran and Dubai defining continental shelf boundaries between the two sides (see Figure 4.7)[37]. Iran ratified the agreement on 15 March 1975, but the United Arab Emirates has not.

This boundary needs to be continued to the east and to the west. An eastward extension will be complicated by the uncertainty resulting from claims of full sovereignty over the whole of Abu Musa Island by both Iran and the UAE.

The 1974 agreement established a boundary, 39.2 nautical miles in length, that appears to be equidistant from the respective mainlands and ignores the influence of islands. One section of the boundary follows the 12 nautical mile territorial sea drawn for the Iranian island of Sirri. Using all territories the boundary is situated nearer to either the island of Abu Musa or Sharjah's island of Sir Bu Noair than to any other Dubai territory.[38]

A draft agreement also exists between Iran and Abu Dhabi defining the two sides' continental shelf boundaries in the Gulf. Ratification of this boundary agreement is prevented by the boundary complications which exist between Abu Dhabi and Saudi Arabia on the one hand, and Iran and the United Arab Emirates on the other.

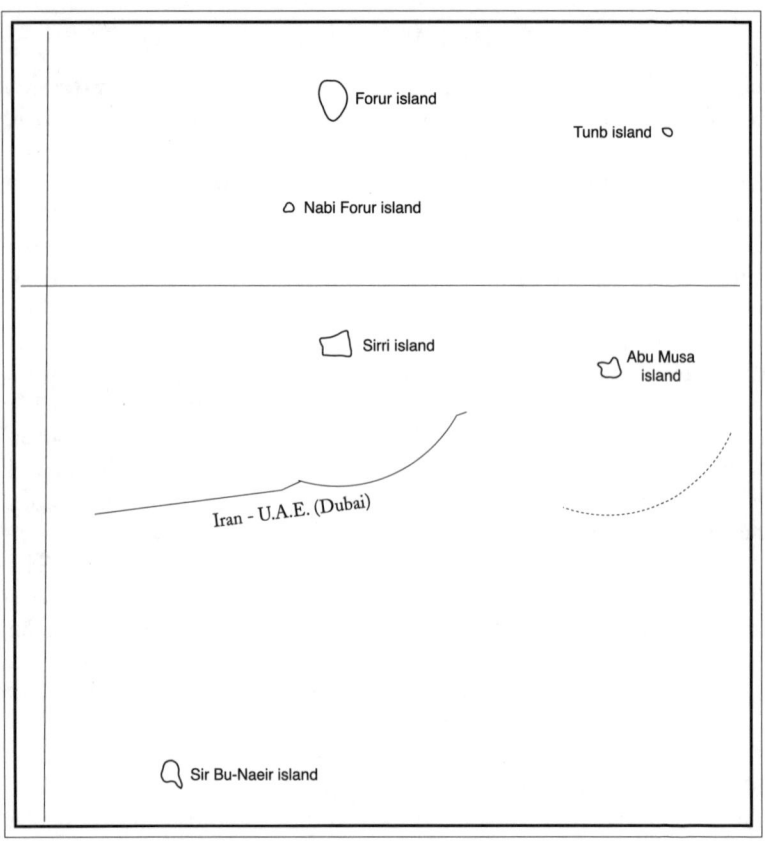

Figure 4.7 The Unofficial Iran–Dubai Continental Shelf Boundary
————— Maritime boundary line
----------- Southern limits of Abu Musa island's territorial sea

The daily Ettelaat of Tehran wrote on this subject in late August 1975:

'The continental shelf delimitation agreement of Iran and Abu Dhabi is ready for signing, but no date has been fixed for it. The agreement with Abu Dhabi is the sixth (continental shelf boundary) agreement that Iran is signing with the countries of the Persian Gulf region. Iran signed the latest agreements with Oman and Dubai. The agreement with Abu Dhabi should have been signed long before this, but Abu Dhabi's disputes with Saudi-Arabia on the oil rich Buraimi Oasis prevent it'.[39]

Finally, in Tehran, foreign ministers of Iran and Pakistan signed a maritime boundary division agreement on 16 June 1997. The agreement, which defines the two countries' continental shelf boundaries, in the Gulf of Oman as far northeastward as Gwatar Bay, is described as a means of maritime co-operation between the two countries. The draft of this agreement was prepared in 1992 by the political and marine experts of Iran and Pakistan on the basis of international laws governing the division of seabed and sub-soil resources.[40]

APPENDIX

I Act on the Marine Areas of the Islamic Republic of Iran in the Persian Gulf and the Oman Sea, 1993

Part I Territorial sea

Article 1: Sovereignty

The sovereignty of the Islamic Republic of Iran extends, beyond its land territory, internal waters and its islands in the Persian Gulf, the Strait of Hormuz and the Oman Sea, to a belt of sea, adjacent to the baseline, described as the territorial sea.

This sovereignty extends to the airspace over the territorial sea as well as to its bed and subsoil.

Article 2: Outer limit

The breadth of the territorial sea is 12 nautical miles, measured from the baseline. Each nautical mile is equal to 1,352 metres.

The islands belonging to the Islamic Republic of Iran, whether situated within or outside its territorial sea, have, in accordance with this Act, their own territorial sea.

Article 3: Baseline

In the Persian Gulf and the Oman Sea the baseline from which the breadth of the territorial sea is measured is that one determined in Decree No. 2/250–67 dated 31 Tir 1352 (22 July 1973) of the Council of Ministers (annexed to this Act);[41] in other areas and islands, the low water line along the coast constitutes the baseline.

Waters on the landward side of the baseline of the territorial sea, and waters between islands belonging to the Islamic Republic of Iran, where the distance of such islands does not exceed 24 nautical miles, form part of the internal waters and are under the sovereignty of the Islamic Republic of Iran.

Article 4: Delimitation

Wherever the territorial sea of the Islamic Republic of Iran overlaps the territorial seas of the states with opposite or adjacent coasts, the dividing line between the territorial seas of the Islamic Republic of Iran and those states shall be, unless otherwise agreed between the two parties, the median line every point of which is equidistant from the nearest point on the baseline of both states.

Article 5: Innocent passage

The passage of foreign vessels, except as provided for in article 9, is subject to the principle of innocent passage so long as it is not prejudicial to the good order, peace and security of the Islamic Republic of Iran.

Passage, except as in cases of *force majeure*, shall be continuous and expeditious.

Article 6: Requirements of innocent passage

Passage of foreign vessels, in cases when they are engaged in any of the following activities, shall not be considered innocent and shall be subject to relevant civil and criminal laws and regulations:

(a) Any threat or use of force against the sovereignty, territorial integrity or political independence of the Islamic Republic of Iran, or in any other manner in violation of the principles of international law;

(b) Any exercise or practice with weapons of any kind;

(c) Any act aimed at collecting information prejudicial to the national security, defence or economic interests of the Islamic Republic of Iran;

(d) Any act of propaganda aimed at affecting the national security, defence or economic interests of the Islamic Republic of Iran;

(e) The launching, landing or transferring on board of any aircraft or helicopter, or any military devices or personnel to another vessel or to the coast;

(f) The loading or unloading of any commodity, currency or person contrary to the laws and regulations of the Islamic Republic of Iran;

(g) Any act of pollution of the marine environment contrary to the rules and regulations of the Islamic Republic of Iran;

(h) Any act of fishing or exploitation of the marine resources;

(i) The carrying out of any specific research and cartographic and seismic surveys or sampling activities;

(j) Interfering with any systems of communication or any other facilities or installations of the Islamic Republic of Iran;

(k) Any other activity not having a direct bearing on passage.

Article 7: Supplementary laws and regulations

The government of the Islamic Republic of Iran shall adopt such other regulations as are necessary for the protection of its national interests and the proper conduct of innocent passage.

Article 8: Suspension of innocent passage

The government of the Islamic Republic of Iran, inspired by its high national interests and to defend its security, may suspend the innocent passage in parts of its territorial sea.

Article 9: Exceptions to innocent passage

Passage of warships, submarines, nuclear-powered ships and vessels or any other floating objects or vessels carrying nuclear or other dangerous or noxious substances harmful to the environment, through the territorial sea is subject to the prior authorisation of the relevant authorities of the Islamic Republic of Iran. Submarines are required to navigate on the surface and to show their flag.

Article 10: Criminal jurisdiction

In the following cases, the investigation, prosecution and punishment in connection with any crimes committed on board the ships passing through the territorial sea is within the jurisdiction of the judicial authorities of the Islamic Republic of Iran:

(a) If the consequences of the crime extend to the Islamic Republic of Iran;

(b) If the crime is of a kind to disturb the peace and order of the country or the public order of the territorial sea;

(c) If the master of the ship or a diplomatic agent or consular officer of the flag state asks for the assistance and investigation;
(d) If such investigation and prosecution is essential for the suppression of illicit traffic in narcotic drugs or psychotropic substances.

Article 11: Civil jurisdiction

The competent authorities of the Islamic Republic of Iran may stop, divert or detain a ship and its crew for the enforcement of attachment orders or court judgements if:

(a) The ship is passing through the territorial sea after leaving the internal waters of Iran;
(b) The ship is lying in the territorial sea of the Islamic Republic of Iran;
(c) The ship is passing through the territorial sea, provided that the origin of the attachment order or court judgement rests in the obligations or requirements arising from the civil liability of the ship itself.

Part II Contiguous zone

Article 12: Definition

The contiguous zone is an area adjacent to the territorial sea the outer limit of which is 24 nautical miles from the baseline.

Article 13: Civil and criminal jurisdiction

The government of the Islamic Republic of Iran may adopt measures necessary to prevent the infringement of laws and regulations in the contiguous zone, including security, customs, maritime, fiscal, immigration, sanitary and environmental laws and regulations and investigation and punishment of offenders.

Part III Exclusive economic zone and continental shelf

Article 14: Sovereign rights and jurisdiction in the exclusive economic zone

Beyond its territorial sea, which is called the exclusive economic zone, the Islamic Republic of Iran exercises its sovereign rights and jurisdiction with regard to:

(a) Exploration, exploitation, conservation and management of all natural resources, whether living or non-living, of the seabed and sub-soil thereof and its superjacent waters, and with regard to other economic activities for the production of energy from water, currents and winds. These rights are exclusive.

(b) Adoption and enforcement of appropriate laws and regulations, especially for the following activities:

(i) The establishment and use of artificial islands and other installations and structures, laying of submarine cables and pipelines and the establishment of relevant security and safety zones;

(ii) Any kind of research;

(iii) The protection and preservation of the marine environment;

(c) Such sovereign rights as granted by regional or international treaties.

Article 15: Sovereign rights and jurisdiction in the continental shelf

The provisions of article 14 shall apply *mutatis mutandis* to the sovereign rights and jurisdiction of the Islamic Republic of Iran in its continental shelf, which comprises the seabed and sub-soil of the marine areas that extend beyond the territorial sea throughout the natural prolongation of the land territory.

Article 16: Prohibited activities

Foreign military activities and practices, collection of information and any other activity inconsistent with the rights and interests of the Islamic Republic of Iran in the exclusive economic zone and the continental shelf are prohibited.

Article 17: Scientific activities, exploration and research

Any activity to recover drowned objects and scientific research and exploration in the exclusive economic zone and the continental shelf is subject to the permission of the relevant authorities of the Islamic Republic of Iran.

Article 18: Preservation of the environment and natural resources

The government of the Islamic Republic of Iran shall take appropriate measures for the protection and preservation of the marine environment and proper exploitation of living and other resources of the exclusive economic zone and the continental shelf.

Article 19: Delimitation

The limits of the exclusive economic zone and the continental shelf of the Islamic Republic of Iran, unless otherwise determined in accordance with bilateral agreements, shall be a line every point of which is equidistant from the nearest point on the baseline of two states.

Article 20: Civil and criminal jurisdiction

The Islamic Republic of Iran shall exercise its criminal and civil jurisdiction against offenders of the laws and regulations in the exclusive economic zone and continental shelf and shall, as appropriate, investigate or detain them.

Article 21: Right of hot pursuit

The government of the Islamic Republic of Iran reserves its right of hot pursuit against offenders of laws and regulations relating to its internal waters, territorial sea, contiguous zone, exclusive economic zone and the continental shelf, in such areas and the high seas.

Part IV Final provisions

Article 22: Executive regulations

The Council of Ministers shall specify the mandates and responsibilities [powers and duties] of different ministries and organisations charged with the enforcement of this Act.

The said ministries and organisations shall, within one year after the approval of this Act, prepare the necessary regulations and have them approved by the Council of Ministers.

Pending the adoption of new executive regulations, the existing rules and regulations shall remain in force.

Article 23

All laws and regulations contrary to the present Act, upon its ratification, are hereby abrogated.

The above Act, comprising 23 articles, was ratified at the plenary meeting of Tuesday, the thirty-first day of Farvrdin, one thousand three hundred and seventy-two (20 April 1993), of the Islamic Consultative Assembly and was approved by the Council of Guardians on Ordibehesht 12, 1372 (2 May 1993).

II Protests from States and Communication

1 Protest from the United States of America, 11 January 1994

The Permanent Mission of the United States of America to the United Nations presents its compliments to the United Nations and has the honour to advise that the government of the United States of America has studied carefully the legislative acts of the Islamic Republic of Iran setting forth the Islamic Republic of Iran's maritime claims, including the Act on the Marine Areas of the Islamic Republic of Iran in the Persian Gulf and the Oman Sea of 2 May 1993, and Decree-Law No. 2/250–67, 31 Tir 1352 [22 July 1973] of the Council of Ministers, taking into account the relevant provisions of international law as reflected in the 1982 United Nations Convention on the Law of the Sea, which will enter into force on 16 November 1994.

The United States is of the view that certain provisions of these acts are inconsistent with international law, and the United States reserves its rights and the rights of its nationals in that regard.

The United States wishes to recall that, as recognised in customary international law and as reflected in the 1982 United Nations Convention on the Law of the Sea, except where otherwise provided in the Convention, the normal baseline for measuring the breadth of the territorial sea is the low water line along the coast as marked on large-scale charts officially recognised by the coastal state. Only in localities where the coastline is deeply indented and cut into, or if there is a fringe of islands along the coast in its immediate vicinity, may the coastal state elect to use the method of straight baselines joining appropriate points in drawing the baseline from which the breadth of the territorial sea is measured.

The United States notes that, notwithstanding the fact that the Iranian coastline is rarely deeply indented or fringed by islands, the Islamic Republic of Iran has employed straight baselines along most of its coastline and that, in the vicinity of most segments, the Iranian coastline is quite smooth. Consequently, the appropriate baseline for virtually all of the Iranian coast in the Persian Gulf and the Gulf of Oman is the normal baseline, the low water line.

While the Convention does not set a maximum length for baseline segments, many of the segments set out in Iranian law are excessively long. In fact, 11 of the 21 segments are between 30 and 120 miles long. The United States believes that the maximum length of an approximately drawn straight baseline segment normally should not exceed 24 nautical miles.

The United States also wishes to recall that islands may not be used to define internal waters, except for situations where the islands are part of a valid straight baseline system, or of a closing line for a juridical bay. Article 3 of the 1993 Marine Areas Act of the Islamic Republic of Iran asserts that waters between islands belonging to the Islamic Republic of Iran where the distance of such islands does not exceed 24 nautical miles form part of the internal waters of the Islamic Republic of Iran. This claim has no basis in international law. The United States notes that article 19 (2) (h) of the 1982 Law of the Sea Convention provides that 'any act of wilful and serious pollution contrary to this Convention' may be considered prejudicial to the peace, good order or security of the coastal state. In specifying activities in its territorial sea that the Islamic Republic of Iran does not consider to be innocent, article 6 (g) of the 1993 Marine Areas Act includes 'any act of pollution of the marine environment contrary to the rules and regulations of the Islamic Republic of Iran'. The United States assumes that the relevant Iranian rules and regulations will conform to the accepted rule of international law set out in article 19 (2) (h) of the 1982 Law of the Sea Convention.

The United States recalls that, under articles 21 and 24 of the 1982 Law of the Sea Convention, a coastal state may adopt laws and regulations relating to innocent passage relating to the design, construction, manning or equipment of foreign ships only if they are giving effect to generally accepted international rules or standards, and may not adopt requirements that have the practical effect of denying or impairing the right of innocent passage or of discriminating in form or in fact against the ships of any state or against ships carrying cargoes to, from or on behalf of any state.

The United States notes that the Islamic Republic of Iran's claim in article 7 of the right to adopt 'such other regulations as are necessary for the protection of its national interests and the proper conduct of innocent passage' cannot confer upon it any greater rights than those authorized under international law.

The United States also notes that international law permits a coastal state to suspend temporarily in specified areas of its territorial sea the innocent passage of foreign ships if such suspension is essential for the protection of its security, and that such suspension may take effect only after having been duly published.

Article 8 of the Islamic Republic of Iran's 1993 Marine Areas Act cannot be accepted as removing the requirements that any suspension of innocent passage through parts of its territorial sea be temporary and that it take effect only after being duly published.

Article 9 of the 1993 Marine Areas Act impermissibly seeks to require foreign warships, and vessels carrying dangerous or noxious substances harmful to the environment, to obtain prior authorization from the Islamic Republic of Iran to pass through the Islamic Republic of Iran's territorial sea.

Such a requirement has no foundation in the provisions of the 1982 Law of the Sea Convention, and the United States will continue to reject, as contrary to international law, any attempt to impose such a requirement on the exercise of the right of innocent passage of all ships.

The United States assumes that the Islamic Republic of Iran will not seek to exercise criminal jurisdiction, pursuant to article 10 of the 1993 Marine Areas Act, on board ships other than merchant ships and government ships operated for commercial purposes, or to exercise civil jurisdiction, pursuant to article 11 of this Act, in situations not contemplated by article 28 of the 1982 Law of the Sea Convention.

The United States further recalls that the scope of a coastal state's authority in its contiguous zone, a maritime zone contiguous to and seaward of the territorial sea in which freedoms of navigation and overflight may be exercised, is limited to the exercise of the control necessary to prevent and punish infringement of its customs, fiscal, immigration and sanitary laws and regulations committed within its territory or territorial sea, and that the authority of the coastal state to enforce its environmental laws seaward of its territorial sea is as prescribed in article 220 of the Convention.

The claim in article 13 of the 1993 Act to adopt measures in the Islamic Republic of Iran's contiguous zone necessary to prevent infringement of its security, maritime and environmental laws exceeds that permitted by international law.

Although a coastal state may establish, in accordance with article 60, paragraphs 4 and 5, of the 1982 Law of the Sea Convention, safety zones of a radius not exceeding 500 metres around artificial islands and other installations and structures located within its

107

exclusive economic zone, international law does not authorize a coastal state to establish so-called security zones in such areas. Article 14 (b) (1) of the 1993 Marine Areas Act impermissibly asserts the right to do so. That provision also appears to claim more authority to control the laying of submarine cables and pipelines on the Islamic Republic of Iran's continental shelf than is permitted by international law as reflected in article 79 of the 1982 Law of the Sea Convention.

Further, international law permits a coastal state to regulate only marine scientific research in its exclusive economic zone, not 'any kind of research' as claimed in article 14 (b) (2) of the 1993 Marine Areas Act. In particular, hydrographic surveys conducted seaward of the territorial sea are not marine scientific research and are not subject to coastal state jurisdiction.

The United States notes that, to the extent article 16 of the 1993 Marine Areas Act seeks to prohibit in the Iranian exclusive economic zone the exercise by foreign warships and military aircraft of their freedoms of navigation and overflight, it contravenes international law. The United States has previously protested the Islamic Republic of Iran's claim in this regard, and will continue to operate its ships and aircraft consistent with its rights under international law.

The government of the United States wishes to assure the government of the Islamic Republic of Iran that its objections to these claims should not be viewed as singling out the Islamic Republic of Iran for criticism, but is part of its worldwide effort to preserve the internationally recognized rights and freedoms of the international community in navigation and overflight and other related high seas uses, and thereby maintain the balance of interests reflected in the Convention.

This is only one of a number of United States protests of those claims by coastal states which are not consistent with international law as reflected in the 1982 United Nations Convention on the Law of the Sea.

The government of the United States requests that this note be circulated by the United Nations as part of the next *Law of the Sea Bulletin*.

2 Comments from the Islamic Republic of Iran concerning the viewpoints of the government of the United States of America regarding the Act of Marine Areas in the Persian Gulf and the Oman Sea

The government of the Islamic Republic of Iran took careful note of the viewpoints of the government of the United States of America regarding the Act on the Marine Areas of the Islamic Republic of Iran in the Persian Gulf and the Oman Sea as expressed in the latter's note of 11 January 1994, and would like to make, in this respect, the following comments:

In the note of the United States, reference was repeatedly made to customary rules and regulations of international law as embodied in the United Nations Convention on the Law of the Sea of 10 December 1982; and it appears that the United states believes that the provisions of the Convention are of a customary nature, the observance of which being obligatory to all States whether or not they are parties to the Convention; and on this basis some provisions of the Marine Areas Act have been considered as inconsistent with the rules of international law.

In this regard, it is necessary to explain that the Islamic Republic of Iran, unlike the United States, does not consider all provisions of the Convention as customary law and believes that many of them which are the result of years of negotiations in the framework of the Third United Nations Conference on the Law of the Sea and preparation of regulations in the form of a package deal, are of contractual nature the binding force of which depends on the entry into force of the Convention on the Law of the Sea for the States Parties. The Islamic Republic of Iran had already declared, at the time of signing the Convention on 10 December 1982, that:

> Notwithstanding the intended character of the Convention being one of general application and of law-making nature, certain provisions are merely [the] product of *quid pro quo* which do not necessarily purport to codify the existing customs or established usage (practice) regarded as having an obligatory character. Therefore, it seems natural and in harmony with article 34 of the 1969 Vienna Convention on the Law of Treaties, that only States Parties to the Law of the Sea Convention shall be entitled to benefit from the contractual rights created therein.

It is also to be noted that the United States, in its note, referred to 16 November 1994 as the date of the entry into force of the Convention, a reference which will be necessary if the provisions of the Convention were of a customary nature.

It is quite clear that making a distinction between customary and conventional rules of international law is a complicated task and as long as a general belief on the binding force of a particular conduct is not definitely realized, one may not speak of it as a custom. From the viewpoint of the Islamic Republic of Iran, the adoption of different laws by states on their rights and jurisdiction in seas, which are in many cases inconsistent with the 1982 Convention, is an indication of the fact that as yet no definite custom has been formed.

The method of decision-making on some of the provisions of the Convention in the proceedings of the Third United Nations Conference on the Law of the Sea also demonstrates the uncertainty of their customary nature. For instance, reference can be made to the issue of the right of coastal states to enforce regulations for their security in the territorial sea which was emphasised in the course of the Conference by the Group of 27 (including the Islamic Republic of Iran) and a proposal was submitted for amendment of article 21 of the preliminary draft Convention. Although, on the request of the Chairman of the Conference, the Group agreed not to insist on voting for the proposal, in his statement of 26 April 1982, the Chairman stated that:

> the sponsors of the amendment have persisted that this decision would not in any way damage the right of littoral states in taking necessary measures for the safeguard of their security interests according to articles 19 and 25 of the suggested text of the Convention.

Until the enactment of the recent Act in the Islamic Republic of Iran, there existed several laws and regulations, each one of them covering a part of issues relating to the Law of the Sea matters, while in some cases developments in such rules concerning the expansion of states' jurisdiction were not provided for. The Marine Areas Act was therefore prepared and approved with the aim of compiling all relevant regulations in a single comprehensive text so as to replace previous laws and at the same time to include the most recent developments of the Law of the Sea. A list of the relevant laws and regulations is attached to the present note.[42]

Decree No. 2/250–67, dated 31 Tir, 1352 (22 July 1973) is amongst such regulations approved and put into force nearly 20 years ago. Usage of the straight baselines is in one way considered as an unusual measure, as other states, too, use the same method under similar circumstances. The reason for further emphasis on the Decree of 1973 was that since its enforcement and in spite of its international circulation in the collections circulated by the United Nations Secretariat, so far no objections have been received thereto. The Islamic Republic of Iran, therefore, considers this as a recognition of its content by the international community.

As mentioned in the United States' note, there is no criterion in international law to determine the maximum length of parts of the straight baselines; thus the reference made by the United States to 24 nautical miles lacks legal foundation. Instead, in drawing the line, effort has been made to employ those criteria which have been internationally important and were later mentioned in the Convention. Among them is the drawing of straight baselines in a way that they do not depart in any appreciable extent from the general direction of the coast (article 7, paragraph 3), and it has also been taken into account that in determining the straight baselines, the coastal states may consider the economic interests peculiar to the region concerned, the reality and importance of which are clearly evidenced by long usage.

As for the declaration of waters between islands whose distance is less than 24 nautical miles as internal waters it is noteworthy to recall the Act on Territorial Waters and the Contiguous Zone of Iran dated Tir 24, 1313 (July 1934), and its amendment of 22 Farvardin 1338 (11 April 1959), according to which similar rules have been provided in connection with islands belonging to the Islamic Republic of Iran, and in the recent Act the criterion for the distance between islands has been changed in conformity with the extension of the breadth of territorial sea. Moreover, in recent years, the context of some of its provisions, such as the authority of the government of the Islamic Republic of Iran in the field of marine scientific research in areas beyond the territorial sea, while being consistent with the recognised rules of international law, has been observed by other states, and for example marine scientific research in the areas under the jurisdiction of the Islamic Republic of Iran has been carried out after a prior consent has been granted. In this connection, the Islamic Republic of Iran assumes that any kind of scientific research in the exclusive economic zone, because of its effects on the exploration and exploitation of living and mineral resources and economic interests, is directly linked to the rights of the coastal state (in this case Islamic Republic of Iran) and should be conducted with prior authorisation. In accordance with the Law of the Sea Convention, even in cases where the scientific research is conducted exclusively for peaceful purposes and in order to increase scientific knowledge of the marine environment for the benefit of all mankind, the matter has not been excluded from the jurisdiction of the coastal state and under normal circumstances such a state is merely requested to grant its consent without reasonable delay (article 246 (3) of the Convention). Therefore, hydrographic research, even though it falls under this category, would require the authorisation of the coastal state.

In drafting the Act, the ecological and environmental conditions of the Persian Gulf are another main issue which was taken into consideration, to which fundamental importance should be attached. From an environmental point of view, the Persian Gulf as a semi-enclosed sea, is very vulnerable and that is why it has been recognised as a special area in some international treaties relating to the marine environment. The limited width of the Persian Gulf (as the share of each opposite state in the widest parts is less than 100 miles), its shallowness, the volume of economic activities, particularly in the field of fishing and the oil industry, and the scope of navigation traffic have created a situation where the smallest incident inflicts severe enduring pollution of the marine environment. The sinking of a Russian cargo ship, *Kapitan Sakharov*, a few months ago, which brought about hazards and damage, particularly in fishing and navigation, could be set as a good example for the importance of the issue. With regard to this matter, the littoral states of the Persian Gulf have taken co-ordinated measures, in the framework of the Kuwait Convention (1978) and its protocols, to protect the marine environment which, in comparison, have been more comprehensive than the measures taken in other regions.

Some of the objections raised by the United States to the Marine Areas Act of the Islamic Republic of Iran are also in connection with the regulations drawn up with due consideration to this very particularity of the Persian Gulf region, such as not regarding as innocent the passage of ships which, against the laws and regulations of the Islamic Republic of Iran, cause any sort of marine pollution in the territorial sea.

The requirement of obtaining a prior authorisation for the passage of some categories of foreign vessels, especially for ships carrying hazardous substances, was also put in to have more supervision of the traffic of such vessels and with the aim of protecting the marine environment of the region. The same argument applies to the environmental regulations to be enforced in the contiguous zone.

As for the question of a 500 metre zone around oil platforms and installations, it is necessary to emphasize that, due to the high number of exploitation platforms and the volume of shipping traffic, the establishing of such a zone is completely necessary for the security of installations as well as international navigation. As for the competence of the coastal state in laying submarine cable sand pipelines, it is also to be noted that the government of the Islamic Republic of Iran, having due regard to the same considerations, deems a prior permission a necessary requirement: to give an example, it clearly emphasised this point in its reservations, at the time of signing the 1958 Geneva Conventions on the High Seas and on the Continental Shelf. As for article 16 of the Act, attention is to be given to the fact that, due to the multiplicity of economic activities in the region, it is possible that such activities, for which the coastal state enjoys sovereign rights, could be harmed by military practices and manoeuvres; accordingly, those practices which effect the economic activities in the exclusive economic zone and the continental shelf are thus prohibited.

Qatar–Bahrain Territorial And Boundary Disputes

Chapter 5

Emergence and Evolution of Territorial States in Qatar and Bahrain

INTRODUCTION

The two states of Qatar and Bahrain have not been able to delimit their maritime boundaries in the waters separating them. The problem which prevents delimitation of these boundaries is complex involving a number of islands, shoals (*fashts*), and the district of Zubarah in Qatar to which Bahrain lays claim.

Bahrain and Qatar went as far in their disputes as nearly declaring war in 1986 over these disputes. Conflict was averted and relations normalised as a result of intervention by the Gulf Cooperation Council (GCC) of which both states are members.

The current disputes were invoked in the spring of 1986, according to the Bahrainis, when Qatar interfered with works being done on the Fasht al-Dibal and declared the whole area around the Hawar islands a military zone. The GCC intervened and Qatar evacuated Dibal in June that year and the two sides began preparing for the defence of their claims at an international tribunal. The GCC advised its two members in December 1990 to try and settle their differences in an out of court settlement within six months. Not only did the two states not succeed in sorting out their differences within the GCC timetable, but Qatar announced on 16 April 1992 that she had increased her territorial waters in the Gulf from 3 to 12 miles. These extended territorial waters give a new dimension to an already very complicated issue.

With the lapse of the GCC deadline and considering that the problem was deepening as time went by, Qatar decided to make a unilateral application to the International Court of Justice at the Hague.

117

This court announced in an unofficial communiqué[1] in July 1991 that the State of Qatar filed on that date in the Registry of the International Court of Justice an application instituting proceedings against the State of Bahrain in respect of their disputes over the Hawar islands.

The origin of the dispute over the ownership of the Hawar archipelago and Zubarah, however, is as old as the State of Qatar itself, and a background study of the case would demand a look at the history of the evolution of both states and their boundaries.

Bahrain and Qatar's dispute over the Hawar archipelago has probably been the most important factor in the two states' relationship, and has played a major role in the evolution of the two states' territorial and boundary differences.

It is also noteworthy that during the discussions in this section special reference will be made to the former claims of Iran to Bahrain for two reasons: firstly because examination of the geographical dimension of Iran's former claims will prove to be most relevant to the present state of territorial disputes between Bahrain and Qatar; and secondly because the legally binding and internationally respected settlement of those claims needs to be specially projected for the benefit of historical records concerning the evolution of the independent 'State' in Bahrain.

Finally, as each country sees its territorial extension and boundary limitation in the image of the evolution of its own territorial state, and since territorial and boundary claims and counter-claims are normally made on the basis of what is seen in each country as historical evidence, the study of these disputes necessitates a brief examination of the history of evolution of state and boundary in each case.

HISTORICAL BACKGROUND – EMERGENCE OF BAHRAIN

Archaeological discoveries in the Bahrain archipelago provide evidence of the existence of different civilizations in these islands and the nearby coastal regions of Hasa and Qatif. Throughout most of the Islamic era the name Bahrain embraced these coastal regions (now eastern provinces of Saudi Arabia) as well as the Bahrain islands and Qatar peninsula. In pre-Islamic antiquity, Bahrain is said to be identifiable with the Dilmun of the Assyrio–Babylonian text, and with Tylos of classical Latin and Greek texts. It is also identifiable with Aval of the Persian text of the Achaeminian era (sixth century BC), and with Haggar of the same text of the Sassanian period (224–685 AD).

Some archaeological discoveries made near the village of Abu Ali on Bahrain's main island, Manamah, suggest a Phoenician connection. Either they had originated from this part of the world, or they regularly traded with these islands through which they left their mark in a number of places in the Persian Gulf, including Kuwait and the Bahrain islands.[2]

One of the early steles discovered in Bahrain suggests that Sennacherib, King of Assyria (707–681 BC) had attacked northeast Arabia and captured the Bahrain islands. The Achaemenian federative empire of Iran united the greatest part of the civilized world of the time and by constructing roads and developing communication systems via land and sea, encouraged trade links between various parts of their empire. Bahrain was included in the Achaemenian empire at the time of Darius the Great when most other civilized parts of the world were contained within the borders of that empire. This was the time when Darius organised a naval unit to explore sea routes between India, Persia and Egypt which eventually led to the construction of a canal between the Red Sea and the Nile.[3]

These Achaemenian undertakings were part of their plan for the creation of an enduring world-wide federation, a goal for the attainment of which Alexander the Great led his troops to the eastern lands.

Following the fall of the Achaemenians, Bahrain and other parts of the lower Gulf as well as Iran itself were occupied by Macedonian forces. At the apex of Sassanian power in the fifth and sixth centuries, trade prospered in the Gulf and the Indian Ocean. Bahrain had already been reincorporated into the realms of Iran. In fact, it was Artaxeres (Ardshir Papakan, 225 – 241 AD) founder of the Sassanian empire who had defeated Satiran and regained Bahrain.[4] He appointed his son Shapur I as governor of Bahrain. Shapur constructed a new city there and named it Batan Ardeshir after his father.[5]

Bahrain constituted at this time a separate province in the political organisation of the Sassanian empire and was subdivided into the three districts of Haggar, Batan Ardeshir and Mishmahig.[6] The Haggar district included what is now known as the al-Hafuf province of Saudi Arabia, a name later pronounced by the Arabs as Hajar. Batan Ardeshir, was also on the Arabian coast where it is now known as al-Qatif,[7] and Mishmahig included the Bahrain archipelago which was earlier called Aval, but later, in the Islamic era, became known as Bahrain.

Roman Emperor Trajan, whose forces reached the shores of the Gulf in 116 AD, ravaged the coasts of Iran and Arabia, apparently as retribution for the raids carried out by the coastal people of Arabia.[8] His forces were defeated by the Parthian King Arshak XXIII. He was the first and the last of the Roman emperors to enter in the Gulf.

Iran's first renaissance under the Sassanians allowed her to regain the position she once possessed under the Achaemenians in the Gulf, and retained this ascendancy until the Arab conquest of Iran in the seventh century AD.[9]

When Shapur II came of age, the Arabs from inner Arabia raided Iranian possessions on the southern coasts of the Gulf. These raids continued and provoked strong Sassanian retaliations against them. Shapur's forces cleared the whole of Bahrain, Qatif and Hasa of the Arab raiders. Much has been said of Shapur's brutality in these retaliatory measures. Exaggeration sometimes overshadowed reality. Stories have been repeated throughout history of an incredible nature. Even some modern European writers have repeated these exaggerations without thinking of their natural and physical possibility. An example of these exaggerated stories is one repeated by Sir Arnold T. Wilson in his book *The Persian Gulf*. He quoted this story from Caussin de Perceval who, in turn, had quoted others and so on. This story is as follows:

> Coming down to the early part of the fourth century we find, during the minority of Shapur II (309–25 AD), the tribes of Arabs from Bahrain (embracing at this time Hasa and Qatif) and Yamama made various raids on the territory. Shapur attacked and massacred them in large numbers, some of the survivors taking refuge in Mesopotamia, while those from Bahrain retired again to their own country. Wishing to get hold of these latter, Shapur embarked with his army upon the Persian Gulf, landed at Qatif, and put to sword great numbers of the inhabitants of Bahrain. He seized Hajar, exterminated the greater part of the Abd al Qais tribe, wreaked a terrible vengeance on the Bajila Khatam, and fell upon the Tamim. When tired of killing he ordered his men to pierce the shoulders of the vanquished, tie them with ropes, and bring them as prisoners. This brutal treatment earned for Shapur the title in oriental history of Dhul Aktaf, or 'man of the shoulders Bahrain then became an appanage of Fars.'[10]

This is an example of a situation in which exaggeration gets out of hand. Piercing the shoulders of a group of people and tying them together by rope run through the pierced holes in their shoulders, and taking them from Arabia to Iran as prisoners in their slow means of transportation would take months, and suggesting that they were still alive, does not correspond to any law of nature. Either the vanquished were men of extraordinary and unnatural physics, or the entire story is but a sham made up to discredit the Sassanians. There is a general consensus among historians that Shapur II treated the raiding Arabs brutally, but there is little room in the intelligent mind for such unlikely stories.

Shapur II was a young man at the time with an athletic figure and broad shoulders as is evident from his life-size statue in Cave Shapur in Kermanshah. His broad shoulders earned him the title Zol Aktaf or 'possessor of shoulders'.

From the time of the emergence of Arab caliphates of Umayyad and Abbasid, Bahrain gradually became the centre of attention for political movements against the domination by Damascus and Baghdad of various peoples in the region. The Khawarej were the first to rebel in the Gulf. They were followed by the Zangian (followers of Sahib az-Zang), and the Qarmatians followed them. The Qarmatians expanded their authority far beyond the limits of both maritime and coastal Bahrain, well into Arabia proper.

Following the downfall of the Qarmatians, the Ayounis succeeded in creating the first local state in Bahrain in 467 AH (1074 AD). The Ayouni state survived until 636 AH (1238 AD) when it paved the way for the rise into local prominence of the Bani Oqail bin Amer who established the state of Asafir, or Bani Asfoor which survived for about 150 years[11] and included coastal Bahrain and Najd as well as maritime Bahrain. They were followed by another local state – the Jaboor – whose authority extended to al-Hasa, Qatif, Najd, and Hormuz.[12]

Bahrain was occupied by the Portuguese in 1522. This was the time when the power and influence of the Safavid empire in Iran was on the rise. The Safavids defeated the Portuguese in the Strait of Hormuz ports and islands of Iran and drove them out of Bahrain in 1602. From this time until 1783, Bahrain remained under the uninterrupted control of Iran.

The Arabs of Muscat, commanded by Imam Sultan bin Saif II (1708–21) attacked Bahrain in 1717 or 1718 with the vessels he had at his disposal, and conquered the archipelago. Evidently the domination by Muscat Arabs of Bahrain did not last long and after their departure, the archipelago went under the Sheikh of Zubarah, the chief of the powerful Bani Hawalah tribes. Although the Sheikh of Zubarah (northwest corner of Qatar peninsula) was nominally an

Iranian subject, he was dauntless and independent of the feeble rule of Shah Sultan Hussein, the last of the Safavids, in Isfahan.[13]

Under Nader Shah Afshar, commander Lotf-Ali Khan left for Bahrain with 4000 warriors. Iranian forces opened the forts of Bahrain one after the other, and returned Bahrain to the realms of Fars in AH 1140 (1737 AD). Lotf-Ali Khan's military camp was organised by Mohammad Taghi Khan Zand, governor of Fars, on behalf of Nader Shah. Affairs of Zubarah were settled because the Sheikh of Zubarah, ruler of Bahrain, was in secret collaboration with the Arabs and used to cause inconveniences to Iran. The last governor of Bahrain was Shaikh Nasr Khan who represented Karim Khan Zand, ruler of the southern provinces of Iran after Nader Shah's assassination in 1747.

ARRIVAL OF AL-KHALIFAH IN BAHRAIN

Bahrain's political fortunes began to change with the arrival of the Al-Khalifah in the archipelago. The Al-Khalifah clan of the Utoobi tribes had arrived originally from the interior of Arabia and first settled in Qurain (now Kuwait) in about 1710.

. . . Utoobee conquerors of Bahrain, who reduced it in 1194 AH (1779), came originally from Koweit or Gran. They were formed by intermarriage of three large tribes of Arabs, the Beni Sabah, under Shaikh Solaiman bin Ahmad, the Beni Yalahima (Jalahimah) under Shaikh Jaber bin Utoobee, and the Beni Khalifah, under Shaikh Khalifah bin Mohammad.[14]

On the union of these tribes, for the purpose of resisting attacks of more powerful tribes in the neighbourhood of Kuwait, they determined to become at once merchants and agriculturists in an economically self-sufficient self rule, and that the profit arising from these activities would be equally divided among them. This arrangement was observed with success for about 50 years, when the mercantile federation of the three tribes determined to end the federation in favour of independent life of each for its own.

With this in mind, Shaikh Khalifah Bin Mohammad, the highly intelligent chief of the Al-Khalifah branch of the league, persuaded other members of the union to permit him to leave Al-Qurain for the more attractive pearl shores of Bahrain which then extended from the Bahrain archipelago to Jolfar (now Ras al-Kheimah). This was agreed upon and the Al-Jalahimah branch of the federation conveyed their tribal cousins to Zubarah in Qatar peninsula where they completely succeeded in their object and after a while refused to continue the economic ties of the original league.[15] Iranian governor of the locality Shaikh Nasr Khan decided at this time to bring the unruly Shaikh of Zubarah under control. The Al-Khalifah had already made themselves masters of Zubarah. Shaikh Nasr Khan besieged the settlement at Zubarah but sustained heavy casualties. He despatched the intelligence of the event to his son whom he had put in charge of the Bahrain islands, and charged him to be resolute and vigilant against foreign attack until he returned from Bushehr with reinforcements. With this message Shaikh Nasr Khan appears to have been aware of an imminent attack on Bahrain by the tribes of Zubarah who had defeated him. The boat conveying his despatch was intercepted at sea by the Al-Sabah forces who, having heard of the events at Zubarah, came to the assistance of their Al-Khalifah brethren. Aware of the defenceless state of the Bahrain islands, the amalgamated forces of the Utoobi Arabs immediately proceeded to attack and gained possession of Bahrain's principal posts before Shaikh Nasr Khan's fleet arrived on the scene. Finding the enemy in possession of the islands, he realised that he had to return to Bushehr hoping that a much larger army could evict the Utoobis from Bahrain, a hope which never materialised.

This event took place in 1783 and the Al-Khalifah who were by then living in Zubarah, made themselves masters of the Bahrain archipelago, with Zubarah still being an important part of their state, in fact it was the political centre of the Al-Khalifah state, the same as it was under Iranian control. Five years later, the Wahhabis, led by Soleiman bin Asifan, conquered the Qatar peninsula and remained there for some years. When in 1808 Sultan of Muscat conquered Bahrain, the Al-Khalifah, assisted by the Wahhabis, succeeded in driving the Muscatis out in 1809. Another attack on Bahrain took place in 1816 by the Sultan of Muscat. The Sultan had signed an agreement with the Iranians in 1811 whereby Bahrain was leased to him. The Al-Khalifah were defeated as they had no support from anyone. They had in 1810 driven the Wahhabis out.[16]

It was around this time that Captain G. B. Brucks of the Indian Navy studied the areas of the Gulf and gave the following account of the Hawar archipelago in 1829:

Warden's Islands is a group of eight or nine islands and rocks, extending from latitude 25° 46' 25" N, longitude 50° 55' E, to latitude 25° 33' N, longitude 50° 53' 20" E. The principal is called Hawahk, and is about 4 miles long. It has two fishing villages on it and belongs to Bahrain.[17]

During the occupation of the neighbouring territories of Hasa by the Egyptians in the 1830s Mohammad Ali Pasha, Khadiv (Viceroy) of Egypt who waged a campaign in Arabia against the Wahhabis on behalf of the Ottoman Sultan, had his envoy write to the people of Bahrain:

> If you are subjects of the Government of Persia obey the Shahanshah, otherwise, why is it that you neither consider yourselves as the subjects of Shahanshah nor do you obey Mohammad Ali Pasha?[18]

In order to avoid an Egyptian attack, Shaikh Abdullah, Ruler of Bahrain, claimed to be the subject of the Shah of Iran.[19] Despite this move, and in spite of protests on the part of the British, Bahrain fell under the influence of the Egyptians and so remained until their retirement in 1840 when the islands again came under Wahhabi control.

When in 1860 the British began to increase their interference in the affairs of Bahrain, Mohammad bin Khalifah wrote two letters to the Iranian authorities; one on 20 Ramazan 1276 (12 April 1860) to Nasser ad-Din Shah Qajar; and the other to Mirza Mehdi Khan, Foreign Minister of Iran on 18 Shavval 1276 (10 June 1860). In the former he declared:

> I, my brother Ali, and all Al-Khalifah and the people of Bahrain are subjects of the Government of Iran . . . and Bahrain is a part of the territories of the Iranian government.[20]

In the second letter, he reported to the Iranian Foreign Minster that English Captain Jones had arrived in Bahrain and asked him to meet the captain in his vessel, but he declined awaiting instruction from Tehran on whether or not to do so.[21] Shaikh Mohammad bin Khalifah, a shrewd leader, clearly hoped to play the British off against the Iranians, and to expand his realms to Hasa and Qatif.

Having thus secured the Iranian authorities' support, he attacked Qatif with the firing power of two vessels and captured that territory, then under the rule of Shaikh Mohammad bin Abdullah who was defeated in the attack and was driven out of Qatif.[22]

Shaikh Mohammad bin Khalifah's action apparently caused much anger amongst the British. He was unlucky as his British match happened to be Colonel Lewis Pelly, a very shrewd politician with superior skill and resolution. Colonel Pelly, then British Political Resident at Bushehr, arrived in Bahrain in force, and imposed upon Shaikh Mohammad a treaty on 31 May 1861 (21 Zilqadah 1277) which consisted of a preamble and four articles. By signing this document, Shaikh Mohammad undertook in Article II:

> . . . to abstain from all maritime aggression of every description against neighbouring Shaikhs, from prosecution of war, piracy and slavery by sea, so long as he should receive the support of the British government in the maintenance of the security of his own possessions against similar aggressions directed against them by the chiefs and tribes of the Persian Gulf.[23]

In Article III, he undertook:

> . . . to make all such aggressions and depredations on himself, known to the British Resident in the Persian Gulf as the arbitrator, in such cases, and to promise that no act of aggression or retaliation would be committed at sea by Bahrain on any other tribes, without the consent of the British government.[24]

After signing this treaty, Colonel Pelly imprisoned Shaikh Mohammad bin Abdullah of Qatif in Damam and left Qatif under Bahrain's sovereignty. Further agreement, signed between the Al-Khalifah rulers of Bahrain and the British in the 1880s and 1890s, made Bahrain an official protectorate of Great Britain.

EMERGENCE OF THE STATE OF QATAR

The history of the creation of the State of Qatar is tied up with the history of the Al-Thani gaining paramountcy in the peninsula in mid-nineteenth century.

Al-Thani is a branch of the Ma'adhad clan of the famous Bani Tamim tribe which lived in the area even at the time of the Iranian federative empire of the Sassanians (224–685 AD). The descent of Bani Tamim is traced to Mudar bin Nizar. This historical figure – whose tribe was considered as one of the oldest in Arabia – achieved statesmanship, chivalry and poetry and earned his tribe a place in Arab and Islamic history.

The Al-Thani inherited their name from their great ancestor, Thani bin Mohammad bin Thamir bin Ali, whose eleventh great grandfather, Ma'adhad bin Mushrif ruled the oasis of Yibrin.[25] He was said to have come from the Washm district of Yamamah in the seventeenth century. Others date the arrival in Qatar peninsula of the great grandfather of Thani back to 1750 AD.[26]

The northwestern town of Zubarah in Qatar had, for centuries, been the site of Iranian or local governments of Bahrain (old Bahrain which embraced coastal areas as well as the archipelago). The peninsula, once an arena of territorial contention between the Iranians and the British in the nineteenth century, attracted the attention of others from the outset of the twentieth century because of its sensitive position in the territorial contentions between the British and the Ottomans which continued until 1913. Before the Al-Thani, the southern half of the Qatar peninsula was said to have been ruled by Beni Muslim tribe. Early in the nineteenth century the Al-Thani was, most of the time, a dependent of the ruler of Bahrain. An Iranian government document states:

> The Al-Thani shaikhs – ancestors of present ruler of Qatar – in order to be safe from the incursions and plunder of Al-Khalifah and other tribes, on several occasions – in the first half of the nineteenth century – declared themselves as subjects of Al-Khalifah shaikhs and paid a tax of 900 qarans[27] every year to the shaikhs of Bahrain and some of the time a member of the Al-Khalifah family ruled in Qatar.[28]

Changes of great consequence which shaped the present political geography of the lower Gulf, especially that of the Qatar peninsula, began in the mid-nineteenth century. Within the context of Qatar, this change was the outcome of two major developments: adoption of Wahhabi religious reforms and the rise in the commercial value of pearling activities in the vicinity of the peninsula.

Mohammad bin Thani – the able ruler of the shaikhdom of the Ma'adhad in Fuwairit – resolved to invest his wealth in pearling and the pearl trade. This enterprise proved to be well timed and brought the Al-Thani prosperity of the measure they needed in their struggle for a greater political role in the peninsula. Starting with only one large boat, the tribe was soon in possession of a considerable fleet of fishing craft.

The Qatar peninsula was, at the time, controlled by Zubarah authorities nominally dependent on Iran, but each one of the tribes of the peninsula almost constituted almost an independent political entity. These included: Al-Naim, Al-Sudan, Al-Mossallam, Al-Salatah, Al-Buinin, Al-Mahandah, Al-Kholaifi, Al-Amamarah, Al-bin Ali, Al-Mahrah, and Al-bu-Kuarah.

The Al-Thani gradually became involved in the contest for supremacy in the peninsula. In 1849 Shaikh Mohammad Al-Thani moved his tribe, Ma'adhad, from the north to Doha which, in time, became the capital of the emirate of Al-Thani.

The Al-Khalifah Shaikh Mohammad's attack on Zubarah in 1861 and his defeat by the British opened up the opportunity for the Al-Thani to extend their authority in the peninsula. Sheikh Mohammad bin Thani, leader of the House of Thani gained patrimony of the tribe in 1864. The Qataris consider this date as the date of the birth of the emirate of Qatar and Shaikh Mohammad bin Thani is regarded by them as the founder of the Al-Thani dynasty and the founding father of the State of Qatar.

Shaikh Mohammad's success has been attributed to his personal qualities such as deep insight, calm judgement, enlightened religious knowledge and tactful guidance.[29]

The birth of the state of Al-Thani however, was given recognition first by the 1868 maritime treaty with Britain which was signed by Shaikh Mohammad bin Thani and Colonel Lewis Pelly, British Political Resident in Bushehr.

In the early twentieth century the Al-Thani claimed the whole of the Qatar peninsula, but the northwest of the peninsula, namely the district of Zubarah, was still strongly claimed by the Al-Khalifah of Bahrain. In fact Al-Thani rule did not go much beyond Dhohah, Wakrah, Dha'Sim and Khawr al-Mohadradah. This was on the whole a principality heavily dependent on British support on the one hand and on Ibn Saud of Arabia on the other. A report on the state of affairs in the Qatar peninsula in 1934 remarks:

> Shaikh Abdullah claims the whole of the Qatar peninsula bound on the south west by a line drawn from Nakhsh towards the east, al Gabal, Wadi al Gaiban to the Subkah, and coming out on the east coast on the northern shore of Khor Odaid Udayd. Beyond the frontier mentioned is a neutral zone of several miles in breadth, one part being between Qatar and the Oman tribes on the southeast, and the other part being between Qatar and the Saudi territory on the southwest. The neutral zone and the frontier between the Qatar and Oman tribes is recognised by all, but that between Qatar and the Saudi government is only recognised as on sufferance from Ibn Saud . . .
>
> Ibn Thani is definitely dependent on the goodwill of the Ibn Saud and his Hassa governor, Ibn Jalloui, for the safety of his lands from the raids of the Nejd tribes, specially from the Manasir.
>
> I believe it irks Ibn Thani to be so much dependent for his safety on Ibn Saud, but to strengthen himself by hiring a body of mercenaries

from the tribes of Bini Hajar and Al Murra, other than the few dozen men he has at present, would cost him much and more than he could well afford.[30]

BRITISH PROTECTION FOR QATAR AND BAHRAIN

The people of the port of Zubarah revolted in 1867 against Shaikh Hamad, Agent of the Ruler of Bahrain there. Shaikh Mohammad bin Khalifah asked Colonel Lewis Pelly for assistance in accordance with Articles 1 and 2 of the treaty of May 1861 between them. Pelly apparently took some time to decide to assist Shaikh Mohammad. As the revolt in Zubarah increased, Shaikh Mohammad sought assistance from the governor of Fars.[31] But, before receiving any assistance from the British fleet or from the Iranians, Shaikh Mohammad mobilised his own forces and with the help of Shaikh Zaied bin Khalifah Al-Nahyan, Ruler of Abu Dhabi, suppressed the rebellion in Safar 1284 (1867).

This undertaking proved to be fatal for Shaikh Mohammad. Colonel Pelly, then Political Resident in the Gulf, appeared before Bahrain with the British navy and blockaded the islands. Shaikh Mohammad's correspondence with Iran for assistance was intercepted at sea, and cannons were fired over the fort from which Iranian flags were flying. Several Bahraini vessels were burnt and Shaikh Mohammad was dismissed by force from the emirate of Bahrain, after a penalty of 10,000 Iranian tumans was extracted from him.[32]

Pelly then appointed Shaikh Ali, a brother of Shaikh Mohammad, in his place as the new Ruler of Bahrain.[33]

Almost immediately after succeeding his brother, Shaikh Ali followed his policy by sending his agent, an Iranian by the name of Khalil Merrikhi, to Prince Hessam as-Saltana, governor of Fars, and to the Shaikh of Bandar Lengeh (a Qasemi Shaikh governing Lengeh as a subject and official of the Iranian government), seeking support and soldiers.[34]

People of Lengeh extended assistance to Shaikh Ali bin Khalifah. This act angered the British who sent a warship to Lengeh and threatened them (the people of Lengeh) with penalty and punishment.[35]

Shaikh Ali bin Khalifah, disappointed with the Iranian Government for their lack of decisive action, entered into a treaty with Colonel Pelly in 1868 which formed the basis for Bahrain to become a British protectorate at a later date. This treaty put a final end to the brave efforts of Shaikh Mohammad and his brother Shaikh Ali for the preservation of Bahrain's independence from the colonial ambitions of Colonel Pelly. They did their utmost and explored every possibility available to them, such as flying Iranian flags over their forts hoping that it might deter Colonel Pelly. But it was the colonial era, and brave, intelligent, and freedom-seeking leaders were treated as the most dangerous of enemies.

Colonel Pelly, however, signed in the same year (1868), a tribute agreement with Shaikh Mohammad bin Thani in Qatar whereby the Al-Thani were to pay tax to the ruler of Bahrain.

As the Turks annexed Al-Hasa in 1871, they expressed desire for sovereignty over the surrounding areas including Bahrain. This became a source of irritation to both the British and the Iranians, neither of whom failed to protest vigorously to the Porte whenever occasion evinced a disposition by the Porte to interfere in Bahrain politics. Turkish authorities on more than one occasion expressed the intention of rebuilding the town of Zubarah and establishing a military post there, but Shaikh Isa bin Ali of Bahrain invariably protested against this Turkish design.[36]

The Iranians, at this time confronted by the Turkish pretensions over areas of their interest, found themselves and the British in the same position *vis-à-vis* the Porte, and saw the British interference in the affairs of Bahrain to be to their benefit. Haji Mohsen Khan Moin al-Molk the Ambassador to London, for instance, wrote in 1871 to the Iranian Foreign Ministry:

> . . . (Porte) will await the opportunity to implement its designs on Bahrain, especially that it has entered its warships in the Persian Gulf, and has recently demonstrated its control of the Najd regions, and finally, I have the honour to submit that, although for temporary political expediency at present the interference of the English government in the safekeeping of Bahrain is desirable, but, on the whole, the leaders of the excellent government must not consider it sufficient . . .[37]

The Porte was frequently informed by the British government that no hostile settlement would be permitted at Zubarah. In 1893, having objected to the British authorities taking up instances of Bahrain's suffering from the piracy of certain Arabs in the Gulf, the Porte was informed that Bahrain was under British protection. Later the same year, a claim was put forward by the Ottomans to the right to treat the people of Bahrain as Turkish subjects within Ottoman territory. This claim was immediately protested against by the British Resident in the Gulf. Later the Turks occupied the small island of Zakhnuniyah, a dependency of Bahrain, but subsequently evacuated it after a British protest. Later on 29 July 1913 a convention was concluded between British government and the Ottomans in which the Porte renounced all claims to Bahrain. In a secret clause added to this convention which was never ratified, the Porte expressed the desire to obtain the island of Zakhnuniyah by paying £1000 to the Shaikh of Bahrain for this purpose.[38] This money was never paid and the Shaikh of Bahrain did not renounce claims to Zakhnuniyah.

In the month of Ramazan 1312 (March 1895) a rebellion against Shaikh Isa bin Ali, the new ruler of Bahrain, erupted in Bahrain and Colonel Sir Arnold T. Wilson (author of *The Persian Gulf*), then Political Resident in the Gulf who had returned from Muscat, was present in Bahrain. The French Consul at Bushehr wrote to his government on 23 March:

> Reports that I have received from reliable sources suggest that the British Political Representative in the Persian Gulf is in Bahrain for a few days now, but I do not know as yet, the reasons for Colonel Wilson's trip.[39]

Many of the people of Bahrain were apparently killed in this rebellion. The rebellion increased and eventually the rebels emigrated to Zubarah towards the end of Moharram 1313 (July 1895). Since the Ottomans were then active in northern Qatar, quarrels erupted between the Shaikh of Bahrain and the Ottomans. Four hundred Turkish troops were sent to Zubarah in a warship. This move made the British intervene by sending a representative to Zubarah asking the migrant tribes to return to Bahrain.[40] This incident caused the Ottomans to increase their activities in the northern Qatar peninsula.

A retaliatory action by the migrant tribes on Bahrain was expected. Led by Al-bin Ali and supported by the Ottomans, they invaded Bahrain in 1895 and motivated military intervention by the British. On the discovery of a large number of Qatari boats at Zubarah armed and prepared for sea, British vessels, after warning, opened fire, disabled a great number and destroyed or captured many others. The Al-bin Ali sued for peace and finally relations with Qatar were restored the following year.[41] This was the year in which the emirate of Al-Thani of Qatar began to emerge as a political entity independent of others in the region.

Treaties and agreements of 1880, 1892, 1898, 1909, 1912 and 1914 that the British signed with the rulers of Bahrain completely alienated them from their right to conduct their own foreign policy. Meanwhile, the Al-Thani of Qatar signed in 1916 a treaty with the British Political Resident in the Gulf whereby the British government guaranteed Qatar against threats from the chiefs of the region.[42]

THE CONTINUED IRANIAN CLAIMS OF SOVEREIGNTY TO BAHRAIN

Iran's historical claims to Bahrain entered a new and vigorous phase in the twentieth century. Describing Iran's renewed claims to Bahrain, *The Times* of London (21 December 1927) claimed that Bahrain was 'an island country which included five islands').[43] *The Times* of 5 January 1928 also described Bahrain as 'a country formed of one large island and four smaller'.[44] The Iranian parliament passed a bill in November 1957 by virtue of which Bahrain was announced officially as Iran's fourteenth province,[45] with two special seats reserved in the Lower House of the Majlis for the representatives of the so-called fourteenth province. From then on, the declared policy of Iran was to leave any international organization which accepted Bahrain as a member state. This policy created great complications in Iran's international relations, especially those with Britain and some Arab states, notably with Saudi Arabia which took upon herself to block, whenever possible, the Iranian claim.

This Saudi Arabian protectionist policy towards Bahrain was the reason for Iran's protest against the signing of the Saudi Arabian–Bahraini continental shelf boundary delimitation agreement of 1958. Iran was then convinced that the agreement was signed deliberately in defiance of her claims to Bahrain. Iran, on the other hand, began negotiating with Britain in London in 1965 for the delimitation of her continental shelf boundaries with the Arab countries and emirates of the Persian Gulf, but soon it became clear that with the existing territorial differences, including Iran's claims to Bahrain, offshore boundary delimitation was not possible.

Relations between Iran and Saudi Arabia improved dramatically after King Faisal of Saudi Arabia visited Iran in late 1965. The two countries agreed, among other things during this visit, to delimit their continental shelf boundaries in the Persian Gulf.[46]

To return the Saudi King's visit, Mohammad Reza Shah Pahlavi of Iran was invited to pay a state visit to Saudi Arabia in 1967, but this visit was called off[47] because the Saudis had welcomed the Ruler of Bahrain as a 'head of state', only one week before the Shah's own proposed state visit to their country. The scheduled visit was cancelled in protest and for a while relations between the two countries became frosty,[48] until King Hassan of Morocco intervened and reconciled the Shah with King Faisal of Saudi Arabia.[49]

The Shah visited Saudi Arabia in November 1968, a month after the signing of the continental shelf delimitation agreement between the two countries. This visit ended in the rapid improvement of bilateral relations in all aspects. Friendship and co-operation became so close and productive that it led many to suspect that the two sides had made a secret deal on the issue of the Bahrain islands. One source claims:

> Because the chemistry during that meeting was right, with the Shah in a good mood, King Faisal gave him two billion barrels of oil reserves in the disputed (continental shelf) area. In return, the Shah gave up his claim to Bahrain . . .[50]

This rumour is completely baseless, because Iran–Saudi Arabian continental shelf boundary agreement was concluded a month before the Shah's meeting with King Faisal in Saudi Arabia, and also, because the agreement was reached wholly under the influence of a sense of urgency for the settlement of territorial disputes and delimitation of maritime areas between the two countries at that time. King Faisal's conciliatory and compromising posture in this respect had nothing to do with the issue of Bahrain, it was because of the greater urgency of preparing the ground for much-hoped for Iran–Saudi Arabian cooperation in the Persian Gulf for the preservation of peace and security in the wake of imminent British withdrawal from the region.[51] Meanwhile, although the above rumour has no base, the parallel secret negotiations between Iran and Britain on the subject of Anglo–Iranian territorial disputes in the Gulf gave rise to the rumour that the two sides, in conjunction with 'some'[52] Arab governments, agreed on a trade-off agreement by giving Abu Musa Island to Iran in return for Iran's withdrawal of claims to Bahrain.[53] This rumour was more credible because of its background history. The British had endeavoured since 1928 to come to a similar arrangement with Iran on the issue of Bahrain and the islands in the Strait of Hormuz.

The Shah's Court Minister and his closest adviser, Amir Asadollah Alam, writes in his confidential diary of Sunday 23 March 1969:

... The British Ambassador called. I told him we can reach no settlement in respect of Bahrain until we know the fate of the Tunbs and Abu Musa. In that case, he declared, we have all been wasting our time. 'So be it ', I said . . .[54]

Amir Khosro Afshar, Iran's chief negotiator in the issue of Bahrain, the three islands and Shatt al-Arab, confirmed in a discussion with this writer, on Wednesday 2 January 1991, that:

There was no trade-off deal with the British during our negotiations on the separate issues of Bahrain and the three islands of the Strait of Hormuz.'

What is undoubtedly true, however, is that the Iranians tried hard to link the two issues of Bahrain and the three islands. Reviewing his memoirs, Sir Denis Wright, British Ambassador to Iran between 1963 and 1971 who unofficially negotiated with the Iranian leadership on the subject of Anglo–Iranian disputes over Bahrain and the three islands of Greater Tunb, Lesser Tunb and Abu Musa, asserts that during the said negotiations; 'At one point I had to reject an Iranian proposal that agreement on Bahrain must be subject to agreement on the islands . . .[55]

Nevertheless, it appears that the Iranians did not lose hope for such a compromise until the last moment. Amir Asadollah Alam asserts in his confidential diary of Sunday 23 March 1969:

. . . I reported that he (Ambassador Denis Wright of Britain) expresses more hope and offers more assistance than he did the other day, that if the issue of Bahrain was settled first, then we can discuss the issue of the islands. That is to say when [Iran] supports the Federation [of the Emirates then scheduled to include Bahrain], can take these places [the three islands] even in the name of defending the federation without any [unpleasant] reaction from the Arabs . . .[56]

It was with the background of an understanding of this nature on the part of the Iranians that the Shah appeared to have been determined to link the two issues, even as late as the time when the UN Secretary General was asked to test the will of the people of Bahrain. In his confidential diary of Wednesday 30 April 1969, Amir Asadollah Alam indicates:

. . . I reported the comments of the British Ambassador, who tells that the delay in negotiations with Bahrain springs from the Shaikh's reluctance to allow the UN Secretary General U Thant to send a fact-finding mission to the island at the invitation of Britain and Iran. This has come as a real surprise. According to His Imperial Majesty, 'we shall accept no compromise on Bahrain until the status of Abu Musa and Tunbs has been clarified'. I told him that I had already made this point clear to the Ambassador, but HIM instructed me to make it doubly clear . . .'[57]

Iran and Britain finally agreed to submit their differences over the issue of sovereignty of the Bahrain islands to the UN Secretary General. The British claim that the initiative was originally theirs,[58] though all indications point to the Shah of Iran's great desire to settle territorial disputes in the Persian Gulf before the British left the region at the end of 1971. The Shah announced in January 1969 at a press conference in New Delhi at the end of his state visit to India that:

We cannot accept an island separated by the English from our country to be given to the others, by them but on our account. This is the principle that Iran cannot ignore . . . Iran, on the other hand, has always adhered to its policy of never resorting to force for obtaining territories or territorial concessions against the will of the people of those territories. I want to say that if the people of Bahrain do not wish to join our country we shall never resort to force, because it is against the policy of our government to use force for capturing this part of its territory . . . Our policy and philosophy is to oppose occupation of other territories by force . . . Anything that could somehow demonstrate the will of the people of Bahrain to us and to you and to all world is good.[59]

Recently disclosed British Foreign Office confidential documents reveal that the Shah was contemplating the withdrawal of Iran's claim to Bahrain as early as 1965–66, at least four years earlier than the time this claim was officially withdrawn. This is clearly stated in the following two documents.

1. *Confidential letter of 2 September 1966 from the British Ambassador in Iran to the British Foreign Office*

Senator Abbas Mas'udi (1964 Personalities No. 118), who is Iran's most influential newspaper proprietor and is planning to visit Kuwait, Doha, Abu Dhabi and Dubai beginning next week, called at my house yesterday afternoon. After discussing his coming trip, which will be his first to the Gulf area outside Kuwait, he came to the purpose of the visit, which was to ask whether I had any suggestion about the handling of the Bahrain problem.

In speaking to me Mas'udi indicated that he shared the Shah's privately expressed view (as recently as 27 August the Shah had told Clare Hollingworth of the *Guardian* off the record that Bahrain was of little interest to him, given that the oil was running out and the pearls had already run out – the line he took in London last year, as you will remember) that the Iranian claim to Bahrain was an embarrassment but one which was difficult to abandon because of the sensitivity of public opinion. He told me that the Shah knew he would be speaking to me about his coming trip to the Persian Gulf and I think it unlikely that Mas'udi would have dared to make this approach to me about Bahrain without the Shah's blessing. . . . Mas'udi also enquired whether HMG had any plans for giving independence to Bahrain, arguing that if so it might be relatively easy for the Iranian Government to recognise Bahrain's independence simultaneously with HMG doing so.[60]

2. Confidential letter of 29 September 1966 from the British Residency in the Persian Gulf to the Arabian Department of the Foreign Office

During August Aram[61] told H.M. Ambassador in Tehran that 'as far as Iran was concerned, Bahrain had little or no value' and that Iran might 'give up her claim to Bahrain in return for a *quid pro quo* on the other islands' (presumably Tunb, Abu Musa and Sirri) which they consider of strategic value.[62]

While expressing their own delight and great interest and that of the Bahrainis on these hints, the British Political Residency's advice to the British government on the Iranian Foreign Minister's operative hint about a *quid pro quo* on the islands of Tunb, Abu Musa and Sirri was to kill the idea. The Residency's confidential letter reads:

If it turns out after all this that the operative hints in Aram's reference (paragraph 2 (a) above) to a *quid pro quo* over the 'strategic' islands belonging to or claimed by Sharjah and Ras al-Khaimah, we shall obviously be driving up a cul-de-sac.[63]

However, following the new developments, the Shah's government wrote to the Secretary General of the United Nations in early 1970 requesting the use of his good office for determining the will of the people of Bahrain.

U Thant, UN Secretary General wrote to the governments of Iran and Britain on 20 March 1970 informing Tehran and London of his willingness to carry out the wishes of the government of Iran in Bahrain.[64] He assigned Signor Vittorio Winspeare Guicciardi, Director General of the UN Geneva Office as his personal envoy to ascertain the will of the people of Bahrain. Subsequently, both governments of Iran and Britain wrote to the UN Secretary General informing him that they would accept the finding of a UN delegation to Bahrain, provided it was approved by the UN Security Council.

Signor Guicciardi's mission to Bahrain began on 30 March 1970 and lasted for about two weeks. He informed the UN Secretary General in UN Document No. 9772 of his findings in Bahrain. Paragraph 57 of his report indicates:

> The results of the investigation have convinced me that the overwhelming majority of the people of Bahrain are in favour of their territory being officially recognised as an independent country of complete sovereignty, with the freedom of determining their relation with other nations.[65]

Signor Guicciardi's report was circulated to the United Nations Security Council. The Council met on 11 May 1970 to debate this report and approved it unanimously[66] (see Appendix I). The Council then issued its resolution 278 (1970) of 11 May 1970 (see Appendix I for text of the resolution) in which the will of the people of Bahrain for independence was confirmed.

The UN Security Council's said resolution was conveyed to the governments of Iran and Britain. The Iranian Government reported the result of the United Nations' finding and resolution to the Lower and Upper Houses of the Majlis on 14 and 18 May 1970 respectively (see Appendix II for the original Persian text of the bill) which was debated and approved by the Majlis. The British government too revoked on 24 August 1971 its special agreements of the late nineteenth century with Bahrain, paving the way to Bahrain's subsequent declaration of independence. Iran and Bahrain established diplomatic relations on 29 August 1971. A remarkable feature in the documents related to the Iranian claims of sovereignty over Bahrain and the documents related to the settlement of these claims is the absence of any geographical description of the areas and territories claimed. Iran's geographical description of claims never went beyond the term 'Bahrain islands'.

GEOGRAPHICAL DIMENSIONS OF IRAN'S FORMER CLAIMS TO BAHRAIN

An examination of Iranian government documents shows that there was no direct reference to the geographical extent of Iran's claims of sovereignty over the Bahrain islands. Nevertheless, these documents, from the earliest time, describe the archipelago as being of 33 islands. Considering that the number of islands of Bahrain's immediate archipelago does not exceed 16, which when calculate together with the 17 islands of Hawar archipelago totals 33, it seems that the Iranian government had, from the beginning of the claim, considered Hawar archipelago as part of its claim to Bahrain.

This particular Iranian way of considering the areas of claims to Bahrain has continued throughout the history of the claim and became an established geographical convention in the Iranian studies of the Persian Gulf. The following examples of this, are two documents from the Iranian governments of before and after the Islamic Revolution. The first document is a booklet called 'Bahrain' which was published by the Foreign Ministry of the Imperial Iranian Government in 1975 in which, Bahrain is described as being an archipelago of '33' islands, and its geographical situation is described as:

> Bahrain is an archipelago in the Persian Gulf, situated between al-Hasa and Qatar peninsula, and is composed of 33 islands great and small. The largest of these is called Manameh which is 30 miles in length from north to south, and its breadth is 10 miles. On the south of Bahrain and west of Qatar is situated the archipelago of Hawar.
>
> Bahrain's area of land is estimated at 247 square miles. This . . .[67]

The second document is also a booklet called *Bahrain*, similarly published by the Ministry of Foreign Affairs of the Islamic Republic of Iran in 1989, in which Bahrain is described as being composed of 33 islands and, Hawar archipelago is listed as being number five in the list of Bahrain's major islands, albeit the text mentions that ownership of this archipelago is being contested by the two states.[68] It is on the basis of this traditional geographical description of Bahrain that not only do all books published in Iran or by the Iranians around the world describe the Bahrain archipelago as being composed of 33 islands, but many of them clearly refer to the Hawar islands as being a part of Bahraini territory. As an example, *Encyclopaedia Iranica*, a notable work of Iranian studies, which is being published by the US University of Columbia under the supervision and editorship of

(Iranian) Professor Ehsan Yarshater, describes Hawar archipelago as being 'part of the State of Bahrain'.[69] On the other hand, Iran has always considered the eastern extreme of its claims on Bahrain to be the northwestern corner of the Qatar peninsula, if not the entire peninsula itself. This geographical description includes all islands situated between Qatar peninsula and Bahrain's main island. This tradition is an old one. Hamdollah Mostofi, a famous fourteenth century Iranian geographer, for instance, states:

> The foundation of Bahrain was laid by the hands of Ardeshir (Artaxerxes) Babakan of the Sassanids (224 AD). In the ancient times, Bahrain, al-Hasa, Qatif, Khatt-e Azar, al-Arreh, Faruq, Yanuneh, Sabun Darian, Zubarah, were all calculated to be within the Arabic Sultanate which were Iran's protectorates and belonged to the province of Fars (Persia).'[70]

In modern times too, the geography of Iran's ownership of Bahrain has been described as starting from Zubarah on the Qatar peninsula. A noted Persian publication of the 1960s states:

> Eventually Bahrain was rescued from the clutches of the Portuguese and until the end of the Safavid era Bahrain's governorship was in the hands of the Shaikh of Jabbarah of Hawlah on behalf of the Imperial Court of Iran.[71]

It is noteworthy that 'Jabbarah of Hawlah' was an Iranian terminology of the nineteenth century used in reference to Beni Hawalah tribe ruling Zubarah on behalf of the Iranian government.

An official correspondence from the Iranian Government in the first half of the nineteenth century to the British Legation in Tehran states:

> . . . and 50 years ago Shaikh Nasr, Governor of Bahrain, was governing the said (Bahrain) islands . . .[72]

Considering the fact that Shaikh Nasr Khan was Iran's last governor of Bahrain, who governed the archipelago of Bahrain from Zubarah, this document leaves no doubt that Iran then, as ever before and after then, considered Zubarah and the vicinity, including the Hawar archipelago as part of Bahrain, all being claimed by Tehran as one province. Similarly a recent work of political geography published by the Institute of Political and International Studies of the Ministry of Foreign Affairs of the Islamic Republic of Iran gives the following brief history of Bahrain together with Zubarah and Hawar archipelago from an Iranian perspective:

This territory (Bahrain) returned to the Iranian authorities from the time of the Dailamids (936–978 AD), and at the time of restoration of state and boundary in Iran of the Safavid era (1501–1722 AD) it was a province dependent of Bushehr governorship, and the town of Zubarah (Jabbarah) which was the most important locality of the Qatar peninsula, was considered as the centre of the state of Bahrain. In 1717 the Arabs of Muscat attacked Bahrain and the Hawar islands via the sea but the state of Bahrain did not remain in their hands for long. The governorship of Bahrain was held by the Shaikh of Zubarah who was from the powerful Hawalah tribe of Iranian origin. He nominally adhered to Iranian sovereignty but in practice had no fear and was almost independent. At the time of Nader Shah's rule, Lotf-Ali Khan, Governor of Fars (Persia), attacked the Shaikh of Zubarah in 1737 with an army from Bushehr, and by occupying Bahrain, made that locality subject to the Governorate of Fars. Shaikh Nasr Khan, the last of Iranian governors of Bahrain, was there on behalf of Karim Khan Zand (1757–99). The Al-Khalifah clan of the Utoobi tribe of Unaizah Arabs moved from within Arabia . . .

At this time, not only Zubarah (on the northwest corner of the Qatar peninsula) but the Hawar islands were parts of Bahrain and all these coasts and islands were still officially subject to the government of Iran . . .[73]

The idea of Zubarah, in the Qatar peninsula, being a part of the state of Bahrain, captured Iranian imagination to the extent that once, whilst reporting on the letter of undertakings by Shaikh Ali Al-Khalifah of Bahrain to Colonel Lewis Pelly, British Political Resident in the Persian Gulf (1868), Mohammad Ali, Chief of the Passport Office of the Iranian Ports, suggested (in brackets) – where the said letter speaks of the people of Qatar being subjects of the Shaikh of Bahrain – that:

. . . (here the government of Iran can capture Qatar as well) . . .[74]

The notion of Qatar (Zubarah) being part of the Bahrain of Iranian claims continued for such a long period of time that even in 1956 the Iranian Ministry of Justice asked the Ministry of Foreign Affairs on behalf of the Bandar Abbas Court of Justice, whether the Emirate of Qatar was also part of Iranian territory or not. In reply to this enquiry the Ministry of Foreign Affairs stated that Iran had no territorial claim on Qatar.[75]

QATAR AND BAHRAIN DECLARING INDEPENDENCE

Almost immediately after the British revoked their special agreements with Bahrain in August 1971 the State of Bahrain declared her independence. This was at least three months before Pax-Britannica was formally withdrawn from the Gulf in December 1971.

Bahrain delimited her continental shelf boundaries with Saudi Arabia in 1958 which was the first agreement of its kind in the Gulf region. Bahrain's continental shelf boundary with Iran was delimited in 1971 and ratified in 1972; the only other continental shelf boundary to be delimited is that with Qatar which is being prevented by the Hawar, Dibal and Jaradah disputes.

Qatar declared her independence in September 1971. Its only inland boundary was delimited with Saudi Arabia in 1965. This settlement was arrived at after some decades of intense dispute. The dispute principally involved the two important localities of Jabal Nakhsh and Khor al-Udayd. The Saudis endeavoured for many years to secure a corridor of access to the Gulf in the Khor al-Udayd area which was recognised by the British in the nineteenth century as belonging to Abu Dhabi. The Westerners at one time, were allegedly prepared to pay the Shaikh of Abu Dhabi a sum of £25,000 in return for the cession to Saudi Arabia of a strip of territory on the Gulf coast of Khor al-Udayd in the form of lease. 'The Americans whose interests in the oil deposits of Arabia had grown considerably by then, proposed that the British government actually pay for the sale of the said territory'.[76]

The Americans once again approached the British for settlement of the disputes in that area. The main stumbling block at this time (1944) was the issue of Jabal Nakhsh. The Saudis had by then lost their interest in Khor al-Udayd mainly owing to the development works continuing extensively at Ras Tanurah, albeit they eventually managed to obtain a corridor of access from Abu Dhabi at Khur al-Udayd in 1974.

Jabal Nakhsh was an important part of Qatar's Dokhan district where large oil reserves were expected to be found. After World War II, the enormous oil reserves of both Qatar and Saudi Arabia began to be recognised and exploited. The new discoveries opened up fresh possibilities for rapid development in the region and pushed boundary disagreements to a secondary position of importance for the time being. The two sides eventually succeeded in settling their territorial differences and in delimiting their mutual boundaries at the southern end of the Qatar peninsula in 1965.

Border clashes erupted between Qatar and Saudi Arabia in late September and early October 1992 resulting in a number of casualties on both sides. The Saudis claimed that the incident was a local one involving cross-border tribes including the Al-Morrah tribe, whereas Qatar maintained that the Saudis had for some time been pushing their boundary northwards into the Qatar peninsula and the incident was the latest instance of Saudi aggression.

Qatar delimited her continental shelf boundaries with Abu Dhabi in 1969 and with Iran in the same year. Qatar's continental shelf boundary with Bahrain is not delimited because of disputes with Bahrain over the question of sovereignty over the Hawar archipelago, *fashts* of Dibal and Jaradah, and Zubarah district.

Chapter 6

Qatar–Bahrain Disputes in The Twentieth Century

INTRODUCTION

The period between 1895 and 1939 was a period of relative lull in Bahrain–Qatar territorial disputes. Yet, territorial differences between the two states gained new twists and turns in the early decades of the twentieth century. The expanded territorial differences between Bahrain and Qatar in the twentieth century included the district of Zubarah as well as the islands of Hawar and the *fashts* or shoals of Dibal and Jaradah, and the seabed between the two states and their territorial waters.

In this chapter efforts will be made to study each of the above mentioned cases separately with the hope that this approach will make appreciation of the very complicated Qatar–Bahrain territorial disputes easier.

ZUBARAH

Zubarah, now a seemingly worthless ruin lying on the northwest coast of the Qatar peninsula, was the original bone of territorial contention between Bahrain and Qatar in the early decades of the twentieth century. Zubarah was the first territory in the vicinity of Bahrain upon which the Al Khalifah clan descended and apparently retains an enduring symbolic significance for them. The locality is of sentimental value for the Al Khalifah as Shaikh Khalifah bin Mohammad, the first Ruler of the Al Khalifah of Bahrain, is buried there. Zubarah had been Al Khalifah's headquarters since their arrival in Qatar from Qurain (Kuwait) in 1766 until they moved to Manama in 1870. It was from Zubarah that the Al Khalifah attacked and

142

captured Bahrain from the Iranians in 1783.[1] The Al Khalifah continued ruling Bahrain from Zubarah until 1870 and from this date, they continued claiming ownership of the locality, albeit their claims have varied in substance with the passage of time and in accordance with the dictates of the British political representatives in the region. Admittedly, however, it is hard to understand this intense sentimental attachment of the Al-Khalifah of Bahrain to the district of Zubarah. After all, it was only a temporary home for them in the eighteenth century. Sir Charles Belgrave, who acted as the adviser to the Ruler of Bahrain in the 1930s and 1940s, has made some references to this sentimental attachment of the Al Khalifah to Zubarah. He confesses to being continually surprised by the intense reaction in the Al Khalifah at the mere mention of the name Zubarah. He said:

> When Shaikh Hamad died in 1942, I remember the words which were attributed to Queen Mary Tudor, when I am dead . . . you shall find Calais lying on my heart, but in this case the word would have been Zabarah.[2]

Zubarah continued to be controlled directly by the rulers of Bahrain until late Nineteenth century, whereas its inhabitants, notably the Naim tribesmen, continued to recognise the sovereignty of the ruler of Bahrain until the Al-Thani seized the district by force in 1937. Even in 1934, Hajji Abdullah Williamson, a British Moslem officer of the former Anglo-Persian Oil Company stated in his memorandum of January that year:

> Ibn Thani, other than the 60 odd members of his own family, has no tribe which he can claim as his own in Qatar. There are a few scattered semi nomads of the Naim tribe on the peninsula dating back to the time of the Bini Muslim who were the rulers in Qatar before the Thani family. Ibn Thani depends for his fighting force on men drawn from the Bini Hajar and Bini Murra, two of the three tribes pasturing along the border of Qatar. The third is al-Monasir. Ibn Thani is definitely dependent on the good will of Ibn Saud and his Hassa Governor, Ibn Jalloui, for the safety of his lands from the raids of the Nejd tribes, specially from the Manasir.'[3] and [4]

Bahrain's initial claims to Zubarah were claims of full sovereignty. Beginning in 1920 Abdullah bin Isa, son of the ruler of Bahrain officially asked the British representative for permission to open a port at Zubarah. The government of India firmly refused his request and

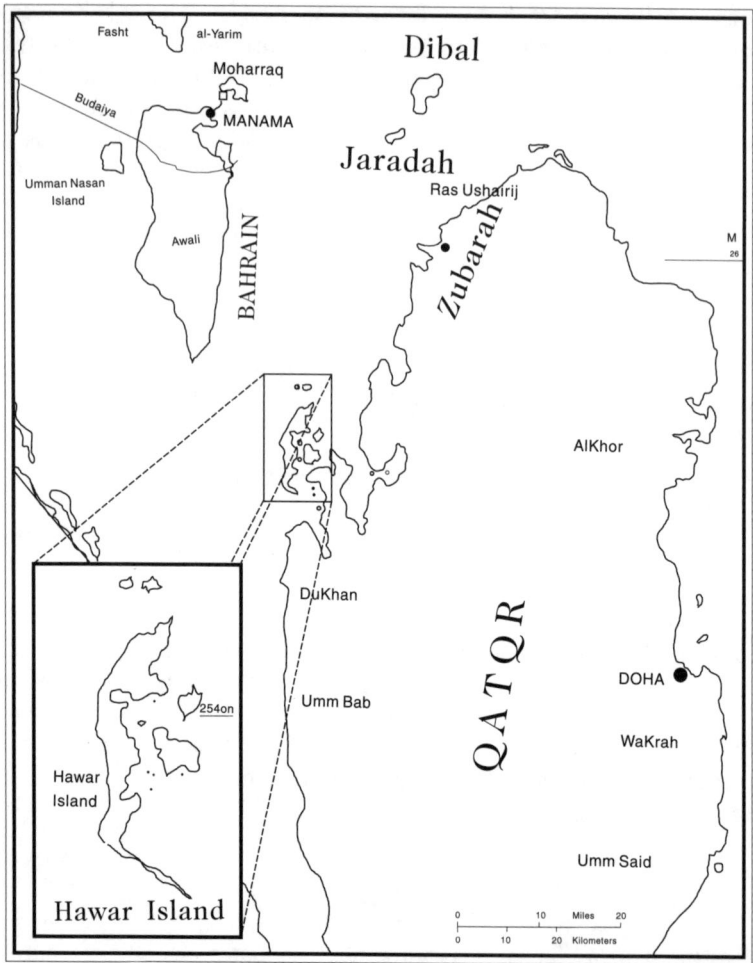

Figure 6.1 Qatar–Bahrain Areas of Territorial Differences: Zubarah, Hawar, Dibal and Jaradah

reminded him of a warning by the Political Resident to the State of Bahrain in 1875 not to interfere in the affairs of Zubarah.[5] Early in 1936 Petroleum Concession Limited endeavoured to obtain from the ruler of Bahrain an oil exploration concession for all territory (including territorial waters) not already leased to the Bahrain Oil Company. Major Holmes contacted the ruler of Bahrain for the

144

purpose but he made a number of amendments to the draft concession presented to him.[6] As doubt arose at this juncture on the actual ownership of the Hawar archipelago, the Indian government was asked to clarify the situation. Replying to a letter from Mr Longrigg of Petroleum Concession Ltd, the India Office acknowledged that Hawar Island was to be considered as Bahrain territory.[7] This acknowledgement was once again reaffirmed on 14 September 1936 by the India Office.[8]

Earlier, when the Anglo–Persian Oil Company's concession in Qatar was secured and representatives of Petroleum Concession Ltd (also a subsidiary of APOC) visited Zubarah with a view to carrying out a preliminary survey for a port on the western coast of Qatar peninsula, Bahrain found it necessary to bring her age-old claims on Zubarah to the attention of all concerned. At the same time, quarrels between two factions of the Naim tribes of Zubarah erupted and in the event involved both Bahrain and Qatar.

It was around this time that Bahrain resumed claims of sovereignty to Zubarah. An Iranian government document of 1937 states:

> The governorship of Lengeh has reported to the governorate of the southern ports, on the basis of a statement from a passenger arriving from Bahrain, that disputes have erupted between Shaikh Hamad, son of Shaikh Isa Shaikh of Bahrain, and the Shaikh of Zubarah, as a result of claims made by Shaikh Hamad as to the ownership of Zubarah which have ended in quarrelling and fighting, and have resulted in many casualties, and Shaikh Hamad has not as yet been able to succeed in proving his claims.[9]

This was before the Al-Thani Shaikh seized Zubarah in 1937. The Bahrainis, as a result of the development of this quarrel, sent three guards to hoist their flag in Zubarah.[10] The British Political Resident in the Persian Gulf supported Al-Thani of Qatar and secured from Bahrain a promise not to press for the ownership any further provided that Qatar preserved the *status quo* in Zubarah.[11] Shaikh Abdullah Al-Thani of Qatar defeated the warring factions of the Naim tribes and made them submit to Qatar.[12] This development which occurred as a result of British efforts to pacify the Bahrainis, further complicated the issue of Bahraini claims of sovereignty over Zubarah district.

Shaikh Hamad of Bahrain was so angered at this point that he decided to consult his solicitors in London. But the Political Resident informed him that the warning of 1875 was the final verdict of the British government.

In the 1940s the British negotiated an agreement between the rulers of the two states whereby 'the ruler of Qatar undertook that Zubarah would remain without anything being done in it which did not exist in the past'. This was to be from consideration and reverence to Al Khalifah, ruler of Bahrain. The ruler of Bahrain also undertook 'not to do anything that might harm the interest of the ruler of Qatar in Zubarah'.[13]

By the early 1950s the British seem to have concluded that Bahrain's claims of sovereignty over Zubarah should be rationalised as a price for the British decision to give Bahrain the ownership of the Hawar islands and Dibal and Jaradah *fashts*. The British Political Agent in Bahrain, C. J. Pelly, wrote to the ruler of Qatar on 26 January 1950 stating, among other things:

> . . . His Highness the Shaikh of Bahrain does not claim sovereignty over Zubarah or any other part of Qatar territory, nor does he claim rights to oil or any material there in. He merely wishes to send his dependants with their flocks for grazing to the Zubarah area without supervision from anyone and without the imposition of customs or other controls on such people as was the custom in the past . . .[14]

The highly obscure terms in which the wishes of the ruler of Bahrain about Zubarah were described needed further clarification. This clarification came in 1954. Early that year, John W. Wall, British Political Agent in Bahrain wrote to the ruler of that state pointing out:

> . . . I understand Your Highness's claims on Zubarah to be as follows:
>
> a. Property – the Al Khalifah claim to possess certain immovable property in Zubarah, consisting of dwelling houses, and Your Highness claims the right of all members of the Al-Khalifah, together with their dependants and servants to enjoy their properties there without interference by the authorities of the Qatar government and without being subject in any way to the control of that government and its officers.
>
> b. Freedom of entry – Your Highness claims the right for all your followers to enter freely into Zubarah and the surrounding area, for the purpose, as regards the Al Khalifah, of enjoying their property there, and, as regards your tribal followers for the purpose of grazing their flocks; and Your Highness claims that right of your followers to take into Zubarah and its surrounding areas, free of customs duty or control by the Qatar authorities all such provisions and materials and animals as they need for their own use and consumption Your Highness defined the word 'followers' as:

I) All Bahrain subjects.

II) All persons of whatever nationality who are in your service or in the service of the Bahrain government.

III) All those tribesmen who are recognised as owing allegiance to the ruler of Bahrain or who take any kind of pension, subsidy or stipend from him.

c. Sovereignty – Your Highness claims jurisdiction over all your followers as defined above while they are in Zubarah or the area surrounding it.

Your Highness said in our conversation yesterday that you did not claim sovereignty over the land, that you made no claim to any oil that there might be in the ground of Zubarah, do not affect in any way any agreement made between the ruler of Qatar and the Qatar Petroleum Company . . . .[15]

The Political Agent subsequently informed the ruler of Bahrain of the agreement of the ruler of Qatar with the terms of the claims in section (a) above but disputed the question of sovereignty over all people entering Zubarah on the part of Bahrain.

Furthermore, government authorities in Qatar had expressed a desire for the establishment of a police post in Zubarah which was deemed by Bahrain to be in clear contravention of the 1944 agreement between the two states whereby Qatar undertook not to do anything in Zubarah which did not exist in the past. This question, however, remained unsettled.

In a letter to the British Political Resident in the Persian Gulf, Shaikh Ali bin Abdullah Al Thani of Qatar wrote to the British on 14 May 1954 stating that he wished to reopen the fort at Zubarah for the periodic visits from his police patrols.[16] He did not, however, rule out his intention of establishing a permanent police post in Zubarah. What he said in his letter was that 'at present' he had no intention of maintaining a permanent police post at Zubarah.[17] The ruler of Bahrain also complained in July and September of 1956 to the British Political Resident in the Gulf that the Qatar authorities had compelled his subjects to take passports which was in contravention of the 1944 agreement between the two states.

This was a new addition to the complicated dispute over the district of Zubarah and the situation remained the same until 1957 when, after years of trying to persuade the ruler of Qatar to allow Bahrain to enjoy some freedom of access to Zubarah, British Gulf authorities gave up their futile efforts.

The British Political Resident in Bahrain, Sir Bernard Burrows, ruled in August 1957 that 'Bahrain should entertain no further hopes of being granted any extraterritorial privileges at Zubarah'.[18]

Not much has been heard of the dispute since 1957 and the ruins of the Zubarah settlement remained under Qatari control and has been treated as an integral part of that state as anywhere else along Qatar's northwestern shorelands. In 1970, during the legal process of Iran's withdrawal of claims to Bahrain, the Prime Minister of Bahrain told an Iranian Foreign Ministry official that:

> We ourselves have border disputes with Qatar over the district of Zubarah and have decided to recover this part of Bahrain territory from the Qataris.[19]

Even now Bahrain has not completely given up what she deems to be her rights in that locality and has invoked this claim in the recent reference of her territorial and boundary differences with Qatar to the International Court of Justice.

HAWAR ISLANDS

When in 1907 fighting broke out between Ahmad bin Shahin Al-Dosari, of Baharinah origin and of substantial influence in Hawar Island, and Batii bin Salman the headman of a neighbouring village in Hawar Island, the dispute was referred to and adjudicated by a Bahraini court of justice and verdicts were issued by the Al-Khalifah ruler of Bahrain solely because there was no other court of justice in the vicinity for the case to be referred to.[20] The Al-Thani emirate of Qatar was, at that time, known as the Al-Thani of Doha. In his acclaimed *Gazetteer of the Persian Gulf*, Lorimer listed the Hawar islands as belonging to Qatar – clearly because of the archipelago's geographical proximity with the Qatar peninsula – Lorimer explained in the following words that certain tribesmen of Bahrain had some form of connection with Hawar main island:

> Hawar, due west of the point of Ras Aburuk and about 5 miles from it, is about 10 miles long, north and south, and roughly parallel to the Qatar coast. There are no wells, but there is a cistern to hold rainwater built by the Dawasir of Zallaq in Bahrain, who have houses at two places on the island and use them in winter as shooting boxes. Fishermen are also frequent in Hawar. The island is adjoined on the north by Jazirat Rubath and on the south by Jazirat Suwad, in the channel between it and the mainland.[21]

Hawar is an archipelago consisting of 17 islands, islets and rocks which are situated in the waters separating Bahrain from Qatar.

The main island – Hawar Island – is the largest, 11 miles long and 2 miles wide with about 17 square miles in total land area. There are two hamlets on Hawar Island: one situated in the northern section and one in the southern section, each with a small population of about ten families. There is also water storage on the island created by the Bahrainis and the State of Bahrain stationed a military garrison on the island in the mid-1930s.

The other 16 islands are:[22] Southern Swad, Al-Waqrah, Al-Waqrah, Al-Waqrah, Bu Sadad (island), Bu Sadad (four rocks), Bu Sadad, Bu Sadad, Bu Sadad, Al-Mahzurah, Northern Swad, Al-Hajiyat, Al-Hajiyat, Ajirat, Rubadh, Al-Motaradh.

Although the Hawar islands were mentioned in the 1925 correspondence relating to oil activities of British companies, the issue of Hawar disputes arose in 1936 when the Bahrain Petroleum Company (BAPCO) and Petroleum Concession Limited (a subsidiary of the Anglo–Persian Oil Company) entered into negotiations with the ruler of Bahrain for exploration rights in seabed areas between Bahrain and the Qatar peninsula.

These developments encouraged the ruler of Bahrain to demonstrate his ownership of the Hawar islands. He had placed a military garrison on the main island in 1935. The ruler of Qatar protested against this action and claimed that the island of Hawar was part of Qatar.

Bahrain's flag was also hoisted on Hawar Island and on *fashts* or shoals of Dibal and Jaradah. The company directors wrote to the India Office for their assessment of the situation.

In a letter dated 14 July 1936 the British confirmed Bahrain's ownership of the islands but began to play with the wording which would, at the same time, cast a shadow of doubt or uncertainty on the subject.

In reply to a letter from Mr Stephen H. Longrigg of Petroleum Concession Limited, for instance, Mr M. J. Clauson of the India Office wrote in September 1936:

> We are very much obliged to you for your letter of 11 September, summarising your company's proceedings, actual and intended, on the Arab side of the Persian Gulf.
>
> . . . There is only one point to which I feel it is desirable to refer at the moment. You mentioned that the question of the ownership of the

Hawar group of islands has been referred to the India Office, who have replied that it should be considered as Bahrain territory. In order that there may be no misunderstanding, may I refer to Walton's letter to Skliros, dated the 14 July. It is important that the company should clearly understand that His Majesty's Government's position is as stated in the last sentence of that letter, namely, that, on the basis of the evidence at present before them, it appears to them that Hawar belongs to the Shaikh of Bahrain and the burden of disproving his claim would lie on any other potential claimant. Perhaps you will be kind enough to drop me a line to confirm that the company appreciates the limited nature of the decision given by His Majesty's Government in regard to this group of islands.[23]

Nevertheless, the British repeated their recognition of Bahrain's ownership of the Hawar group of islands in their official correspondence of 1937 and 1938 between the governments of India and the states of Bahrain and Qatar and the British Foreign Office.

The British Political Agent filed a report to the Political Resident in May 1938 in which he stated that because of the 1936 move by Bahrain for the control of these islands, Bahrain rightly possesses a *prima facie* claim to Hawar.[24] This report formed the basis on which the Political Resident, Mr. Fowle officially declared in 1939 that the Hawar islands (except for the island of Janan in the south which was recognised in 1947 as belonging to Qatar) as belonging to the state of Bahrain.[25]

The new Political Resident, C.G. Prior who replaced Fowle in September 1939, confirmed Fowle's decision albeit he expressed the view that he might not personally agree with it, and maintained that reversing Fowle's decision would not be 'Practical Politics'.[26]

In 1947 the British introduced a line dividing the seabed between the two states. The government of Bahrain made inquiries with the British government of India regarding the status of the Hawar islands. Later, when writing in reply to a letter from the ruler of Bahrain in April 1949, C. J. Pelly, British Political Agent in Bahrain, gave an explanation on the 1947 division of the seabed between Bahrain and Qatar, and pointed out officially once again that:

. . . in 1939 His Majesty's Government recognised the Hawar group of islands as appertaining to Bahrain . . .[27]

In 1964 Bahrain not only claimed that Hawar islands and the *fashts* of Dibal and Jaradah belonged to her, but claimed a new line of delimitation of the seabed boundary of the two states.[28] This claim was rejected by Qatar.

FASHTS (SHOALS) OF DIBAL AND JARADAH

Bahrain's flags of ownership were hoisted on the *fashts* (shoals) of Dibal and Jaradah in 1936. These two *fashts* were considered by the British maritime boundary award of September 1947 as Bahraini enclaves.

The decision recognised Bahrain's 'sovereign rights' in the areas of these *fashts, but the view was expressed that the shoals should not be considered to be islands having territorial waters.*[29]

The Geneva Convention of 1958 on territorial sea, however, regulated internationally binding guidance for boundary delimitations in the maritime areas of the world.

Article 10 of the Geneva Convention of 1958 defined an island as 'a naturally formed area of land surrounded by water, which is above water at high tide'.[30]

A year later (1959) when expansion of commercial activities in the seabed areas between Qatar and Bahrain began, changes in, or clarification of, geographical description of shoals of Jaradah and Dibal became necessary for the British. In a letter to their Bahrain representative, the British Foreign Office decided that Jaradah was an island with its own territorial sea.[31]

Although the decision was described with the adjective 'undoubtedly', the letter was full of doubt about describing the geographical character of Jaradah as 'an island'.

The new definition for Jaradah, however, contradicted the British decision of 1947 (pages 224 and 225 of P.G. 53 – FO 371/140194) whereby Jaradah was awarded to the ruler of Bahrain without territorial waters. In fact the British authorities had expressly informed the ruler of Bahrain that Dibal and Jaradah should not be considered to be islands and having territorial waters.[32]

The new definition for Jaradah was based on an unscientific method of observation or casual sighting:

Since this 1947 award, the Navy have made constant visits to Dibal and Jaradeh to ascertain that they were still shoals, being covered by water at high tide, and not islands. Jaradeh was first reported three years ago (1956 to be above water at high tide, and frequent visits, a report on the last of which by the Commodore Arabian Seas and Persian Gulf I enclose, have confirmed that Jaradeh is apparently now an island.[33]

What the Foreign Office had ignored was that paragraph 3 of Article 6 of the Geneva Convention of 1958 underlined the principle that once a boundary had been laid down (or an award made) this would remain in force whatever subsequent geographical changes may take place or refinements may be made in more modern charting.

The changed geographical description of Jaradah, from the point of view of the British Foreign Office, necessitated the 1947 award to revision 'in the event of more exact geographical data being forthcoming at a later date'. But this provision had been superseded by the terms of above-mentioned Article 6 of Geneva Convention of 'more exact geographical data'.

Even as an 'island' with territorial waters of three miles, Jaradah and its territorial sea would still be on the Qatar side of an equitable median line between that state and Bahrain.

The British had also endeavoured without success to define the territorial sea for the Dibal shoal while clearly acknowledging it as a shoal not an island. The magical solution was that because the southernmost part of Dibal is within three miles of Jaradah, 'the giving of territorial waters to Jaradeh will mean that territorial waters will leapfrog and have to be given to Dibal also'.[34] To this end the Foreign Office asked the British Admiralty for their expert opinion on the geographical description of Jaradeh. The Hydrographic Department of the Admiralty, in reply, confirmed that it was sure of the permanency of the islet at Jaradah, in spite of the fact that this 'storm island' had been in existence for the previous three years.[35] The Admiralty further doubted validity of the claim that the islet created at Jaradah could be considered as a naturally formed island. It, nevertheless, suggested that works carried out on Jaradah by the Bahrainis be considered as a basis for arguing a 'naturally formed' islet on Jaradah shoal. The Hydrographic Department of the Admiralty suggested:

> It could perhaps be argued that it is a naturally formed accretion of sand built up *as a result of* a man-made well-head or beacon.[36]

The expert view of the British Admiralty, however, favoured limitation of Bahrain's claim to the 1947 award on the basis of 'sound' geographical arguments. The Admiralty argued:

> It is noticed that about 6½ miles south of Katah ad Jaradeh a coral mound 9 feet high is charted. This lies on the Qatar side of the line division. If it be naturally formed it is entitled to a belt of territorial sea.

A tongue of shallow water extends about 1½ miles northward of it and terminates in a shoal of 4 feet depth, while a shoal of 5 feet lies a further mile northwestwards should either or both these shoals also built up and at same time emerge above the low water level, these will extend the limit of the territorial sea from the coral mound. Such an extension would overlap the limit from Katah ad Jaradeh resulting in a median line limit there and consequent reduction of area of territorial sea appertaining to Katah ad Jaradeh.

5½From the above it will be seen that there is a good case for limiting the sovereignty rights of Bahrain to that of the 1947 award, namely the areas which were *then* above spring tide low water level. Even if an islet exists there, it would not seem essential for it to have a territorial sea for, there are at least two precedents where HMG does not admit of a territorial sea for a foreign low-water coastline.[37]

An official British naval report in 1959 described the geographical status of Dibal as:

No part of the shoal, other than the artificial island and beacon, shows above sea level at high water spring.[38]

The government of Bahrain claimed in 1964 that the shoals of Dibal and Jaradah were islands with territorial waters. These claims were rejected by Qatar in 1965.[39] The authorities in Qatar requested international arbitration in these disputes as early as 1965 a suggestion which was rejected by Bahrain.

The state of Bahrain continued the work of elevation construction in Dibal and Jaradah. Erection of a number of buildings and Bahrain's coastguard station on Dibal in 1986 led a contingent of Qatari forces reportedly to land on Dibal on 26 April 1986 and to arrest up to 29 ex-patriate workers who were immediately released.[40]

Subsequent to these actions, the state of Qatar declared Dibal and Jaradah shoals along with Hawar islands as military zones.[41] Four days later Bahrain denounced these moves as 'a violation of good neighbourliness'. A serious conflict was about to break out when the armed forces of both states were called to readiness, but a decisive intervention by the leaders of Oman, Saudi Arabia and the United Arab Emirates averted a conflict. Leaders of the Gulf Cooperation Council succeeded in brokering a temporary settlement between the two states (also members of the GCC) whereby the two sides agreed on returning the situation of Dibal and Jaradah to the *status quo ante*. A monitoring group, set up by the GCC to ensure implementation of the agreement, made sure that the two sides adhered to the letter of the agreement. Qatar evacuated Dibal in June 1986.

The situation remained tense in 1986 and 1987 in spite of an exchange of visits between top officials of the two states. However, a joint committee for the study of all matters related to this dispute was created on a proposal by Saudi Arabia in December 1987. This committee was to determine whether the parties were able to settle their disputes and if such a settlement was found to be impossible, the dispute to be referred to international arbitration.

By 1989 all attempted mediation by the GCC leaders failed to bring the two sides closer to each other on these disputes. It was decided at the GCC summit meeting of December 1990 that the two states would be given until 15 May 1991 to settle their dispute or their differences would be referred to the International Court of Justice.[42]

THE SEABED AREAS

Territorial and boundary differences between Bahrain and Qatar continue in the continental shelf areas separating the two states, which include seabed and subsoil resources.

In their efforts to settle territorial differences among their protégé states, and in order to facilitate exploitation of oil resources in the disputed areas, the British decided in December 1947 to divide the seabed between the two emirates with a line running along the following points:[43]

Position	True bearing	Nautical Miles from	
A	015°	3.00	North point of Rabadh Island
B	056½°	3.20	Northeast corner of Ajaira Island
C	064°	2.06	East corner of No. 3A1 Wakara Island
D	058°	1.14	East corner of No. 3A1 Wakara Island
E	163½°	1.23	East corner of No. 3A1 Wakara Island
F	141°	0.81	No. 9 Bu Sa'ada Island
G	168°	1.20	No. 9 Bu Sa'ada Island
H	159°	0.30	Southeast corner of Hawar Island
I	298°	7.31	Southeast corner of Hawar Island
J	241°	4.77	West corner of A1 Mataradh
K	291°	2.36	West corner of A1 Mataradh
L	324½°	3.28	West corner of A1 Mataradh

This award also recognised the ruler of Bahrain as having sovereign rights in the areas of the Dibal and Jaradah shoals which are above spring tide low water level only. The British also informed the ruler of Bahrain that these shoals should not be considered to be islands having territorial waters. Both states rejected the verdicts, albeit Qatar's rejection of this continental shelf award was especially directed to the two exceptions concerning the Hawar islands and Dibal and Jaradah shoals.

Bahrain argued that its authority should properly include the entire seabed lying to the west and northwest of the Qatar peninsula on the basis of a maritime boundary drawn to the east of the Hawar islands. Qatar argued that the award gave Bahrain the shoals of Dibal and Jaradah which are situated in the seabed areas allotted to Qatar.

With regard to the delimitation of the maritime areas of the two states, it was stated in the letter informing the rulers of Qatar and Bahrain of the 1947 decision that, the British government considered that the line dividing 'in accordance with equitable principles' the seabed between Bahrain and Qatar was a median line based generally on the configuration of the coastline of the Bahrain mainland and the Qatar peninsula.[44]

The letter further specified two exceptions: one concerned the status of Dibal and Jaradah shoals; the other that of the Hawar islands giving them to Bahrain while situated in the section of sea allotted to Qatar.[45]

Having refused the 1947 maritime boundary, Bahrain claimed in 1964 a boundary line delimiting the seabed areas of the two states. Qatar did not accept this claim and invoked 'customary international law and local practices and customs' to determine the new line of division.[46]

The British Political Agency in Bahrain decided in February 1966 to intervene in the dispute between Bahrain and Qatar on the delimitation of their mutual seabed for the purpose of defining operating limits of oil companies in that part of the sea. The Qataris made it clear to the British at that time that they preferred arbitration.[47] They also stipulated that the Hawar islands should be included in the scope of the proposed arbitration.[48] The Bahrainis responded to this by proposing to freeze the problem by informing the British officially that they would not accept arbitration on Hawar or Jaradeh and Dibal.[49] They argued that whatever way the arbitration opinion might go, one side or the other would regard itself as the loser. This would be bound to lead to a deterioration in relations.[50] This response postponed the issue for over twenty years.

Qatar announced on 16 April 1992 that her territorial waters were officially extended to 12 nautical miles from her low tide coastline. This announcement added a new dimension to the already very complicated dispute of territorial and maritime boundaries between Bahrain and Qatar.[51] The Foreign Ministry of Bahrain rejected in an official declaration on 16 April 1992, articles 1, 2 and 3 of Qatar's declared decision[52] and officially expanded in early 1993 Bahrain's territorial waters to 12 nautical miles.

MEDIATION AND COMPLAINT

Saudi Arabia began mediation efforts between Bahrain and Qatar on these disputes in the wake of the withdrawal of Pax-Britannica from the region in 1971. Seven years later (1978) the king of Saudi Arabia put forward a series of principles on the basis of which these disputes could be negotiated and settled.

Saudi proposals also included maintenance of the *status quo* and the formation of a tripartite committee to study ways of settling disputes. These Saudi efforts were to be channelled through the Gulf Cooperation Council since the creation of the latter in 1981.

The GCC, however, succeeded in bringing the disputes under control. The Saudi king had put forward a proposal in December 1987 which was accepted by the two states. In this agreement the two states undertook to refer their disputes to the International Court of Justice and to abide by its rulings. Other provisions of this agreement included maintenance of the *status quo* and revival of the tripartite committee to renew efforts in bringing about a settlement to the disputes.[53]

A special committee sitting at the annual GCC summit (Doha) in mid-December 1990, stipulated that, should no out of court settlement be attainable within six months (by 15 May), the dispute between the two states could be referred to the International Court of Justice at the Hague.

Qatar referred the dispute to the ICJ on 8 July 1991,[54] evidently believing that this action was taken because the six month deadline had expired, and that it was agreed to do so at the end of the six-month period without the requisite progress having been made.

In letters addressed to the ICJ Bahrain contested the basis of jurisdiction invoked by Qatar, and claimed that a renewed joint application should have been made. Accordingly, Qatar withdrew in July 1992 her initial application to the ICJ, which was replaced by a new joint reference.[55] The ICJ began consideration of this application as from Monday 28 February 1994.[56] Examination of this case is expected to last for some years.

It was announced on Friday 1 July 1994 that the International Court of Justice decided on that day, by a majority of 15 votes to one, in the proceedings concerning jurisdiction and admissibility in the territorial and boundary differences between Qatar and Bahrain,[57] that the Bahrain formula for proceedings should be adopted. That is to say that the whole of the dispute should be submitted to the Court. This decision permits Bahrain to present its claims in respect of Zubarah as well. This aspect of the disputes was not included in Qatar's original formula.[58]

Iran–UAE Territorial and Boundary Disputes

Chapter 7

Disputes Over Tunb and Abu Musa

Territorial Foundation of States in Iran and the United Arab Emirates

GEOGRAPHY OF ISLANDS IN DISPUTE

Greater Tunb

Seventeen miles southwest of Qeshm, the island of Tunb is situated on the north of the Gulf's median line. This island's distance from the Iranian port of Bandar Lengeh is 30 miles, and it is situated at more than 46 miles from the Emirate of Ras al-Kheimah. The term *tunb* is Tangestani dialect (southern Persian) which means hill. In his book of a journey through Iran and the Persian Gulf, the famous British diplomat James Morier, states:

> On 20 February we were close to the two islands called the Greater and Little Tomb, which bear Persian names of the Persian side, an arid piece of land . . . .[1]

Since Tunb is located relatively far from the entrance to the Persian Gulf, its strategic value, individually, is far from being significant. However, from the perceived Iranian strategic viewpoint, Tunb is highly valuable as it forms part of the Iranian defence line against the entrance of the Strait of Hormuz.

Lesser Tunb

Eight miles southwest of Greater Tunb is situated the 115 foot high rock island of Lesser Tunb. It is an uninhabitable island with some significance as a connecting point secondary to the Greater Tunb in Iran's perceived defence line at the entrance of the Persian Gulf.

Abu-Musa

Abu Musa is situated at the westernmost point of the six islands, forming the last point of the perceived Iranian strategic curved line

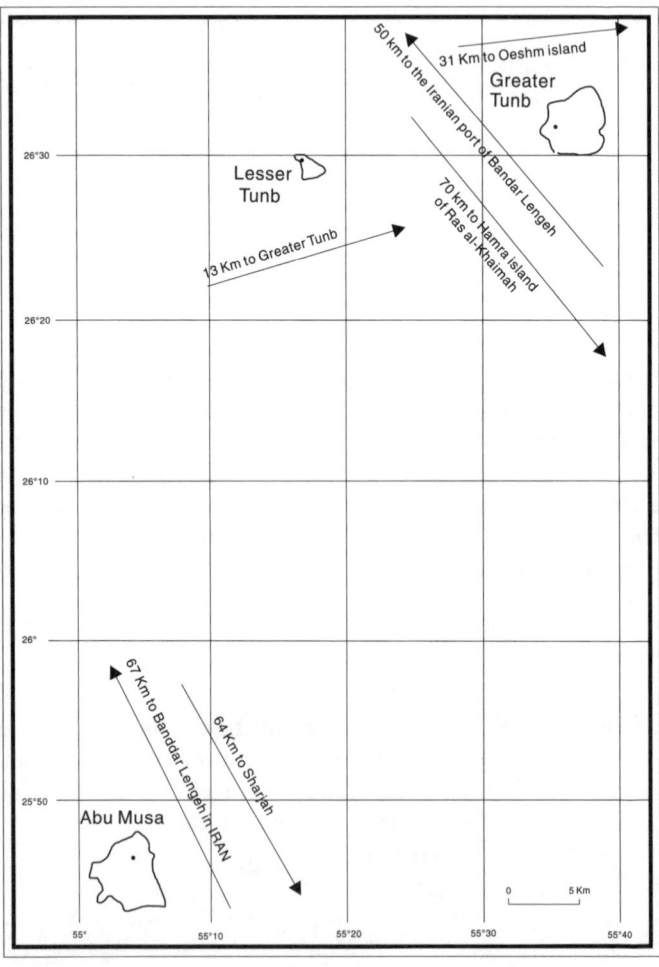

Figure 7.1 Islands of Greater Tunb, Lesser Tunb, and Abu Musa
Based on: TPC H-7D

against the opening of the Strait of Hormuz. It is located between longitude 55°01'E. to 55°04' and latitude 25°51'N to 25°54'N. It is situated 31 miles east of Sirri Island of Iran and 42 miles south of Bandar Lengeh, and its distance from the port of Sharjah is about 40 miles.

Abu Musa is larger than the two Tunbs, almost rectangular in shape, and about 3 miles diagonally between opposite corners. This island is relatively low land consisting of sandy plains, particularly towards the south and centre, with dry grass which is grazed by domestic animals. The surface is uneven, with hills rising high northwards, eventually ending in a volcano-shaped peak known as Mount Halva. This mountain peak is about 360 feet high.

There is fresh water from a number of wells on the island, and plantations of date palms are a familiar sight. Abu Musa is particularly known for its deposits of red iron oxide. The first concession for its exploitation was given to a native of Bandar Lengeh, in the late nineteenth century, by the Qasemi Shaikh of Lengeh in return for an annual royalty of £250. This concession was given to Haj Moin Bushehri, a famous Iranian industrialist of the turn of the twentieth century, after the Qasemi autonomy of Bandar Lengeh was abolished in 1887. Lorimer estimated the number of people (Iranians) working these mines, at around the turn of the twentieth century at 100, adding that 'the amount of oxide removed annually is said to average 40,000 bags'.[2]

There are about 2000 inhabitants working on the Iranian side of the island, under Iranian sovereignty, most of whom are employed by the governorate of Bandar Abbas. These are in addition to the military personnel stationed on the island. Several development projects have been implemented mostly in connection with services for the island including the creation of two small but modern settlements; one for the local fishermen and the other for government employees. These two settlements have necessary facilities including electricity, 16 miles of road and a primitive airstrip. The Northern Fisheries Company of Iran has begun a fishery industry project in the island. Two small farms fruit and vegetables have been created which are still in their early stages. A desalination plant provides fresh, potable and drinkable water for the inhabitants.[3]

On the Sharjah side of the island some development projects have also been implemented for the native settlers of 700 or so. The population of this section increases at the time of year when the weather is more suitable, thus, the village of Abu Musa is gradually becoming a holiday camp for visitors from the emirates. New buildings have been constructed to accommodate newcomers and visitors. The settlement has electricity and a water distillation plant.

Contact between the Iranian and Sharjah populations of the island is rare, but in the event of emergencies such as disfunctioning distillation plants, they assist each other. A small boat *Khater* ferries between the Arab section of the island and Sharjah twice weekly, whereas the Iranian inhabitants are connected to Bandar Abbas by air as well as by regular boat services.

Concession for exploitation of Abu Musa's iron mines was given to the German company Woenckhaus in the recent times. This concession was later (1912) given to the British company Golden Valley Colour Limited, and the Japanese joined in at a later stage. All these concessions were granted by the Shaikh of Sharjah endorsed by Iran following the Iran–Sharjah *Memorandum of Understanding* of November 1971.

Abu Musa's oil is produced from the nearby Meidan-e Mobarak, which is of the best quality produced in the Persian Gulf. Oil is produced from the three wells of the field by Butes Oil and Gas Company, the concession for which was granted by Sharjah and the latest was endorsed by Iran in December 1971 on the understanding that the profit from the exploitation should be equally divided between Iran and Sharjah.

Following the November 1971 Iran–Sharjah settlement, and following restoration of Iran's sovereignty rights to the island, Iran's 12 mile territorial water limit was applied to Abu Musa. Application of this territorial water limit overlapped that of the emirate of Umm al-Quiwain, where exploration concession was given to the Oxidental Oil Company in 1969. A solution was found to the problem which was reportedly based on the allocation to Umm al-Quiwain of 15 per cent of Sharjah's income from Abu Musa's oil output.

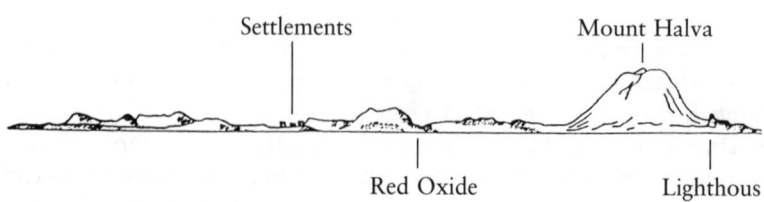

Figure 7.2 South-Western Profile of Abu Musa Island

EMERGENCE OF STATE IN IRAN

The term 'state' assumed a meaning similar to the modern sense of the word in the Persian Gulf when the Achaemenians consolidated their empire in the mid-sixth century BC. The empire included most of the civilised world of the time, stretching from India in the east to Egypt and Libya in the west. This realm included the entire southern side of the Persian Gulf. When the Sassanians (224–685 AD) assumed power in Iran, territorial contentions between the Persian and Roman empires settled Iran's western flanks in Mesopotamia where the Sassanids created their frontier-keeping vassal kingdom of Hirah.

Arab raids on Iranian possessions in the Persian Gulf began in the early Christian era, and by the time the Sassanids consolidated their power, these raids had become frequent.

Shapur I made a naval reprisal in the Persian Gulf which was completely successful. The raids, nevertheless, continued until Shapur II came of age. His reprisals were so effective that an end was put to the problem for a long time. Quoting early Islamic historians and geographers in his highly acclaimed book *The Persian Gulf*, Sir Arnold Wilson notes:

> The reign of Shapur II (309–37 AD) was marked by frequent raids upon the Persian coasts by the Arabs of Hajar, which then included Hasa, Qatif, and Bahrain.
>
> Almost for the first time since the expedition of Sennacherib, we read of a naval expedition against these raiders in the Persian Gulf, commanded by the king himself, which was completely successful.[4]

Almost all Arab and Islamic historians and geographers of the early Islamic era, such as Tabari, Masudi and Yaqubi, confirm that all areas of the Persian Gulf belonged to Iran in the pre-Islamic period.

The first dynasty of the post-Islamic era to revive the dominion of Iran was that of the Buyids, albeit the Iranians began moving towards a revival of their identity and independence almost from the beginning of the emergence of the Arab caliphate. The Samanids and Saffarids, however, revived the state in Iran in the third Islamic century (204 and 253 respectively AH).

Ahmad Moez ad-Doleh (334–356 AH) and his powerful nephew Azad ad-Doleh (356–367 AH) of the Buyids not only added Mesopotamia to their dominions, but restored Iran's control of the southern Gulf. This dominion remained more or less the same throughout the years of the Seljuquids, Ghaznavids, Mongoloids, Atabakis down to the Safavid period (1051–1722 AD).

Nader Shah Afshar (1736–47 AD) brought under control the chaos which followed the downfall of the Safavid empire, and restored stability throughout Iran and in the southern coasts of the Persian Gulf by sending a task force to those coasts.

EMERGENCE OF THE EMIRATES

The tribes of the Musandam Peninsula and other coasts of the lower Gulf, living peacefully for fear of Nader Shah[5] used the opportunity arising from his assassination in 1747 and resumed their activities outside the peninsula. This chaotic situation continued until Karim Khan of Zand's rise into prominence in central and southern provinces of Iran in 1757. Unlike Nader Shah, the Khan of Zand preferred the friendship and co-operation of the Arabs on both shores in his struggle for power in Iran. His leniency towards Arab tribes proved most helpful for the Qasemis (Jawasim) on their way to paramountcy in the subsequent period. They began their organised interference in the maritime trade and commerce in an effective manner. Their sea power had, by the turn of the nineteenth century, grown substantially. The British who had, by then, established themselves as the masters of the eastern waters, deliberated that their control of the Persian Gulf and Strait of Hormuz was essential for the security of India. This policy led the British to move their forces into the Gulf on the pretext of eradicating acts of alleged piracy by the tribes of the Greater Musandam Peninsula. British naval units, commanded by General Sir William Grant Keir, attacked Jolfar and defeated Qasemi forces in 1819.

A peace treaty was signed in February 1820 by the British and five tribal leaders of the Musandam Peninsula whereby these tribes were brought under the control of the British. Articles 3, 6 and 10 of this treaty provided some hint of recognition by the British of these tribal units, for the first time, as political entities independent of each other and of neighbouring states. Article 3 for instance, allowed the tribal chiefs signatory to the treaty to 'carry by land and sea a red flag, with or without letters on it'.[6] This was to become the independent tribes' flag of identity while their progress into territorial states had to wait for nearly a century and a half. In fact, when in 1864 authorities of the Indo-European telegraph line suggested determination of territorial dimension with defined boundaries for the trucial tribes which would ensure security of the said telegraph line, Colonel Lewis Pelly, British Political Resident in the Persian Gulf, opposed the idea on the grounds that implementation of these European concepts in Eastern Arabia at the time was 'inexpedient'[7] and would result in great complications. The well informed and shrewd politician that Pelly was, knew very well that the issue of sovereignty in the Musandam Peninsula did not extend to territory. He knew well what was described by J. B. Kelly a century later. Kelly asserted in 1964:

> The concept of territorial sovereignty in the Western sense did not exist in Eastern Arabia. A ruler exercised jurisdiction over a territory by virtue of his jurisdiction over the tribes inhabiting it. They, in turn, owed loyalty to him . . . . his (the tribesman's) loyalty is personal to his tribe, his shaikh, or a leader of greater consequence, and not to any abstract image of state.[8]

These words were echoes of what Sir Rupert Hay, a former British Political Resident in the Persian Gulf, had stated a decade earlier:

> Before the advent of oil the desert was in many ways similar to the high seas. Nomads and their camels roamed across it at will and, though there were vague tribal limits, there were few signs of the authority of any established government outside the ports and oases.[9]

With this background to the political geography of the Musandam Peninsula in mind it is not too difficult to understand how a tribe exercised independence and loyalty to another authority at the same time, or exercised loyalty to two different claimants of sovereignty seasonally. Writing on the political status of the tribes of northern Musandam, Lorimer asserts:

> From local enquiries . . . it seemed certain that Kumzar and Khasab on the western coast, together with the villages between them, actually acknowledged the sovereignty of the Sultanate of Oman; but some doubts remain as to the status of the inhabitants of Film, Shabus and Shisah on the eastern side of the promontory, who were said to be virtually independent while at home and to become subjects of the Shaikh of Sharjah in the date season . . . [10]

The Qasemis of what was later to become Sharjah, like other tribes of the Musandam Peninsula continued their traditionally vague connection with the rulers of Muscat in the first half of the nineteenth century, whereas the rulers of Muscat themselves had some similar vague arrangement with the Iranians.

While the Sultans of Muscat administered territories around Bandar Abbas and Chah Bahar of Iran's southern coasts in the form of a lease arrangement with the Iranian government,[11] their forces attacked and occupied places in the lower Gulf including the Bahrain islands on behalf of the Iranian government.

The Qasemi Shaikhs signed in 1864 a separate treaty with the British whereby their shaikhdom became a British protectorate and their foreign relations were restricted to those with the British only. This treaty accepted Sharjah's political status as an emirate independent of all others in the region, and the name 'Sharjah' was fashioned from then on. This political status still did not recognise the territorial extension of the Qasemi dominion which had to go through a long process of disintegration and reunification beginning in 1866.

Shaikh Sultan bin Saqar who had ruled since 1803, died in 1866. Before dying, he appointed his sons and brothers as his representatives in the towns of Ras al-Kheimah, Diba, Kalbah, and Khor Fakkan, urging them to obey his elder son Shaikh Saqar in the event of his death.[12]

Ras al-Kheimah was separated from Sharjah a year later (1867) and was reincorporated into Sharjah in 1900. Twenty one years later (1921) Ras al-Kheimah was separated from Sharjah for the second time and has remained so ever since. Fujairah also claimed separation from Sharjah in 1901, but was forced to continue payment of tribute to Sharjah until 1952 when its separation from Sharjah was officially recognised by the British. The eastern district of Kalbah had also claimed independence from Sharjah but was reincorporated into that emirate in 1951. These territorial upheavals encouraged the British to bring stability to the region by introducing European concepts of territorial sovereignty and political boundaries to the region. Exploration of oil resources was an added factor which necessitated territorial and boundary divisions in southeastern Arabia.

In 1954, J.F. Walker, a British arbitrator, was assigned to carry out territorial divisions and boundary delimitation enquiries, and began his work by defining the realm of each emirate and designing boundary lines among them. His work continued until 1961 and his territorial and boundary awards became official in 1962, whereby the emirates assumed territorial status for the first time. This territorial arrangement among the emirates was still an alien phenomenon to the tribal rulers until their collective statehood emerged in 1971. Dr John Wilkinson of Oxford University described this situation in 1977 in the following terms:

This ludicrous partitioning of territory is of recent origin and stems in large measure from the imposing of European notion of territorialism on a society to which they were foreign. The *ad hoc* process by which this happened started a century and a half ago when Britain initiated a series of treaties with the Sultan of Muscat and the coastal shaikhs of northern Oman, with the purpose of limiting their maritime activities and foreign relationships. Subsequently, as Britain sought to develop an exclusive influence in the Gulf and, later still, to favour the claims of particular companies to act as concessionaries for oil exploration, she was forced first into defending the protégé coastal rulers from attack from the hinterland and then of proclaiming their authority over the population and resources of Greater Oman, by dividing it into a number of territories subject to them. This is not to say that the embryonic states she helped create were entirely artificial. Rather it is to imply that from the start the terms of reference by which they came into existence more or less disregarded important aspects of traditional organisation within the region . . .[13]

The seven emirates of northern Oman were, however, merged into a federation created in the wake of the British announcement of 1968 of withdrawing Pax-Britannica from the Persian Gulf. This federation came into official existence on 2 December 1971 with Abu Dhabi as its capital. The new entity was named 'United Arab Emirates' and became a member of the United Nations on 9 December 1971.

QASEMI (JAWASIM) AUTONOMY IN BANDAR LENGEH

No study of the historical background to Iran–UAE differences over Tunbs and Abu Musa islands can escape a brief look at the role of the Qasemi autonomy in Bandar Lengeh. One of the local chiefs in the Persian Gulf who used the opportunity of Nader Shah's death to set up their independence was an Iranian admiral, Mulla 'Ali Shah, who managed to establish himself as autonomous governor of Hormuz. Mulla 'Ali refused payment of tribute to the central government as early as 1747 and sought alliance, by marriage, with the powerful Qasemi shaikhs of Jolfar on the Greater Musandam coast. In 1751 the Qasemi Shaikh sent a fleet to the northern shores of the Strait of Hormuz, seemingly to pay a courtesy call on Mulla 'Ali upon the marriage of his daughter, but in reality to expand his influence to the districts of the northern Gulf. [14] When robbers attacked the British Political Agent's residence in Bandar Abbas in 1759, the East India

Company sought redress from Karim Khan Zand. Shaikh Nasr Khan, Governor of Lar, was assigned to sort out the chaos at Bandar 'Abbas and Hormuz. Inevitably war broke out between his forces and those of Mulla 'Ali Shah. An army of 1000 fighters, commanded by the Qasemi Shaikh of Jolfar himself, landed at Bandar 'Abbas in support of Mulla 'Ali.

As the war dragged on, a branch of the Qasemis managed to establish itself at Lengeh, Laft, Shenas and Qeshm Island. Karim Khan Zand (1757–79) was tolerant towards the autonomous Arab tribes on the northern coasts, actually seeking their assistance in his struggle for power. His leaning towards these Arab tribes, meanwhile, helped the Qasemis of both shores to achieve prominence in the late eighteenth and early nineteenth centuries. In his time, the headmanship *(zabeti)* of Bandar Lengeh was given to Shaikh Saleh, the Qasemi chief of that locality,[15] and was inherited by Shaikh Saleh's sons and grandsons in accordance with Iran's old federative tradition and without in any way contravening Iran's sovereignty over Lengeh and its dependent ports and islands. Kish, Tunb, Abu Musa, Sirri and a number of other islands had always been dependencies of the governorship of Lengeh. Therefore, the Qasemi authority at Lengeh, like all those before it, included these islands as well as the coastal ports of Charak, Mogham and Chiru. A number of French and British official maps confirm this including the French Foreign Ministry's *Carte du Golphe Persique* of 1764, the British *Map of the Empire of Persia* made by D'Anville in 1770, and *A Map of the Empire of Persia*, similarly compiled by D'Anville in 1794.

(For a full list of official British maps – 28 in all – proving Iranian ownership of the Tunb and Abu Musa islands, see Appendix IV.)

On the basis of the agreement of 12 August 1798 between the East India Company and the Sultan of Muscat concerning Bandar 'Abbas and Qeshm, the British General, Sir William Grant Keir moved over 1000 troops to Basidu on Qeshm Island after defeating the Qasemi tribesmen at Jolfar in 1819. Soon after, they established a military depot on Qeshm in spite of clear indications of opposition from the Iranian government. In 1822, having established their control over the Musandam coast, the British decided to send an expeditionary force to Lengeh to subjugate the Qasemis of the Iranian coast. Iranian authorities opposed the idea on the grounds that the Qasemi shaikhs of Lengeh were Iranian subjects.

> To prevent any misunderstanding on the part of the Persian government of the object of the British expedition – particularly operations against

the shaikhs of Lingeh and Charak – a special emissary, Dr Dukes, was despatched in advance with reassuring letters from the governor of Bombay for the governor-general of Fars and the Persian governor of Bushire. Another letter was sent to the British *chargé d'affaires* in Tehran, to enable him to inform the Shah. The Shah, however, was not appeased and the Prince of Shiraz wrote to Keir requesting him to refrain from interference at any of his ports, especially Lingeh. Keir therefore thought it inadvisable to land any troops on Persian soil.[16, 17]

Although the British could have been in no doubt that Lengeh and its dependencies were integral parts of Iran and that the Qasemis of Bandar Lengeh were Iranian subjects and officials of the government of Iran, Grant Keir's forces attacked Bandar Lengeh and destroyed many of the vessels at anchor there. When faced with mounting Iranian criticism and protestations, the British sought an agreement with the Iranian government. This agreement was signed by Mirza Zaki Khan Nuri[18] on behalf of Iran and Sir William Bruce on behalf of the British East India Company. Article 3 reads: 'The representative of the British government must compensate in kind for the damages incurred as a result of the destruction of sailing and non-sailing boats of the people of ports of Lengeh and Charak'.[19]

That the British were in no doubt about Iran's undisputed sovereignty over Bandar Lengeh and its dependent ports and islands at the time when the Qasemi shaikhs were still in control of the Lengeh governorship was also demonstrated in the form of a map produced in 1835 by the acting British Political Resident in the Persian Gulf, Captain S. Hennell. In order to prevent conflicts among the Arab tribes of the southern coasts of the Persian Gulf during the pearl fishing season of that year. Captain Hennell suggested a maritime truce which was signed on 21 August 1835. He drew a line on the map of the Gulf separating possessions of the Arab tribes from those of Iran. His map specified the ports of Lengeh, Laft, Charak, as well as the islands of Qeshm, Tunb and Abu Musa as possessions of Iran.[20]

A similar map was produced later by Major Morrison, who introduced a new line of territorial specification in the region, from Ras az-Zur near Kuwait to the Sharjah island of Sir Bu Na'ir, continuing to Ash-Shams near Ras Musandam. This line too showed the three islands of Tunb and Abu Musa and the Qasemi governorate of Lengeh as within Iran's jurisdiction. On a British Admiralty map of 1881 the islands of Tunb and Abu Musa are the same colour as Lengeh and the rest of the Iranian mainland.

Meanwhile the Qasemis of Lengeh, throughout their time there, demonstrated their loyalty to Iran, assisting various Iranian expeditions against the rebellious Arab tribes of southwestern Iran or against British interference in Iran's dependent territories such as Bahrain in the 1860s.

The Iranian government decided in 1885 that the old Safavid administrative organisation of the country was no longer viable in the modern world. They introduced a new organisation dividing the country into 27 provinces *(ayalat)*, of which the 26th was the Province of the Ports of the Persian Gulf.[21] The same year, Shaikh Yusuf Qasemi, who had ruled in Lengeh since 1878, was murdered by his relative, Shaikh Qadhib bin Rashid, an event which encouraged the Iranian government to put an end to Qasemi autonomy in Lengeh and its dependencies and to include this *velayat* in the 26th province. Tehran's first step was to increase its direct involvement in the affairs of Lengeh. This policy seems to have been adopted by the former governor-general of the 26th province, Amin as-Sultan, who was Prime Minster of Iran in 1887. 'The years 1887 and 1888 were signalised . . . by a spasmodic attempt on the part of the Persian government to assert themselves in the politics of the Persian Gulf'.[22]

In 1886, Prince Mohammad Mirza was appointed Governor-General of Fars, when Sa'd al-Molk was Governor of Bandar 'Abbas and Lengeh. The Prince Governor of Fars demoted Shaikh Qadhib Al-Qasemi's position in Bandar Lengeh from 'autonomous governor' to 'deputy governor'. The next year, when Amin as-Sultan was Prime Minister, Prince Mohammad Mirza added Bushehr and its dependencies to the province of Persian Gulf Ports and Islands under the governorship of Qavam al-Molk, and Brigadier Hajji Ahmad Khan was appointed as the new Darya-Begi (Maritime Frontier-Keeper) in the Gulf. He visited Abu Dhabi and Dubai in the newly purchased Iranian naval vessel *Persepolis*, and continued correspondence with the Shaikh of Abu Dhabi.

On instructions from Amin as-Sultan, in 1887 Shaikh Qadhib al-Qasemi was arrested for the murder of Shaikh Yusof; he was subsequently taken in chains to Tehran where he died. The Qasemi autonomy of Lengeh was thus brought to its end, and Lengeh was entrusted to a new governor, appointed by Amin as-Sultan. Then in 1898, Shaikh Mohammad, son of Shaikh Khalifah bin Sa'id, a former Qasemi governor of Lengeh, seized Lengeh and retained it until he was expelled the following year by the Iranian authorities. Shaikh

Mohammad was later reported to be in the vicinity of trucial Oman trying to muster a force to return him to Lengeh.

The Iranian government asked the British government to prevent any act of aggression from the southern side of the Gulf against Iranian territories at Lengeh or at any other part of the Iranian coasts. The British government accordingly issued warnings to the shaikhs of trucial Oman not to interfere in the affairs of Iran by assisting Shaikh Mohammad. As has been noted, in 1900 Darya-Begi Hajji Ahmad Khan established cordial correspondence with Shaikh Zayid bin Khalifah of Abu Dhabi, with the aim of isolating him from the other rulers of the Trucial Oman and preventing him from joining any attack on Lengeh.

The Shaikh of Abu Dhabi was also concerned, in the relationship, to secure favourable Iranian consideration of claims made by some of his subjects to properties in Iran. The shaikhs of Sharjah and Dubai, apparently still unhappy about events in Lengeh, reported the matter to Khan Bahador Abdol-Latif, British Political Agent in the Persian Gulf, connecting this relationship with a perceived Russian effort to gain a foothold in Trucial Oman. They argued that Shaikh Zayid's friendly correspondence with the Iranian official was in breach of the bilateral agreement of 1892 between Britain and Abu Dhabi, article I of which prevented the Shaikh from 'entering any agreement or correspondence with any party other than the British government' (Lorimer, 1908). The Shaikh of Abu Dhabi was cautioned and his correspondence with the Iranian Darya-Begi ceased. The success of this exercise of inducement on the British representatives in the region encouraged the Qasemi shaikhs of Sharjah to try to salvage as much as possible of the territory formerly administered by their tribal cousins.

Correspondence between officials of the Iranian and British governments confirms Iran's undisputed sovereignty over Bandar Lengeh and its dependent ports and islands, and the fact that the Qasemi shaikhs of Lengeh were subjects and officials of the Iranain government. William Doria, British Chargé d'Affaires in Tehran in 1858, complains in a letter of the conduct of the shaikhs of Lengeh and Moghu and asks the Iranian government 'to prevent them, especially the Shaikh of Lengeh, from bothering His Britannic Majesty's subjects in those vicinities.'[23]

These complaints did not, however, produce satisfactory results, and the British therefore decided to stir up local troubles against the Qasemis of Lengeh. A certain Hajji Mohammad, apparently a British paid agent, began encouraging the Lengeh population to leave for Basaidu on Qeshm Island. By early 1863 about 200 families were reported to have left Bandar Lengeh, effectively abandoning Iranian sovereignty for that of Britain in the occupied Basaidu.[24] Disturbed by this event, Nasser ad-Din Shah suggested to his prime minister that:

> The Foreign Minister should negotiate with the British Minister (in Tehran) on this subject, arguing why should the British agent behave like that and move Arab inhabitants here and there, and send the text of this letter to Qavam ad-Dauleh and to write (instruct) Qavam ad-Dauleh to assign a good governor for Bandar Lengeh. It is not necessary that the governor should be an Arab; a very good governor must be appointed.[25]

However, Nasser ad-Din Shah's instructions do not appear to have been carried out, as the Qasemi shaikh of Lengeh was still in position four years later, when he assisted Shaikh Al-Khalifah of Bahrain against the will of the British in 1867. Almost immediately after being appointed ruler of Bahrain in place of his brother Shaikh Mohammad, Shaikh 'Ali bin Khalifah Al-Khalifah sought military and political support from the Iranian governors of Fars (Prince Hessam as-Saltaneh) and Bandar Lengeh (Shaikh Hasan Khan al-Qasemi) against the policies of the British Resident in the Persian Gulf, Colonel Pelly. The former failed to respond, but the Qasemi Shaikh and the people of Bandar Lengeh extended assistance to Shaikh Ali and the people of Bahrain. This act deeply hurt and angered British officers, who sent a warship to Lengeh and threatened the people there with punishment. The ship caused considerable damage to people and property in Lengeh resulting in strong protests from the government of Iran.[26]

Chapter 8

Recent Developments

In April 1992 the Iranian authorities were reported to have prevented a group of non-nationals from Sharjah from entering Abu Musa Island. These were Pakistani, Indian and Philippino labourers and technicians, and Egyptian teachers. Iran denied that its officials in Abu Musa had expelled UAE nationals and its permanent representative at the United Nations, Kamal Kharrazi, stated at the time that 'those [varying nationals] who have not lived on the island . . . have no right to stay there . . .'[1] Some interpreted this statement as implying that only Sharjah nationals with proven connections to the island would be allowed to reside there in future.[2] Iran's Minister of State for Foreign Affairs, Dr Ali-Akbar Velayati, stated at the same time that the 1971 Memorandum of Understanding gave only Sharjah nationals the right to reside on the island.[3]

The High Council of the United Arab Emirates met on 12 May 1992 to discuss the issue of Abu Musa Island and agreed at the end of the meeting that the commitments of each member of the Union before 1971 were to be treated as commitments of the Union as a whole. A UAE representative visiting Tehran prior to this meeting had suggested that a joint commission of representatives of Iran and the UAE should be formed to study the issue, but Iranian authorities rejected this on the grounds that there was no such thing as the issue of Abu Musa.[4]

Then it was reported on 24 August that Iranian authorities had refused entry to Abu Musa to a party of over 100 people of different nationalities (mainly Egyptian) some of whom had also been refused entry to the island in April that year.[5] Iranian sources made it clear that the reason for their action was that 'in recent months suspicious

175

activities were seen in the Arab part of Abu Musa Island', namely the Sharjah-controlled section, involving a number of individuals from third countries, including Western states:

> Observers believe Iranian guards and agents were watching the comings and goings of foreigners in the island for some time. Reports from military sources in Tehran say that without the permission of the Iranian government, the United Arab Emirates was building new establishments in the non-military part of the island. It seems that with the agreement of certain Arab countries, a number of non-native Arabs are to become residents on the island . . . Iran's worst fears were realised when the GCC foreign ministers at the end of their Jeddah meeting declared that they will support the UAE in regaining sovereignty over the three islands belonging to Iran (10 September 1992).[6]

President Rafsanjani of the Islamic Republic of Iran announced in his Friday prayer of 18 September 1992 that the Iranian authorities had arrested a number of 'armed third party nationals' who were trying to enter Abu Musa illegally, of whom a Dutch national was in prison in Tehran. He then added:

> Iran's policy in the Persian Gulf is not creation of enemies and conflicts, but defence of its territorial integrity and we will act seriously to ensure this.[7]

The United Arab Emirates on the other hand, without officially denying these serious charges of the breach of the spirit and the letter of the 1971 MOU, accused Iran of preventing UAE nationals from entering Abu Musa, demanding visas from them. The UAE also accused Iran of gradual encroachment in Abu Musa by building roads and an airstrip, and of intending to expand its military presence in the island. In short, occupying the island.[8] Commenting on the incident, *The Times* claimed that 'Iran unilaterally reneged on that [MOU] deal, convincing many Western observers that it planned to use the island in the shipping lane which carries half the world's oil as a base for three submarines that it is now purchasing from Russia.' The newspaper repeated the allegation made in Abu Dhabi and Cairo that Iran had asserted her full sovereignty over the whole of Abu Musa.[9]

Tehran denied all these charges and sent representatives to Abu Dhabi to find a peaceful end to the problem. There were unconfirmed reports that Iran and Sharjah were prepared to reaffirm the provisions of the 1971 Memorandum of Understanding in their entirety, but talks came to an abrupt end when the leaders of the United Arab Emirates intervened and the UAE Foreign Minister unexpectedly decided to tie any agreement on Abu Musa to a demand for the 'return' of the two Tunbs to UAE sovereignty.[10] Shaikh Zayid bin Sultan Al-Nahyan, President of the United Arab Emirates, was reported to have noted in London in September 1992 that his government 'was taking the dispute to international arbitration'. The media campaign intensified, and in October, the UAE government distributed a position paper amongst permanent representatives at the United Nations, highlighting what were claimed to be the historical facts about the islands.

As for the would-be visitors to Abu Musa, when they had proved that they were teachers and their families, going there to complete school examinations – the aboriginal inhabitants of Abu Musa village are under Sharjah sovereignty according to the 1971 Memorandum – the Iranians allowed them to enter the island in November 1992. Iran's Foreign Minister reportedly ascribed the incident to a misjudgement by 'junior Iranian officials'.[11]

After the Iranian authorities had admitted the Arab teachers to Abu Musa, other factors helped the easing of tension between the two sides towards the end of 1992: border conflict flared up between Qatar and Saudi Arabia; UAE and Iranian academics had frank exchanges at a round table discussion in London on 18 November; George Bush (perceived as a defender of UAE claims) was defeated in the United States presidential election. But in late December, the closing statement of the thirteenth summit of the Gulf Co-operation Council, announced in Abu Dhabi, called on Iran to 'terminate its occupation of Greater and Lesser Tunb islands, which belong to the United Arab Emirates'.[12]

This new and surprising treatment, from the Iranian point of view, of the arrangement arrived at between Iran and Great Britain on behalf of the emirates some 21 years earlier, upheld by the UAE since its creation in 1971 and by the GCC since its creation in 1981, provoked a strong reaction from Tehran in the form of a statement by President Hashemi-Rafsanjani on 25 December, dismissing the claim as totally invalid and warning the GCC that 'to reach these islands one has to cross a sea of blood'.[13] Yet the GCC reaffirmed the claim in the closing statements of its subsequent summits, and caused the dispute between Iran and the United Arab Emirates to continue.

Matters were not improved when King Fahd of Saudi Arabia, in his message to participants in the 1994 Hajj ceremony, asked Iran to give the islands of Tunb and Abu Musa to the United Arab Emirates. This was unprecedented, but the Arab league also came out in late 1995 on the side of UAE.

Figure 8.1 The islands of Tunb and Abu Musa and shipping Lanes at the Strait of Hormuz

Chapter 9

Legal and Historical Arguments

A LOOK AT SOME OF THE UAE ARGUMENTS

The outstanding points in arguments put forward by the British in the past and by the United Arab Emirates at present, and Iran's counter arguments, are as follows:

Priority in occupation

One of the first arguments put forward by the British in the past and adopted by the UAE is the argument of priority in occupation.

The British Minister in Tehran wrote to the Iranian Foreign Ministry in 1904 arguing: 'What he (the Shaikh of Sharjah) had done was only to hoist his flag in the islands still not occupied by any one of the governments.'[1] The Iranians say that this claim is vague and ignores the following facts:

(i) Iran was the only government in the vicinity of the islands at the time and the statement 'still not occupied by any one of the *governments*' makes little sense.

(ii) Sharjah was not, at the time, a state or 'one of the governments' in the Persian Gulf. The Shaikh was a tribal chief (probably of Iranian origin) under British protection, with a tribal dominion still without territorial dimensions. This is confirmed by all British official documents relevant to the affairs of the emirates, and by several former British political representatives in the Gulf[2] and [3] and authoritative British academics.[4] The British also ignored the fact that their own pretext for taking control in

179

the Gulf was to suppress the activities of these same tribes, then referred to by them as 'pirates' of no political entity, let alone territorial dimension.

(iii) In the nineteenth century, Iran had lease arrangements with Oman, according to which Fath 'Ali Shah in 1811 and Nasser ad-Din Shah in 1856 granted the Sultan of Oman lease title to Bandar Abbas, Minab and southern Gulf coastal regions from east to west as far as Bahrain. If all these areas belonged to Iran, the islands of Abu Musa and the two Tunbs situated in its geographical centre, could not have been 'unoccupied'.

(iv) Marking occupation or ownership of territory by hoisting flags was a new concept introduced to the Persian Gulf region by European powers, whereas Iran's sovereignty and ownership of these islands, as well as all other offshore territories and inland areas of the Gulf region, were traditionally established without the display of flags of identity.

(v) Nevertheless, in 1887 Iran hoisted her flag in Sirri and Abu Musa to mark her ownership of these islands in the wake of the dismissal of the Qasemi deputy governor of Bandar Lengeh[5]

(vi) All descriptions of the Persian Gulf region by Arab and Islamic geographers and historians of the post-Islamic era confirm that all islands of that sea belonged to Iran. The British had only to look at Hamdollah Mostoufi's Nozhat al-Qolub, for instance, to find statements such as the following: 'Islands situated between Sind and Oman and in the Persian Sea belong to Persia, the largest of which are Qis (Qeshm) and Bahrain'.[6] He also mentions 'Kond' island which can be assumed to be 'Tunb' island.

(vii) When the Iranian Prime Minister, Haji Mirza Aqasi, officially proclaimed Iran's ownership of all islands in the Persian Gulf in 1840, it was not officially challenged by Britain or any other government at the time, or at any time thereafter.

(viii) Numerous official British maps of the eighteenth and nineteenth centuries confirm Iran's ownership of the islands of Abu Musa and the two Tunbs. (See appendix IV.)

Prior control

The British also maintained that 'Qasemi control of the southern Gulf and the islands had been established long before the Persian coast was settled.'[7]

The Iranians say that such a claim defies the historical facts of the region, mainly because of lack of clarity as to which branch of the Qasemi family is meant to have established control over the two Tunbs, Abu Musa and Sirri islands 'long before the Persian coast was settled' (ie the 1887 settlement of affairs of Lengeh). If the Qasemis of Lengeh are meant, no doubt they 'controlled' Lengeh governorate and its dependent ports and islands as Iranian subjects and officials long before they were dismissed in 1887. Otherwise, if it is claimed that the main brach of the family 'established control' over the islands before or after 1887, firm evidence is needed to clarify how this control was established, and which country the islands belonged to before being brought under their control. Here other British official documents enable a better understanding of the situation. British, French and Russian official maps of the eighteenth and nineteenth centuries confirm that the islands belonged to Iran. Moreover, the British Minister in Tehran, writing to the Iranian Ministry of Foreign Affairs in 1904, claimed the contrary by stating that what the Shaikh of Sharjah had done 'was only to hoist his flag in the islands still not occupied by any one of the governments' (see Priority in Occupation above, second paragraph). If the islands were not occupied by any government in 1904, claims that the Qasemi's control of these islands was established 'long before the Persian coast was settled' (in 1887) cannot be justified.

Another British government document[8] verifies that, after the establishment of one branch of the Qasemi family at Lengeh or thereabouts, the family occupied the Iranian islands, probably in the 'confused period subsequent to the death of Nadir Shah', but it does not clarify which branch of the family did so. This story, if true, is only another admission that the Tunbs, Abu Musa and Sirri islands belonged to Iran and were illegally occupied by the Qasemis at a time when Iran in practice was leaderless and deeply sunk in confusion. Nevertheless, the British did not in practice recognise the presumptive occupation of the islands by the main branch of the Qasemi family (of Sharjah) until 1903, when they advised them to place their flag there.

Arab origins of the population

Both the British in the past and the UAE today vaguely refer to the 'Arab origin' of the native population of Greater Tunb and Abu-Musa as a factor determining Arab ownership of these islands. Indeed, during the confusion of August and September 1992, the UAE was accused by some Iranian media of trying to move nationals from various Arab countries to the Sharjah controlled sections of Abu Musa in order to create an Arab majority there.

The Iranians say that it is noteworthy, first of all, that the natives of Greater Tunb and Abu Musa islands are of mixed origin. They are partly Iranians of Bandar Lengeh, and partly Arabs from the Sudan tribe of Sharjah (in the case of Abu Musa) and from the Bani Yas of Dubai (in the case of Greater Tunb), with no tribal link with Ras al-Kheimah. At least one inhabitant of Greater Tunb was reported in the official correspondence between Shaikh Yusof al-Qasemi of Lengeh and Mohammad Hassan Khan, Governor of Bandar Abbas and Lengeh in 1885 to be of Iranian descent by the name of Ahmad Tunbi of Lar origin.[9]

Secondly, Iranians were the first inhabitants of all areas of the Persian Gulf. Arab migration to the Persian Gulf began shortly before the advent of Islam, and the process of Arab–Iranian admixture continued in the Persian Gulf for centuries. It is now impossible to say who in the Persian Gulf is of 'true' Iranian origin and who is of 'true' Arab origin.

Furthermore, groups of people known for their Iranian origin are still in the majority in southern Iraq, Hasa and Qatif of Saudi Arabia, and in Dubai, Sharjah, Ras al-Khaimah and Ajman of the United Arab Emirates. Accordingly, presumed origins of the population cannot be the basis for an argument over the ownership of localities in the Persian Gulf, including the islands of Tunb and Abu Musa.

Iran's late claim

British sources, on the other hand, have been implying that Iran claimed the islands of Greater and Lesser Tunb in 1877 and the island of Abu Musa in 1887 or 1888. The Iranians say that what these sources conveniently neglect is the fact that Iran was at this time reminding the British of Iranian ownership of the islands and that the insinuation of earlier Sharjah or Ras al-Khaimah ownership was unfounded.

Nineteenth-century correspondence

Apart from resorting to these old and long exhausted arguments put forward by the British of India during the colonial era, the United Arab Emirates bases its claims over the islands of Tunb and Abu Musa on a number of letters exchanged between shaikhs of Sharjah and Ras al-Khaimah on the one hand, and British political agents and rulers of various tribes of the southern coasts of the Persian Gulf, and the Qasemi shaikhs of Bandar Lengeh on the other. Some of these letters date as far back as 1864. They contain numerous inconsistencies and contradictions, and make fanciful claims on various localities up and down the region. The validity of these claims was not even admitted by the shaikhs of Dubai, who in most cases did not find them worthy of reply.

The most important of these letters was written by Shaikh Yusof Al-Qasemi of Bandar Lengeh to the Shaikh of Ras al-Khaimah (see Fig. 9.1).

The Iranians say that it is misleading to quote this letter in isolation. An examination of the document in the context of the circumstances in which it was written will clarify the nature of its contents. In 1873, when a dispute broke out between the Qasemi shaikhs of Lengeh and Ras al-Khaimah over the issue of grazing local livestock in Greater Tunb, they sought the arbitration of British political agents.[10] On 10 February, Shaikh Hamid Al-Qasemi of Ras al-Khaimah complained to Hajji Abol Qasem, British Political Agent in Lengeh, that Bu-Samaith tribesmen from the Iranian ports of Aslaviyeh, Charak and Lengeh, encouraged by Shaikh Khalifah Al-Qasemi of Lengeh, had prevented his subjects from entering Tunb to graze their animals. Hajji Abul Qasem ruled that Tunb island belonged to Lengeh (Iran) and the Bu-Samaiths had traditional rights to the grazing there.

As further enquiries into the dispute became necessary, the Political Resident in Bushehr, Edward C. Ross, empowered Hajji Abdul Rahman, Political Agent in Sharjah, to carry out more extensive enquiries. Having visited the island and interviewed the Qasemi Shaikh of Ras al-Khaimah and the Qasemi Shaikh of Lengeh, Hajji Abdul Rahman concluded his report by stating that Tunb Island belonged to the Iranian province of Fars and was administered by the governor of Lengeh. On the basis of this report, Mr Ross wrote to Shaikh Qasemi of Ras al-Khaimah on 19 April 1873, stating that Tunb belonged to Lengeh, that the inhabitants of Ras al-Khaimah should refrain from annoying Iranian livestock breeders there, and that they should remove their horses from Tunb.[11] It is intriguing that while in his book on the United Arab Emirates Mohammad Morsy Abdullah describes Hajji Abdul Rahman's opinion on the status of Abu Musa island 'being an Iranian possession' as accurate, he criticises him for his opinion on the status of Greater Tunb 'as belonging to Lengeh (Iran)' alleging without any verification that this opinion was motivated by economic self-interest, a desire to avert an

Arab–Iranian war (a highly unlikely possibility at the time) and a reluctance to appear to be favouring the Qawasim.[12]

Ten years later, when relations were normalised, Shaikh Yusof al-Qasemi of Lengeh, having been encouraged to establish friendly relations with the Qasemi Shaikhs of Ras al-Khaimah, wrote the above letter to the Qasemi Shaikh of Ras al-Khaimah. The statement marked 1 on the Figure 9.1, 'the island of Tunb actually or in reality is for you,' leaves little doubt about the nature of the letter: it is the standard oriental courtesy or compliment, essential for relations to remain friendly.

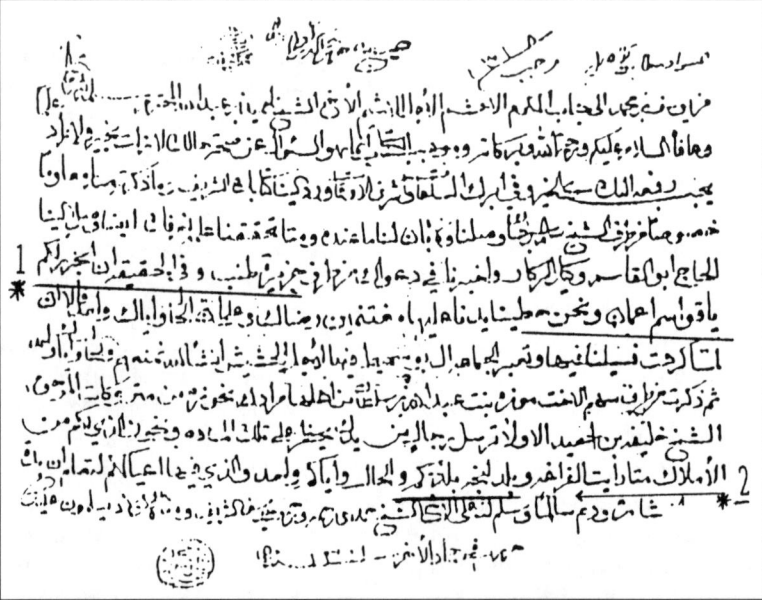

Sentence marked 1 in the text translated means 'the island of Tunb is actually (or in reality) an island for you'.

The sentence marked 2 in the text translated means 'the town of Lengeh is your town'.

Figure 9.1 Letter of 1 Jamadi al-Akhar 1301 (29 March 1884) from Shaikh Yusof al-Qasemi of Bandar Lengeh to Shaikh Hamid al Qasemi of Ras al-Khaimah

A few lines below this statement, Shaikh Yusof adds a further compliment: 'and the town of Lengeh is your town' (marked 2 on Figure 9.1). No one has ever been under any illusion, then or at any other time, that Port Lengeh belonged to any country but Iran; it has always been and still is an indivisible Iranian territory. When this reference to Lengeh as belonging to the Shaikh of Ras al-Khaimah has never been and cannot be taken as anything other than a courtesy compliment, one must ask, how could a similar reference to Tunb island have been, and continue to be, taken literally? Certainly the expression *mi case es su casa* ought not to be.

When in 1929 Abdul-Aziz Al-Saud, king of the new Saudi state in Arabia wrote to Shaikh Hamad Al-Khalifa of Bahrain complaining about the treatment of his subjects in Bahrain, he received a letter of compliment from the Sheikh who states that 'Bahrain, Qatif, Hasa and Nejd were all one and 'belong to Your Majesty'.[13] Certainly inclusion of Bahrain in that list could not have been but pure compliment.

On the other hand, reports for the years 1881–89 from the Qasemi deputy governor to the new governor of Lengeh clearly acknowledge undisputed Iranian ownership of Lengeh and Tunb, and Abu Musa islands. This is also shown in letters of 1885–6 from Shaikh Yusof al-Qasemi, Deputy Governor of Lengeh, to Sa'd al-Molk, Governor of Bandar Abbas and Lengeh, on various aspects of the administration and tax payments, of Lengeh and the dependent ports and islands.[14]

Dual legal status

The British claimed that the islands had been ruled by the Arab governors of Lengeh in their capacity as Qasemi shaikhs rather than as Iranian officials. But how was this 'dual legal status' worked out? How could the governor of Lengeh rule dependent islands of the governorate, not as governor but as holder of another official and legal title?

The Iranians say that apart from masses of British and Iranian documents confirming the legal status of the Qasemis of Lengeh as 'Iranian officials of the Lengeh governorship and loyal subjects of the Iranian government', the British appear not to have taken all the facts into consideration when making the 'dual status' claim. How could they explain what happened when individual Qasemi governors of Lengeh were changed, dismissed or appointed by the Iranian authorities? Would this affect the governor's other mysterious legal or traditional status as 'hereditary Qasemi ruler' *vis-à-vis* Lengeh and its dependent islands? When the Iranian authorities abolished the Qasemi governorship of Lengeh in 1887, what then happened to their other legal or traditional status *vis-à-vis* Lengeh and its dependent islands, and why did the British not protest against continuing direct Iranian jurisdiction over Lengeh and also these islands between 1887 and 1903 (1908 in the case of Lesser Tunb)? Presumably it was on the strength of such questions that when Sir E. Beckett, the legal expert of the British Government at the Foreign Office (who later served as a member of the International Court of Justice at the Hague) was asked to evaluate the legal validity of the claims of dual status for the Qasemi shaikhs of Bandar Lengeh respecting ownership of the islands of Tunbs and Abu Musa, he ruled in 1932 that:

> My conclusion is that unless further evidence is forthcoming that it can be proved that during the period 1880–87 the (Qasemi) Shaikh at Lingah ruled the islands under some title different from that under which he ruled the mainland (I doubt if it will be easy to show this), the Persians did possess sovereignty over Tamb and Abu Musa during those years.[15]

It is important to remember that it was not the first time that the British claimed dual legal status for the Qasemi shaikhs of Bandar Lengeh. They had done the same in respect of Sirri Island after 1887, but as can be seen from the correspondence described later in this Chapter, the British abandoned this futile argument shortly afterwards, and Iran's ownership of and sovereignty over Sirri Island continued relatively unchallenged until 1962, when the Iranian flag was officially hoisted on that island once and for all.

The factor of prescription

One of the legal arguments hinted at by the UAE is the factor of prescription, that is to say that, since 68 years passed between 1903, when Sharjah's flag was hoisted in these islands, and 1971, when they were returned to Iran, and since the rulers of Sharjah and Ras al-Khaimah had, during this period, constructed buildings there and installed official representatives on the islands, the factor of prescription should have overcome any Iranian claim of sovereignty.

The Iranians say that according to international regulations, the factor of prescription stands when occupation of a territory is continued 'uninterrupted', 'undisturbed' and 'unchallenged'. Now, as discussed in previous chapters, it was less than a year after the Emirates occupied the Tunbs and Abu Musa in 1903 that the government of Iran began protesting against and challenging the occupation, and it has done so every year since 1904. Further, not only did Iran exhort Britain to negotiate on several occasions over recognising Iran's rights to the islands, but Iran physically interrupted the occupation on several occasions, and even succeeded in regaining Greater Tunb at the beginning of 1935, albeit for a brief period. There is no doubt that Iran's consistent and vigorous campaign over the 68 years of the occupation of the islands by the Emirates allows little room for the argument of prescription.

Some UAE sources urge that historical facts be ignored in such discussions, because if a historical approach is followed, 'with which we [the UAE] don't agree in international relations, a number of Middle Eastern countries will disappear, will cease to exist'.[16] The Iranians say that this argument has no relevance to the case of the islands of Tunb and Abu Musa, which are not countries.

Territories parted from the Persian or Ottoman empires, which appeared as new countries in the nineteenth and twentieth centuries, were sizeable and populous areas which opted for or achieved independence under some kind of legal façade, and were not occupied and annexed by other states. In the case of the islands in question, they were almost uninhabited at the turn of the twentieth century when they were seized from Iran and annexed by Sharjah. Greater Tunb and Abu Musa are still sparsely populated – the former had 250 inhabitants and the latter 300 in November 1971, when they were returned to Iran – whereas Lesser Tunb was and still is completely uninhabited. These were chunks of Iranian territory seized by Great Britain at the turn of the twentieth century for reasons to do with their perceived security needs at the time. Furthermore, at least two articles of the Memorandum of Understanding of 19 November 1971 between Iran and Sharjah explicitly confirm Iran's sovereignty over Abu Musa Island. Article 2 allows Iran to maintain military units in the northern parts of Abu Musa with full sovereignty – military units with full sovereignty over the areas concerned can only be established in a country's own territory. Article 3 recognises the Iranian law of territorial sea for Abu Musa, whereas the width of Sharjah's territorial sea was, at the time, 3 nautical miles, in accordance with British law.[17]

Duress

The UAE claim now that they accepted the 1971 Memorandum under duress, and recognised the new status of Abu Musa only *de facto*. The Iranians say that they were neither negotiating with Sharjah, nor in a position to impose anything on her under duress. In fact, at the time of the Memorandum, Sharjah was a British protectorate and her foreign affairs were, according to the 1864 and 1892 agreements, the responsibility of the British government. It was Great Britain with whom Iran had arrived at the Memorandum of Understanding, when the former was still a major power in the world, much stronger than Iran, and would in no way have accepted such an arrangement from Iran under duress.

In fact, the reverse argument would be more convincing. Iranians could argue that, by imposing upon Iran an agreement on shared sovereignty over Abu Musa, Britain, a major power acting for the Emirates, prevented implementation of Iran's full sovereignty for the whole of the island. Under duress, Iran had to give the new status of the island *de facto* recognition. Moreover, the UAE contradicted itself (in its position paper of 27 October 1992, distributed in the United Nations):

> According to law, any contract or agreement signed under duress by either party is invalid and considered null and void . . . at times the Emirates government has considered this agreement imposed upon and signed under duress; yet at the same time it has called on Iranian government to execute precisely (her) parts of the document.[18]

This contradiction renders the argument of 'duress' completely null and void. A point in international law suggests *allegans contraria non est audindus*, that is to say, 'he whose statements contradict each other ought not to be heard'.[19]

UAE officials also choose to ignore the high level of welcome extended to the Iranian forces on their arrival in Abu Musa by the Ruler of Sharjah's representative, which hardly suggests Sharjah's acceptance of the Memorandum under duress.

Temporary administrative arrangement

The United Arab Emirates also claim that the 1971 Memorandum of Understanding was a 'temporary administrative arrangement'.

The Iranians believe that there is no time limit on the application of the specifications contained in the Memorandum. On the contrary, no arrangement or agreement defining sovereignty rights, such as the Memorandum specifies for Iran and Sharjah in Abu Musa, can be considered temporary.

In fact, the Iranian side could argue the opposite. Great Britain, acting on behalf of Sharjah, was seeking to put Iran in a tight corner by prolonging the negotiations and playing for time. With time running out, and anxious to avoid the possibility that the emerging federation of the United Arab Emirates would inherit the dispute from the British, a source of friction which would be detrimental to the prospects of regional co-operation for peace and security in the wake of British withdrawal, Iran, despite 68 years of consistent attempts to reassert full sovereignty over the whole of Abu Musa, was left with no alternative but to agree to the British formula for recognising her rights of sovereignty.

Iran accepted this solution only in order to defuse the volatile situation created by the time shortage. Britain was due to leave the Persian Gulf two days later, on 1 December, officially terminating her one and a half centuries of responsibility for the territorial defence and foreign affairs of the tribes which became the Emirates. By accepting the Memorandum, Iran must have hoped that it could later reassert its full sovereignty rights over Abu Musa. This is clearly demonstrated in the preface to the Memorandum, which affirms that Iran (like Sharjah) had not abandoned its claim to full sovereignty over the whole of the island. In other words, while considering the existing Memorandum as valid and legally binding, Iran would have no alternative but to resume, whenever she deemed it expedient, the campaign for recognition of her full sovereignty rights over Abu Musa.

Finally, it is important to note that the ruler of Ras al-Khaimah had returned the island of Greater Tunb to Iran once before, in January 1935, when Iran vigorously demanded its return, but the British intervened and reversed the move. In other words, the British had imposed the occupation of these Iranian islands upon the Emirates, without Ras al-Khaimah being really committed to it.

A LOOK AT THE HISTORY OF IRAN'S CLAIMS

In the nineteenth and first half of the twentieth centuries the British occupied and used a number of Iranian islands in the northern Gulf, either directly or through an assumed sovereignty of the Trucial Emirates. Apart from the Tunbs and Abu Musa, the British disputed Iranian ownership of Qeshm, Hengam and Sirri.

Qeshm was the first Iranian island in the Persian Gulf to be used by the British. As we saw earlier, having crushed the power of Arab 'pirates' of the southern Gulf in 1819, General Grant Keir moved a force, originally 1,200 strong, to Qeshm. The Iranians strongly protested this move, and called on the British to evacuate the island. The British appear to have ignored this protest, and in 1823 they established a naval supply depot at Basidu on the northwestern tip of the island.[20]

When the British decided to establish the Indo–European telegraph line, which had to pass via the coast and islands of the Gulf, they negotiated with the Iranian authorities in 1868 for a cable station on Hengam. For reasons of their own, they closed the station in 1880, but re-occupied the old site 24 years later.[21]

The history of Sirri Island is linked with that of the two Tunbs and Abu Musa. In 1887, when Amin as-Sultan appointed Hajji Mohammad Mehdi Malek at-Tojjar Bushehri as governor of Bandar Lengeh, the latter dismissed the Qasemi shaikhs from the deputy-governorship of Bandar Lengeh. He hoisted the Iranian flag in Lengeh and on the dependent islands of Sirri and Abu Musa (Ashtiani, 1949: 144). The British protested on the grounds of the 'dual legal status' of Sirri. On 11 March 1888, the British Minister in Tehran wrote to the Ministry of Foreign Affairs asking that, since the Qasemi shaikhs' rule of Sirri Island 'was hereditary and not because of their status as Iranian deputy-governors of Bandar Lengeh, why should Iranian authorities hoist their flag in Sirri Island after dismissing the Qasemis in Lengeh?'[22] Replying on the same day, the Iranian Foreign Ministry wrote:

> In reply to the note of the exalted embassy, dated 26 Jamadi ath-Thani, asking for reasons and evidence proving that Sirri Island belongs to the government of Iran; firstly, it is profoundly surprising that the exalted British embassy, being perfectly well informed and aware of [Iranian possession of] all places and areas of the Sea of Oman, specially of the ports of the Persian Gulf,[23] assumes that this matter (of Iranian ownership of these places) needs production of evidence, believes baseless claims of the Jawasim [Qasemi] shaikhs and asks for presentation of evidence; secondly, in complying with the request of the embassy, it is to be stated that according to all laws of progressive countries the strongest evidence of ownership (of places or territories) of a government is 'occupation' and 'possession', and hence there is no need for presentation of any other evidence. The exalted embassy and

agents of the government of India should in good faith and in their own eyes witness that Sirri Island has always been and still is a dependant of Bandar Lengeh and under its governorship have been (and are) assigned by the government (of Iran) to Bandar Lengeh . . . hoisting of flags in the ports of the Persian Gulf has not, from ancient times, been deemed necessary, but not that hoisting them is sometimes deemed necessary, flags were (therefore) hoisted in all those ports. Similar action was accordingly taken in Sirri Island which is a dependant of Bandar Lengeh.[24]

Shortly after, the British Legation wrote back:

It is correct that the deputy-governors of Bandar Lengeh administered Sirri Island, but it was not because (they) were governors of the said Bandar, but because they were the Jasemi (Qasemi) shaikhs that they had control of that island. In consequence, the Government of Iran will note that the Jasemi shaikhs' rule on behalf of Iran was only in Bandar Lengeh. The Jasemi shaikhs had traditional inherited rights to Sirri Island, and no doubt has ever been cast on these rights . . . H.B. Majesty's embassy will be grateful if leaders of the Government of Iran produce evidence proving that Sirri Island belongs to Iran.[25]

Having read this letter, Nasser ad-Din Shah Qajar made the following note in the margin: 'evidence [of Iran's ownership of Sirri Island] is the same as that written previously. What other more important evidence is there to be written?'[26] On 21 July, the Ministry of Foreign Affairs replied that what the embassy had written about the fact that 'the Qasemi shaikhs ruled in Bandar Lengeh on behalf of the government of Iran and that their rule extended to include Sirri Island' was evidence to be added to that already indicated in the Ministry's letter of 26 Jamadi ath-Thani.

If the embassy were to review those (previously introduced) evidences, it would justly and rightly confirm that a territory having been in possession of a government and under the governorship of its representatives and agents for years will naturally be (considered as) the undisputed territory of that government and there is no need for evidence to prove this.[27]

While this correspondence was taking place between Iranian and British government officials, the Qasemi shaikhs made no claim to Sirri and offered no argument in that respect. At the same time, the British appear to have acknowledged Iranian claims:

A War Office map, presented by the British Minister [in Tehran] to the Shah in 1888, showed all the islands [the two Tunbs, Abu Musa and Sirri] in Persian colours: the Persian case was further strengthened with the publication in 1892 of Curzon's two-volume *Persia and the Persian Question* in which the map, prepared by the Royal Geographical Society under Curzon's own supervision, also showed the islands as Persian territory.[28]

Nevertheless, the British continued arguing with the Iranians over what they believed to be the 'rights of the Qasemis to Sirri Island'. In 1894, one of their last communications in this regard provoked the following response from the Iranian Ministry of Foreign Affairs:

> Your letter of 10 Rabi al-Avval 1312 [11 Sept 1894] on the issue of Sirri Island has been received and noted. Your statement that governors of the governorate of Bandar Lengeh were Jawasim [Qasemi] shaikhs and that exercise of their rule in Sirri Island was in respect of their family representation and thus the ownership of the island cannot be of the government [of Iran] is an acceptable argument only if extension of the Bandar Lengeh governorate in Sirri Island was restricted to those times when the governorship of Bandar Lengeh was in the hands of the Jawasim shaikhs and the inhabitants of the island were exclusively from the Jawasim clan, whereas neither was the case, and when the governors of Bandar Lengeh were not Jawasim shaikhs, [the Lengeh governorship] extended to [the island]. The Jawasim shaikhs' deputy-governorship (of Lengeh) was overthrown in early 1306 (late 1887). Two [ten] years before that and since their overthrow, the [non-Qasemi] governorship of Bandar Lengeh has been in power. As you will subsequently see, since the governors listed below were in charge of the Bandar Lengeh governorate [both before and after the overthrow of Qasemi deputy-governorship], they exercised their rule and right of administration in Sirri Island (as well as other dependent territories of Bandar Lengeh) and the inhabitants of the said island have not been exclusively from the Jawasim clan, but are from different clans who have always obeyed the governors (listed below), and the said governors administered affairs there with authority.
>
> (i) Governorship [in Bandar Lengeh] of Nasser al-Molk, under the governorship [in Fars] of Hajj Mo'tamed ad-Dauleh in the year 1293 AH (1876).

(ii) Governorship of Sa'd al-Molk [in Bandar Lengeh] on behalf of Mo'tamed ad-Dauleh in the year 1294 (1877).

(iii) Governorship of Farajollah Khan on behalf of Nasser al-Molk in the years 1295 to 1297.

(iv) Governorship of H.E. Nezam as-Saltaneh until the year 1299 (1881–2).

(v) Governorship of H.E. Sa'd al-Molk, 1300 to 1301 (1882).

(vi) Governorship of H.E. Navvab Mohammad Hosein Mirza, 1302 (1884).

(vii) Governorship of Hajji Mohammad Mehdi Malek at-Tojjar Bushehri, 1303 to 1304 (1885–6).

(viii) Second term of Governorship of H.E. Sa'd al-Molk, 1305 to 1307 (1886–7 to 1888–9). (It was at this time that the Qasemi shaikhs' deputy governorship of Bander Lengeh was abolished).

(ix) Governorship of H.E. Nezam as-Saltaneh, 1308 to 1309 (1889–91 to 1890–1).

(x) Third term of governorship of H.E. Sa'd al-Molk 1310 (1891–2).

(xi) Governorship of Qavam al-Molk 1311 (1893–4).

Apart from all these . . . the embassy will justly confirm that Iran's possession of the said island is in no doubt, and in this case, it is clear that the government of Iran will never remove its flag.[29]

This appears to be the last of the correspondence between British and Iranians on the subject of the ownership of Sirri, and Iran's ownership of and sovereignty over Sirri Island continued relatively unchallenged until 1962, when the Iranian flag was officially hoisted on that island once and for all.

ANGLO–RUSSIAN RIVALRIES AND OCCUPATION OF IRANIAN ISLANDS

British fear of a Russian encroachment in the Persian Gulf intensified at the turn of the twentieth century. In anticipation of such a development, the British decided to occupy the Iranian islands of the Strait of Hormuz, or, at least, fear of Russian designs was the pretext for the occupation of these islands by the British who, brought some of them under their direct control and put some others under the assumed sovereignty of the Qasemi sheikhs of Musandam whose rule in those coasts had not as yet assumed a territorial dimension. In a letter to the Foreign Office in November 1900, the British India Office indicated:

193

. . . In the early part of this year a report was received to the effect that the Russians might land men or hoist their flag at Bandar Abbas. As the outcome of my letter to you, dated the 13 February 1899, authority was given on 14 February . . . under certain conditions, for hoisting the British flag on Hormuz, or Henjam, or Kishm, or whatever island might be considered by the Naval authorities to offer the best advantages for a naval base in that neighbourhood.[30]

In a reply, the Foreign Office wrote to the India Office on 23 November suggesting that 'The islands of Henjam, Kishm and Hormuz' were found most suitable for the said purpose.[31]

Two years went by and the British were still debating the matter of occupying Iranian islands at the Strait of Hormuz in the event of a Russian intrusion in the Persian Gulf. The Russians signed in 1902 an agreement with the Iranians which increased Russian influence in Iran. In a memorandum on Sir A. Hardinge's letter of 14 October 1902 on the subject of Russian threats in the Persian Gulf, the War Office concluded that in the event of a Russian design against Iran:

(a) If Persia is broken up, we must at least, secure Seistan, and keep Russia out of the Persian Gulf.
(b) It would be dangerous for us to risk war with Russia and France . . .[32]

Early in the same year, a secret meeting at the British Foreign Office decided that in anticipation of Russian aggression in the Persian Gulf, the strategic islands at or near the Strait of Hormuz should be occupied. This decision was made known to British political administrators in India and the Persian Gulf in the form of a memorandum, dated 14 July 1902.[33]

An intriguing aspect of these moves was the fact that the islands of Hengam and Qeshm had been under partial British occupation for some years.

The fact that the British had their flag flying on Qeshm and Hengam islands during the time of these debates leaves little doubt that the true aim of their strategic moves was occupation of other Iranian islands in the vicinity of the Strait of Hormuz, ie the islands of Tunb and Abu Musa. This ultimate aim manifested itself about a year later when the government of India sanctioned in a letter in June 1903 occupation of the islands of Tunb and Abu Musa in the name of the Shaikh of Sharjah.[34]

British Foreign Office documents suggest that occupation of these islands took place in late June or early July 1903 in the form of an advice from the government of India to the Shaikh of Sharjah to hoist his flag on Greater Tunb and Abu Musa islands.[35] Ironically, Lord Curzon, Viceroy and Governor-General of India at the time, himself produced a map in 1892 clearly showing the islands of Tunb and Abu Musa as belonging to Iran.[36]

Knowing that these islands belonged to Iran, British Indian authorities made an excuse of tribal relations between the Qasemis of the former governorate of Bandar Lengeh to which these islands belonged, and the Qasemis of Sharjah.

The fact that the British authorities were fully aware that Tunb and Abu Musa islands were Iranian owned and belonged to Iran was reflected in a later date, in the form of a Foreign Office confidential document on the 'Persian Frontiers' which uses without reservation, the term 'occupation' of these islands by the Qasemis. This document indicates:

> In the second half of the eighteenth century the Arabs of the pirate [later called the Trucial] Coast of Arabia occupied the islands of Tanb [also called Tunb, Tamb and Tomb], its dependency Nabiyu Tanb, Abu Musa and Sirri, it seems probable that they did so in the very confused period subsequent to the death of Nadir Shah . . .[37]

Donald Hawley, British Political Representative for the Trucial States between 1958 and 1961, asserts in his book *The Trucial States* that: 'Abu Musa . . . is in the effective control of the ruler of Sharjah, and has been occupied by the Qawasim for several generations . . .'[38]

The week and uncertain nature of the British claim to and occupation of these islands on behalf of the Shaikh of Sharjah can also be seen in a telegram from the British Minister in Tehran to the British Foreign Office, dated 20 April 1904. He states:

> The Government of India's telegram of 18 June 1903, does not appear to have been received here with reference to Tamb and Abumusa, but invalidity of Persian claims to these islands is, I presume, established by it. However, they are coloured Persian in India Survey Map of 1897 and Viceroy's unofficial map of 1892.
>
> It is clear on this presumption, that rights acquired by Shaikh of Shargih must be supported: but before Persian flag is hauled down it would be courteous to give Persian government chance themselves removing it. We could say, if they refused, that we had shown more consideration than they had for Shaikh of Sharjah, and could carry out proposal of government of India. M. Naus might be induced to remove

quietly his flag and guards, and Arab flag then could be re-hoisted after a convenient interval without ostentation. A suggestion that we are acting in a high handed way or to give rise to any violent incident I think is to be avoided.[39]

This suggestion was adopted by British Foreign Office and use of a gunboat in hauling down the Iranian flag, suggested by the Indian government,[40] was avoided, whereas threats of use of a gun boat against Iran's position in Tunb and the Abu Musa islands was made during British officials' contacts with the Iranians.

This policy was put in action and the Iranian government and M. Nauz were persuaded to lower the Iranian flag on these islands. In a later report to the British Foreign Office, Sir A. Hardinge informed that:

> I accordingly called today at the (Iranian) Foreign Office to be informed of His Majesty's decision. M. Naus was present at our interview, and showed me a telegram which he was just sending to Bushire informing M. Damberian that the question of sovereignty over Tamb and Abumusa was a disputed one, and ordering him with the least possible delay to remove the Persian flag from those islands.[41]

Having occupied the islands of Tunb and Abu Musa in 1903, the British continued for about two years still arguing about the need for the occupation of Iranian islands of Hengam and Qeshm in the event of a Russian threat, both of which had already been under partial British occupation. Iran was on the brink of civil war in those years and the authority of the central government was at its weakest. It took the Iranians about one year to realise what had happened to the islands of Tunb and Abu Musa. It was reported in April 1904 that Monseigneur Damberian, a director of the Iranian Customs, of Belgian origin, found out, during his tour of the ports and islands of the Persian Gulf on board the Iranian ship *Mozaffari*, that the Iranian flag was replaced in the islands of Tunb and Abu Musa by the flag of the Shaikh of Sharjah. He lowered that flag and ordered the Iranian flag to be hoisted again in those islands. He also commissioned two Iranian *tofangchi* (armed guards) to Tunb and Abu Musa islands.[42] The British Resident in the Persian Gulf despatched the Royal India Marine Steamer *Lawrence* to visit Tunb island,[43] and having confirmed the news of the action of the Iranian Director of Customs, he suggested to the British Indian officials that the Iranian flag should be hauled down in those islands by use of gunboats and replaced by the flag of Sharjah. He saw in such an action a double blessing as not only would such an action teach Iranians whom they were dealing with, but also:

> This unwarranted infringement by Persia of rights of a chief under British protection may prove useful, should the removal of flagstaff – which stood on plinth of old Henjam telegraph station – give rise to a remonstrance on the part of the Persian government.[44]

When the Qasemis of Sharjah hoisted their flags in Greater Tunb and Abu Musa in 1903 and re-hoisted them in 1904, the island of Lesser Tunb escaped their attention and the attention of the British. The Anglo–Russian agreement of 1907 recognised British encroachments against Iranian territories in the Persian Gulf and removed Russian threats in the Persian Gulf. (The Russians [the USSR] later renounced this by publishing official maps showing these islands as belonging to Iran. See, for example, Figure 9.2.) Yet, when in 1908 the British company Franc C. Strick strove to obtain red-oxide exploitation concessions in Faror, Sirri and Lesser Tunb, the British found it necessary to claim Lesser Tunb also. Major Percy Cox, British Political Resident in the Persian Gulf, suggested in October 1908 that: since Lesser Tunb is of the same name as Greater Tunb, its status would automatically be the same as that of the larger island. This formula was adopted by the British Foreign Office and the company was advised to contact the Shaikh of Sharjah for concessions[45] in spite of the fact that the company had, in its initial studies, reported that the Iranian flag had been in place in Lesser Tunb for years. Hence, Lesser Tunb was occupied by the British protégés in Sharjah in 1908 and their flag was hoisted there.

This transfer of the Iranian possessions in the Persian Gulf over to the Qasemis of Greater Musandam was done on the basis of justification that the islands of Tunb and Abu Musa 'had formerly been ruled by the hereditary Arab governors of Lingeh in their capacity as Qasemi Shaikhs of Lingeh as Qasemi rulers rather than as Persian officials'.[46]

This British undertaking was not taken by the outside world as a serious and lasting arrangement. The German Woenckhaus company, for instance, first obtained a concession from the Iranian authorities and began work in Abu Musa (1907). The Shaikh of Sharjah stopped this work and the company was directed by the British to negotiate a new concession from the Shaikh of Sharjah.[47]

Recovered from the constitutional revolution, Iran found it too late and itself too weak to influence a reversal of the British decision to

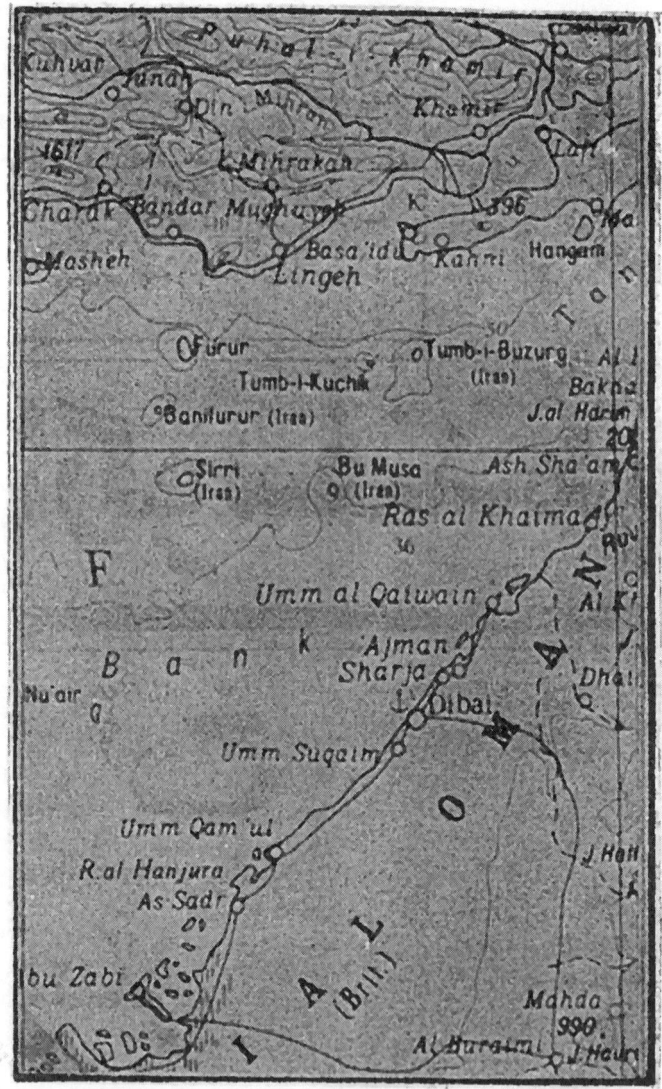

Figure 9.2 An example of official USSR maps confirming Iran's ownership of Tunb and Abu Musa islands.

Copy of a map compiled and published by the Government of Soviet Union in 1967, in which the three islands in question are clearly marked as Iranian. This map was presented to the UN Security Council in December 1971 by Iran, together with a number of other old and new documents.

give these islands to the Qasemis of Musandam. The Iranians remained unhappy about the whole affair, especially as illegal trade through these islands to the Iranian mainland increased.

The Iranian customs office made representations to the government in July 1927, demanding action against illegal trade by establishing observation posts on the three islands.[48] A small fleet of the newly founded Iranian Navy was sent to recover Abu Musa and the two Tunbs and to put an end to the problem there.

THE ANGLO–IRANIAN NEGOTIATIONS OF 1928–9

In the summer of 1928, the Iranian Customs Department began operating a motor boat service from Greater Tunb. This was the outcome of a series of secret contacts with the Shaikh of Ras al-Khaimah, who was prepared to return the two Tunbs to Iran. In August that year, the motor boat seized a sailing boat belonging to the Emirate of Dubai at anchor in the territorial waters of Greater Tunb. The British protested, but the Iranian Foreign Ministry declared that Tunb was under Iranian sovereignty and thus the action was in keeping with international regulations.[49]

When Iran prepared, in 1928, to take her territorial disputes with Britain in the Persian Gulf, especially the issue of Bahrain, to the League of Nations, the British reminded the Iranians of their 1892 treaties with all the chiefs of the Trucial Coast. The Iranians protested that 'the Persian government could not recognise as valid any (British) agreement with the Trucial chiefs which injured or limited the rights and interests of Persia.'[50] The two sides agreed, however, that the status of the Tunb, Abu Musa and Sirri islands should be the subject of negotiations that winter. Protracted negotiations began in January 1929. Sir Robert Clive, British Minister in Tehran, represented Great Britain on behalf of Sharjah, and Taimurtash, Reza Shah's powerful Court Minister, represented Iran.

At the start of negotiations, the British officially claimed compensation of 5,000 rupees for the damage alleged to have resulted from the Iranian motor boat action in seizing the sailing boat of the emirates. When the Iranians ignored this claim, the British concluded that 'owing to the effect produced on the Arab coast by the failure to obtain compensation, His Majesty's government should pay the sum at once in anticipation of a settlement of the claim.'[51]

The matter was never settled, as the Iranians continued to argue that their action was legal according to international law. Taimurtash offered to refer the case to international arbitration. Reporting on their initial discussions, Clive wrote to Foreign Secretary Sir Austin Chamberlain:

> Then we talked about the islands of Tunb and Abu Musa and I asked the Court Minister what benefit did the government of Iran deem to have in taking these islands other than claiming that smugglers in the Persian Gulf are using them as their base for storing goods and smuggling them into Iran. Teimurtache answered that the government of Iran did not see this matter in the same way we do, but their main point is that these islands are indivisible parts of Iran and were occupied by others by force. I answered Teimurtache in accordance with the guideline that you had sent me. The Court Minister said in that case there is no other way but to refer the matter to international arbitration. Replying to His Excellency I expressed hopes that the two sides could settle their differences without having to refer the case to international arbitration.[52]

The negotiations continued until mid-spring 1929 without much progress. Baldwin's Conservative government was replaced in May that year by a Labour government, and Arthur Henderson replaced Chamberlain as Foreign Secretary. Henderson showed a more protective line towards Britain's colonial role in the Persian Gulf and brought Clive's negotiations with the Iranians on the issue of the Tunbs and Abu Musa to an abrupt end. This led the Iranians to try to recover the island in the 1930s through a series of actions.

On 24 February 1930 the Iranian Ministry of War wrote to the Ministry of Foreign Affairs informing them of a report by the Commander in Chief of Iranian forces in the south that:

> A number of flags have been hoisted by the British in the two islands of Tunb and Abu Musa which belong to Iran. Agents were also posted there. This has come as a real surprise to the inhabitants [of the islands]. I beg you to pass on this message to His Imperial Majesty.[53]

On receiving this report, the Ministry of Foreign Affairs wrote to the British Minister in Tehran, Sir Robert Clive, stating:

> Here I would like to inform your excellency that according to information received here the British flag has been hoisted in the islands of Tunb and Abu Musa. The government of Iran considers these islands as belonging to them and find themselves with no alternative but to protest against this action. As far as the Ministry of Foreign Affairs is informed, the government of His Britannic Majesty had no claim to the

ownership of these islands, and hoisting of a flag, which is the manifestation of claim of ownership, has no precedence; your excellency is expected to act for the restoration of *status quo*.[54]

Attached to his letter of protest, the Ministry of Foreign Affairs sent the British Legation a copy of Moshir ad-Dauleh's letter of 14 June 1904, quoted above, to the British Minister in Tehran.

The British denied having hoisted their flag on the islands; but in June 1931 they were said once again to have done so, though the headman of Hengam reported that the Shaikh of Ras al-Khaimah had prevented the hoisting of the British (or his own) flag on Greater Tunb.[55] The Ministry of the Imperial Court wrote to the Ministry of Foreign Affairs at the same time informing them of reports from Bushehr that the British had leased Greater Tunb from the Shaikh of Ras al-Khaimah for a period of 50 years.[56]

On the whole, British Ministers' negotiations with Taimurtash from 1928 onward can be viewed as an attempt to change Iran's protest at Anglo–Qasemi occupation of Tunb and Abu Musa islands, into a position of satisfaction with a legal settlement in favour of the Shaikhs of Sharjah and Ras al-Khaimah. To this end, British authorities in the region prepared a general treaty of the Persian Gulf in 15 articles, within the framework of which a reciprocal deal was offered to Iran.

The outstanding feature of this proposed deal was Iranian withdrawal of claims to Bahrain, Tunb and Abu Musa in return for Britain's recognition of Iranian sovereignty over Sirri Island and the withdrawal of claims to Basaidu (Qeshm) and transfer to Iran of telegraph stations in Lengeh, Bushehr and Hengam Island.[57] The Iranians rejected this package deal on the grounds that Iran's full sovereignty over the places mentioned was undisputed. Consequently, the whole idea of a general treaty of the Persian Gulf collapsed. Finally, during July 1932, Taimurtash told Hoare, British Minister in Tehran, that Iran would renounce the claims to Bahrain in return for British recognition of Iran's sovereignty over Abu Musa and Tunb islands, a proposal which the British rejected.[58] The Anglo–Iranian oil crisis of 1932 intervened and the draft treaty was abandoned by 1934.[59]

Some British sources suggest that, in the latter parts of these negotiations, Teimurtash sent out feelers to test the British position *vis-à-vis* claims of the emirates to Tunb and Abu Musa, by hinting that Iran would renounce the claims to Abu Musa in return for Ras al-Khaimah's dropping its claims to and administration of the Tunbs.[60]

SHAIKH OF RAS AL-KHEIMAH RETURNS THE TUNB ISLANDS

In 1934 the governor of Bandar Abbas and other Iranian officials visited Greater Tunb in a *dhow*. This visit was the result of a secret Iranian arrangement with the Shaikh of Ras al-Kheimah according to which the Shaikh lowered his flag in Greater Tunb and the Iranian flag was hoisted instead. Earlier, a Trucial Coast *dhow* was seized by an Iranian warship in Tunb's territorial waters. On two occasions in 1934, an Iranian warship visited the island and landed a party of Iranians there. These activities attracted the attention of the British who vigorously protested against what was going on in that island. The Iranian government was also orally informed that the British government would as a last resort protect the interests of the Trucial shaikhs by force.[61] Reporting these events to his government, the British Minister in Tehran stated:

> Some mysterious happening took place at Tamb in the early part of the year following on the action of the Shaikh of Ras al-Khaimah at the end of 1934 in having his flagstaff removed. There being grounds for suspicion that the Shaikh had been intriguing with the Iranians, the senior naval officer landed a small guard and, though this was later withdrawn, for some weeks a sloop visited the island at frequent intervals.[62]

However, the British intervened at the end of this episode and reversed that development.

UAE and British sources have endeavoured to justify this action of the Shaikh of Ras al-Kheimah as an undertaking designed to embarrass the British, because he wanted 'to draw attention to the fact that no rent was received from the British for the use of the lighthouse of Tunb'.[63]

The Iranians say that this justification is not comprehensible as never before or after this incident did a ruler give part of his territory to a third country because of financial differences between the colony and the colonial power. The only acceptable explanation of this move can be that the Shaikh of Ras-al Kheimah being aware of unauthorised occupation of these islands, returned the two Tunbs to their rightful owners as a result of a disagreement with the colonial power and as a result of secret arrangements with Iran. Furthermore, whatever the explanation, the undisputed fact is that Ras al-Kheimah returned the two Tunbs to Iran in the mid-1930s when Iran was vigorously campaigning for the recovery of these islands. He did not give these islands to Saudi Arabi, Oman, Sharjah, Abu Dhabi or any other neighbouring Arab states. He gave them back to Iran.

FURTHER DEVELOPMENTS AND NEGOTIATIONS

The Iranians assumed that, while the sovereignty issue remained unresolved, neither side should engage in the exploitation of the iron oxide mines on Abu Musa. The British made no such assumption, and the Iranian Ministry of Finance wrote to the Iranian Ministry of Foreign Affairs on 9 March 1937 reporting that the British were working Abu Musa's red oxide mines.[64]

When, at the end of 1948, the Iranians expressed a wish to place administrative offices on Tunb and Abu Musa, the British ignored it. In 1949 there were rumours, first that Iran was preparing to refer the case to the United Nations, later that they intended to occupy the islands by force. The Iranian government subsequently received a note from the British Embassy in Tehran expressing the British government's 'clear attitude' in that respect.[65] The Iranians in return erected a flagstaff on Lesser Tunb in August that year, which the Royal Navy promptly removed.

In 1953, during Mosaddeq's second term of premiership, there were reports in the Iranian press that an Iranian commission was to be sent to Abu Musa. An Iranian warship landed a party on that island to seek information from the inhabitants. Once again the British notified the Iranians that Abu Musa was subject to the Shaikh of Sharjah. Early the same year the British received reports that the Iranians were contemplating the despatch of troops to occupy the two Tunbs, Abu Musa and Sirri, and for several weeks RAF planes made reconnaissance flights over the islands.[66]

At this time the British were busy in a different game *vis-à-vis* Iran's territorial possessions in the Persian Gulf: the game of launching different and strange claims on other Iranian islands. Apart from the incomprehensible British claims of the ownership by the Shaikh of Dubai over the Iranian island of Hengam in the early 20th century,[67] the British hinted in 1956 at claims of Kuwaiti ownership of Farsi island.

Official British documents suggest that in order to safeguard Ras al-Khaimah's claims to the Tunb islands, the British went so far in 1956 as protesting against Iran's claim of sovereignty over the island of Farsi[68] on behalf of the ruler of Kuwait. In a letter to the British Embassy in Tehran, the Foreign Office explained that 'following the Iranian landing on Farsi in 1956 the British found themselves involved in an exchange of notes with the Iranians about their respective claims to the island which went on for over three years. The reason for this which "applied also in the case of Tunb" was explained to have been: failure to respond to an explicit claim to ownership of the island by the Iranians might have prejudiced the claim of the "rightful owner", in that case the Ruler of Kuwait.'[69]

However, on 18 May 1961, during 'Ali Amini's premiership, a single-rotor helicopter landed on Greater Tunb. As the British authorities made no protest, an Iranian launch made a second landing on 9 August. On the first occasion, the helicopter brought in an Iranian and two Americans, who photographed the lighthouse and adjacent buildings and talked to the lighthousekeeper, but entered no building and accepted no hospitality.[70] On the second occasion, according to a report by British naval officers, the Iranian launch approached the island from the east and landed a party on the eastern coast, but soon withdrew and went round to the south, where they landed a party at the village. The locals described two of the visitors as Americans; the second landing was thought to have been connected with the first, with the purpose of conducting an oil survey.[71]

Confused by these incidents, the British first decided to protest, then to limit their reaction to making it clear to the Iranians that they knew about the incidents and would like an explanation. Finally, on 5 September, the British Embassy in Tehran handed the Iranian Ministry of Foreign Affairs a protest note, on behalf of the Shaikh of Ras al-Khaimah, against the Iranian landings on Greater Tunb.[72]

The Iranian government responded to the protest note on 21 September:

> as the Embassy are aware, the Imperial Iranian Government have never accepted the claim that the island of Tunb is a part of the Shaikhdom of Ras Al Khaimeh or that any other state has a right over it. As has been officially declared to the Embassy on many occasions the Imperial Government of Iran consider the island of Tunb to be part of their own territory over which they have sovereignty. The Imperial Government's sovereignty over the island of Tunb is based on the rules and principles of International Law, and they have never given up their right to it. In the above circumstances the Imperial Ministry of Foreign Affairs do not consider the Embassy's protest as contained in the note under reference to be justified.[73]

The Foreign Office deemed it necessary to repeat the protest in the hope that 'the Iranians will get tired of this sort of exchange before we do'.[74] The British Embassy wrote again to the Iranian Ministry of Foreign Affairs on 13 January 1962, reserving the rights of the Ruler of Ras al-Khaimah in regard to the island of Tunb. In reply, the Iranian Foreign Ministry 'confirmed the contents of their note No. 3052 of the 21 September 1961 reserving all the Iranian rights in respect of the Iranian island of "Tunb" in the Persian Gulf'.[75]

While continuing their arguments and negotiations with the British government on the subject of ownership of the islands of Tunb and Abu Musa in the early 1960s, the Iranian government began a policy of improving friendly relations with the emirates of the Arab coasts of the Persian Gulf.[76] This policy entered a very active phase in 1962 and continued until 1971.

The British had suspected that the helicopter which took a party of Iranians and Americans to Greater Tunb was American, but investigation showed the helicopter to be British owned and hired by Iranians.[77] A year later, during the premiership of Amir Assadollah Alam, Iran successfully completed the task of restoring her full sovereignty over the island of Sirri by applying its law of '12 miles territorial sea' to the island and excluding all non-Iranian activities in and around the island. The move was not objected to by the British or any other government.

Chapter 10

Seizure of the two Tunbs and Restoration of Sovereignty in Abu Musa

Determined to prevent the Arab Emirates inheriting from the British the dispute over ownership of the Tunbs and Abu Musa islands which would prevent co-operation between Iran and her Arab neighbours in the Gulf, government authorities in Iran resumed as from early 1970 demands for the 'returning of Tunbs and Abu Musa to Iran'. After the settlement of the Bahrain issue that year, there were rumours that Iran had withdrawn its historical claims to Bahrain principally because it believed, at the time, that its greater interest centred on the strategic Strait of Hormuz, and in the islands at the mouth of the Persian Gulf, and that Iran was reassured by the British, in conjunction with 'some' Arab governments, of getting Abu Musa and the two Tunbs, in return for Bahrain.

No doubt Iran had been endeavouring to connect the two issues of sovereignty over Bahrain and the three islands of the Strait of Hormuz, but there is no evidence at all suggesting such an agreement between Iran and Britain. The Shah of Iran visited Saudi Arabia in November 1968, a month after the signing of the continental shelf delimitation agreement between the two countries. This visit ended in the rapid improvement of bilateral relations in all aspects. Friendship and co-operation became close and productive which led many to suspect that the two sides had made a secret deal on the issue of the Bahrain islands.

Although these rumours were baseless, the parallel secret negotiations between Iran and Britain on the Anglo–Iranian territorial disputes in the Persian Gulf which were taking place at the same time, gave rise to the rumours that the two sides, in conjunction with some Arab governments,[1] agreed on a trade-off deal by giving Abu Musa Island to Iran in return for Iran's withdrawal of claims to Bahrain.[2] This rumour could have been more credible because of its background history. The British had endeavoured since 1928-9 to come to a similar arrangement with Iran on the issue of Sirri Island and the islands of Tunb and Abu Musa.

However, the announcement by the Iranian government of the policy of withholding official recognition of the emerging federation of Arab emirates which would include territories belonging to Iran severely complicated the task of creating this federation. Saudi Arabia had similarly declared that it would not recognise the federation owing to the territorial disputes in Buraimi and Liwa regions with Abu Dhabi while Iraq's hostile attitude towards British designs concerning those small monarchies in the Persian Gulf was known. The British had, therefore, concluded that creation of the union of the small emirates without the goodwill of the regional powers would put this powerless union in a risky position. Recognition of this fact was the main driving force behind the British decision to try to reach some kind of compromise with Iran, the most powerful country of the region, by reluctantly recognising her rights to the three islands.

From the Iranian point of view, time was running out and British intransigency forced her to come to an arrangement of shared sovereignty with Sharjah clearly against her declared policy concerning Abu Musa. The Iranian government, nevertheless, officially declared that Iran's rights of sovereignty over the whole of Abu Musa would not be affected by the terms of the Memorandum of Understanding which could be a mere instrument of a *de facto* recognition of the *status quo* in Abu Musa and thus a temporary measure which would only postpone finalisation of the restoration of Iran's full sovereignty over the whole of Abu Musa.

A vigorous campaign of legal, political and historical arguments was launched by Tehran aiming at making it known both to Great Britain and Arab quarters in the neighbourhood of the Persian Gulf that she had resolved to leave no stone unturned in making her repossession of the three islands a reality. This campaign appears to have made the intended impression as sympathy for Tehran increased internationally. Even the British seemed to recognise the fact that Iran's rights to these islands could not be ignored completely.

In his confidential diary for 18 February 1969 Iran's Court Minister Alam indicate:

> ... British Ambassador (Sir Denis Wright) ... told me very confidentially that the case of Tunb Island is practically settled and will definitely be given to Iran, for we have told the Shaikh of Ras al-

Kheimeh that if you don't come to some sort of arrangement with Iran – as these islands are situated above the median line (of the Persian Gulf) – Iran will lawfully, and if that was not possible, will forcefully take these islands, and the Shaikh agreed to make a deal over them. I said: what about Abu Musa? He said: this island is situated below the median line. I said: and our power is sufficient enough to put a step below the line . . . He said: (if you resort to force) your relations with the Arabs will be harmed. I said: to hell with it . . ..[3]

Even at this stage some former British officials in the Persian Gulf would express doubt about Sharjah's and Ras al-Kheimiah's 'legal' and 'legitimate' ownership of these islands. While using clearly positive terminology in describing the ownership of the islands of the Persian Gulf, Donald Hawley, British Political Agent for the Trucial States between 1958 and 1961, describes the ownership of the islands of Tunbs and Abu Musa in his book as having 'been occupied by the Qawasim'.[4]

By comparison, the Iranian press were putting forward a vigorous argument on Iran's 'indisputable' ownership of these islands. *Kayhan International* of 30 May 1970, for instance, put forward a legal argument on Iran's sovereignty of the three islands, adding:

> The three islands have belonged to Iran since time immemorial and have always formed an integral part of the country. About 80 years ago, the British government, for imperialistic considerations, unlawfully and temporarily separated them from Iran by preventing Iran from exercising its established sovereign rights over them.[5]

These arguments were a reiteration of the points that the Shah himself made earlier in 1970 and repeated thereafter. In an interview which took place during his flight to Switzerland in early February 1971 for instance, he stated:

> These islands belong to the nation, and we have British Admiralty maps and other documents which prove this. We will – if necessary – regain them by force, because I don't want to witness my country to be put up to auction.[6]

In a second interview with the Indian magazine *Blits* on 24 June 1971 the Shah declared that the islands belonged to Iran; they had been 'grabbed some 80 years earlier at a time when Iran had no central government'; and that his 'father had sent gunboats to recover them, but the British assured Iran that no flag of sovereignty would be hoisted until the question was settled'. The Shah then added: 'I hope this happens now. Otherwise, we have no alternative but to take the islands by force'.[7] The Shah's men put more emphasis on the strategic imporance of these islands to Iran; on 27 June 1971 Amir Abbas Hoveida, the then prime minister, told the people of the strategic Gulf port of Bandar Abbas that:

> Iran was by no means indifferent to the future of the Persian Gulf, because it constituted its vital access route. Iran needed these islands for its security and prosperity, a goal for the attainment of which Iran would fight with all its might should it fail to settle this problem by peaceful means.[8]

Earlier having emphasised Iran's sovereignty rights to the islands, Foreign Minister Ardeshir Zahedi expressed similar concerns by drawing attention to the activities of Communist elements in the south of the Strait of Hormuz:

> Look to the Chinese Communists in Aden. If these islands go, all our (regional and Western) interests will be damaged. Iran, therefore, is determined to seize the islands (if necessary) for the following reasons:
>
> (i) Freedom of navigation in this waterway at all times is essential, for Iran, unlike Saudi Arabia and Iraq, depends upon the Persian Gulf as the only outlet for its oil exports.
> (ii) Iran needs to exploit its offshore oil resources and to protect not only its extensive oil installations at Khark Island and elsewhere, but its oil cargoes for the entire length of the waterway.[9]

By the summer of 1971 the Iranian authorities began vociferously warning that they would use force if a peaceful settlement of the question was not made possible.

Despite these warnings of the use of force, Iran continued negotiations with the British as the year 1971 was drawing to its close.

Some sources suggest that on 21 November 1971 it was believed in Tehran that the last round of negotiations would not take place.[10] Iran's chief negotiator, Amir Khosro Afshar (then Iran's ambassador in London), confirmed to this author on Sunday 10 April 1994 that negotiations between him and Sir William Luce of Great Britain continued to the full, the last round of which took place in London only a few days before the landing of Iranian forces on the islands. On the method of negotiations he explained:

> Sir William Luce and I used to negotiate in London. Having reached certain points of understanding, we would go to Tehran and discuss them

before the Shah. Having heard the Shah's views, Sir William Luce would go to the emirates discussing the points with rulers of Sharjah and Ras al-Kheimah, from there going to London to brief his government. We then resumed the talks in London, repeating the same procedure.

Mr Afshar also disclosed to this author on the same date that, Saudi Arabia and Egypt were aware of the negotiations. He said:

I met and discussed our intention of repossessing the three islands once with King Faisal, and three times with Prince Fahad (now King Fahad) in London. I had also discussed the matter with Mahmud Riyadh, Egyptian Foreign Minister, during a meeting at the United Nations. Several times I discussed the matter with Shaikh Zaied of Abu Dhabi who was to become the President of the Emerging UAE. My last talks on the subject with him took place at the Iranian Embassy in London in the summer of 1971. Shaikh Zaied's suggestions included prosecution of this Iranian intention after the formation of the UAE was officially announced. I explained that Iran wanted co-operation with the emerging UAE and other neighbours in the Persian Gulf in the wake of British withdrawal from the region. This issue constituted long standing disputes between Iran and the British and had to be settled with them before they left the region. Should we allow this matter to remain unsettled after the departure of the British, the UAE inheritance of the dispute will prevent regional co-operation. He had nothing to say to this argument. Moreover, six hours before landing troops on the three islands, on the instruction of the Shah, I informed King Faisal, through Saudi Ambassador in Tehran, of our imminent move to repossess the three islands.'

Mr Afshar also disclosed that he met Shaikh Saqar of Ras al-Kheimah and his heir-apparent separately in London discussing the issue of the two islands of Tunb. No agreement was reached on the subject he said, but some months after Iran's move into the islands, the Saudis intervened asking him to meet the Shaikh and to see to his financial needs. He stated:

I met Shaikh Saqar in the Iranian Embassy in London and told him that we were prepared to extend financial assistance to Ras al-Kheimah provided that he officially renounced his opposition to the reassertion of Iranian sovereignty on the two Tunbs. He said he saw no sense in not doing so, but such an official declaration would put his life in jeopardy with the fanatics.

Equally important is the fact that some 24 hours before the Iranian military action took place, Sharjah announced an agreement with Iran, according to which Iranian forces were to take possession of the strategic areas of Abu Musa.

The announced Memorandum of Understanding between Iran and Sharjah included the following points:[11]

Neither Iran nor Sharjah will give up its claim to Abu Musa nor recognise the other's claim. Against this background the following arrangements will be made:

1 Iranian troops will arrive on Abu Musa. They will occupy areas the extent of which have been agreed on the map attached to this memorandum.

2 (a) Within the agreed areas controlled by the Iranian troops, Iran will have full sovereignty and the Iranian flag will fly.

   (b) Sharjah will retain full jurisdiction over the remainder of the islands. The Sharjah flag will continue to fly over the Sharjah police post on the same basis as the Iranian flag will fly over the Iranian military quarters.

3 Iran and Sharjah recognise the breadth of the island's territorial sea as 12 nautical miles, (according to Iran's law of territorial waters).

4 Exploitation of the petroleum resources of Abu Musa and the seabed and sub-soil beneath its territorial sea will be conducted by Butes Oil and Gas Company under the existing agreement which must be acceptable to Iran. Half of the governmental oil revenues hereafter attributable to the said exploitation shall be paid directly by the company to Iran and half to Sharjah.

5 The nationals of Iran and Sharjah shall have equal rights to fish in the territorial sea of Abu Musa.

6 A financial assistance agreement will be signed between Iran and Sharjah.

November 1971

The financial agreement referred to in the above MOU concerned payments by Iran to Sharjah of one and a half million pounds sterling annually for a period of nine years. This was to cease should Sharjah's oil revenue reach £3 million per annum.[12] Other sources, however, incorrectly imply:

The statement concluded a provision that one half of the oil revenues from the island and its continental shelf, should be allocated under special arrangement for the welfare of the people of Sharjah.[13]

Since Sharjah was still a British protectorate at the time and, in accordance with the terms of the special treaties of 1864 and 1892 with Great Britain, did not have the right to sign an official agreement or treaty with any foreign power except Great Britain, it is noteworthy that the above Memorandum of Understanding between that emirate and Iran cannot be considered but as a British sponsored pact between the two sides.

Sharjah gained its independence, within the framework of the United Arab Emirates two days later (1 December 1971).

Document 5 of the MOU is a letter signed by Dr Abbas-Ali Khalatbary, then Foreign Minister of Iran, and addressed to Sir Alec Douglas Home, British Foreign Secretary, warning that if Iran felt, at any time, activities occurring in the Sharjah-controlled section of Abu Musa aimed at threatening Iran's interests and sovereignty and security in that island, the government of Iran would reserve for themselves the right to implement their full sovereignty over the whole of Abu Musa. Replying to this letter, the British Foreign Office informed Iran that the contents of the above letter were communicated to the Shaikh of Sharjah. An Iranian Foreign Ministry official who wished to remain anonymous told this author on 26 April 1972 that a similar letter to the President of the UAE (December 1971) motivated a positive response.

Abu Musa's 12 mile territorial waters overlapped those of the Emirate of Umm al-Quiwain. In a settlement between Sharjah on the one hand and Umm al-Quiwain on the other, it was arranged for the latter to receive a 15 per cent share of the oil revenue from the Sharjah's share of profit.

The understanding between Iran and Sharjah, declared by the ruler of that emirate on 29 November 1971 was undoubtedly one of the most positive results of the Anglo–Iranian negotiations going on prior to Iran's repossession of the three islands.

The Memorandum of Understanding with Sharjah, however, left the overall matter of ownership of Abu-Musa undefined. In an interview with an *Al-Ahram* correspondent in Sharjah, on 7 December 1971, the then ruler of the Emirate of Sharjah stated that 'Sharjah did not believe that its agreement with Iran adversely affected its sovereignty over the island', and that 'the agreement was temporary and was an instrument for overcoming crisis and preventing bloodshed'.[14] This statement totally contradicted an earlier statement by the Iranian premier to the Iranian Majlis (parliament). Premier Hoveida had stated on 30 November 1971:

The Iranian flag was unfurled on Mount Halva, the highest peak on the island of Abu Musa. I deem it necessary to declare on this occasion that the government of H.I.M. has in no conceivable way relinquished or will relinquish its sovereign rights and incontestable jurisdiction over the whole island of Abu-Musa, and hence, the presence of local agents (ie Sharjah officials) in a segment of the island of Abu-Musa should in no way be viewed or interpreted as contradictory to this declared policy.[15]

Arab reaction to the Iranian action was mixed. Radical Arab states adopted vociferous policies both domestically and in the United Nations, while the moderates preferred prudence. The Arab League was urged by the radicals to lodge a collective Arab complaint with the United Nations Security Council, signed by all 21 member states of the time. The proposal was opposed by the majority of the member states. Instead, they agreed to condemn Iran's action individually by issuing statements in their own capitals. All Arab states issued this statement of condemnation except Jordan, while leaders of Egypt, Morocco, Tunisia, Lebanon, Saudi Arabia, Oman, Qatar and Bahrain apologised privately to the Iranian leadership for having to issue such statements.

The radical Arab states, Algeria, Iraq, Libya and former South Yemen, took their complaint to the United Nations Security Council. The Council met on 9 December 1971 to examine the case. Representatives of these four countries were joined by representatives for Kuwait and the United Arab Emirates, the latter becoming a member of the United Nations on the same day.[16]

Talib al-Shibib, representing Iraq, alleged in his account of the event that:

Iran had claimed the whole Gulf, but 'such ludicrous blanket claims' had been reduced to claims on Bahrain and later to the Tunbs and Abu Musa.[17]

He asserted that his government had received a cable from the Shaikh of Ras al-Kheimah claiming that the two Tunbs had belonged to Ras al-Kheimah since ancient times.[18]

Whereas the UAE representative made a very mild and conciliatory statement,[19] Abdullah Yaccoub Bishara, representing Kuwait, claimed that the islands of Greater Tunb and Lesser Tunb had belonged to Ras al-Kheimah 'for centuries'.[20] a similar statement made by the UAE Foreign Minister at the United Nations General Assembly on 30

Abu Musa Island – 30 November 1971

Having welcomed the Iranian naval representative to the island of Abu Musa on behalf of his brother, His late Highness Shaikh Khalid bin Mohammad Al-Qasemi, the then ruler of Sharjah, Shaikh Saqar bin Mohammad Al-Qasemi, brother of present ruler of Sharjah, is being welcomed on board of the Iranian naval vessel off Abu Musa island.

September 1992, also alleged that the islands of Tunbs and Abu Musa had belonged to the emirates 'since the beginning of history'.[21]

It is worth observing, however, that the tribal entity of Sharjah was created in 1864, the tribal entity of Ras al-Kheimah was created in 1921 and the United Arab Emirates came into being in 1971.

In his statement to the UN Security Council meeting of 9 December 1971 Abdellatif Rahal of Algeria presented a more rational historical account of this case by saying:

> There had been conflicting claims to those islands over the years, but it was undeniable that during the whole period of British control the islands had been part of the territory that had become the United Arab Emirate.[22]

This statement, albeit more rational than those made by representatives of Kuwait, Iraq and Libya, was not in complete harmony with the facts of history, that the British control of the lower Gulf

214

Representatives of Iran and the United Arab Emirates at the special session of the UN Security Council of 9 December 1971, each defending his country's position on the issue of the Arab complaint against Iran's regaining sovereignty control of the islands of Tunbs and Abu Musa which resulted in the complaint being shelved.

territories began in 1820 while Abu Musa and the two Tunbs were seized from Iran and given to the Qasemi tribal entity of Sharjah by the British in the year 1903.

For his part, Amir Khosro Afshar, representing Iran at the hearing, made a relatively short statement rejecting the charges against Iran as baseless, and said the question was essentially an internal matter for his country (UN 1972: 48).

Finally, Abdul Rahman Abby Farah, representative of Somalia, a member of the Arab League, proposed that the Council should adjourn consideration of the complaint allowing third party efforts at mediation to take place. The Council agreed without objection to that course, and thus the case was let to rest.

215

Conclusion

Territorial differences have existed in the Gulf region for centuries without necessarily posing serious threats to peace and stability of the region. This is not, however, true with some instances of territorial disputes still prevailing which are almost entirely created in the wake of introduction of Western concepts of territoriality and precise boundaries to the region. These disputes have been left behind by the withdrawal of pax-Britannica for the regional states to settle them among themselves. A highly complicated example of these disputes is the case of territorial contentions between Qatar and Bahrain, currently reviewed by the International Court of Justice at the Hague, and those between Iran and the UAE.

The nature of Bahrain's claim to Zubarah is very complicated. This complication was made worse by the British interpretation of the issue in the 1950s, especially when they endeavoured to show that Bahrain's claims to Zubarah, in reality, were not territorially oriented, but concerned jurisdiction over the inhabitants (the Naumi tribesmen) who are considered as subjects of Bahrain.

Although in their official correspondence the British reasserted repeatedly Bahrain's sovereignty over Hawar islands and fasht of Dibal and qit'at of Jaradah, they were never able to avoid uncertainties surrounding their expressed views. This was typical of their attitude towards territorial differences all over the region. In their treatment of seabed boundary between the two states, they implicitly suggested that the Bahrain – Qatar median line was to be measured from the coasts of Qatar Peninsular and Hawar islands.

It is the norm in the practice of international maritime laws that the median line between two states is drawn half-way between the two opposite coasts by giving full effect, and if that is not possible, giving half effect to the major islands of the two states situated outside the limits of their respective territorial waters. A good example of this is the delimitation of Iran – Saudi Arabian continental shelf boundary which was measured on the basis of giving half effect to the situation of the Iranian island of Khark and full effect to the Iranian island of Farsi situated in the middle of the sea. But in the case of Bahrain and Qatar, Hawar islands were considered by the British as a part of Bahraini mainland, not as an archipelago belonging to Bahrain with full or half effect.

The British nevertheless, continued until the end of their presence in the region reaffirming somewhat half-heartedly Bahrain's sovereignty over Hawar islands, and over the fasht of Dibal, qit'at of Jaradah, and her right to the ownership of properties in Zubarah and the right of access for the Bahrainis to travel to Zubarah without the supervision of Qatar authorities.[1]

This dispute, largely resulting from the lack of adequate commitment on the part of the British to the just and peaceful settlement of differences between Bahrain and Qatar, continued throughout the years until the Government of the State of Qatar filed on 8 July 1991 an application instituting proceedings against the Government of the State of Bahrain in the Registry of the International Court of Justice at the Hague.

Confident of her position vis-a-vis this move, Bahrain applied in 1992 to the International Court of Justice for adjudication. The Court asked the states of Bahrain and Qatar to reply to the court by 29 December 1992 and 28 September 1992 respectively.[2]

Whereas Qatar concentrates her arguments on the ownership and sovereignty over Zubarah, Hawar islands, Dibal and Jaradah fashts and their related territorial waters and seabed boundaries on the basis of their geographical proximity, Bahrain's claims of ownership and control of these islands, fashts, seabed areas and their territorial waters are based on historical justification.

Though both Bahrain and Qatar have been building military power since their independence in 1971 and although the military powers of both states are now reaching a stage when one could inflict damage on the other, they are both members of the GCC and their close relationships with larger powers inside the GCC and outside it in the region and outside the region would probably prevent a crisis of serious nature to engulf the two states.

This conclusion, however, is not designed to prove or disprove sovereignty rights to the areas of land and sea disputed by regional states in favour of one or the other. Documented facts are demonstrated as clearly as possible in the main text of the book, and I leave the final conclusion to the readers. What I would like, in the meantime, to argue here is that during their colonial rule in the Persian Gulf, the British approached issues of sovereignty and territoriality with great inconsistency resulting from the way their interests were identified at the time of each case. The outcome of such an inconsistent approach could not have been but numerous territorial and boundary disputes in the region.

Territorial disputes between Qatar and Bahrain on the one hand, and between Iran and UAE on the other, provide perhaps a fine example of how the British gave a territory to one state without complete regard for the arguably compelling evidence in support of claims of the other state. They did so presumably because their interests would be more closely identified with those of one at the time rather than those of the other. In the case of Qatar-Bahrain disputes, when the new officer who replaced the author of an earlier award on Hawar islands, is asked to make his opinion on the decision of his predecessor known, he openly acknowledges that the decision was not fair, but he could not reverse it because such a reversal of the decision was not 'practical politics'.

Similarly, in the case of the shoals of Dibal and Jaradah, the British awarded them to Bahrain in 1947 and in spite of openly acknowledging the fact that they were situated five nautical miles within the Qatar side of the median line of the sea in that vicinity. When legal affirmation of this award felt necessary in the wake of the Geneva Convention of 1958 on the 'territorial sea', British Foreign Office began an endeavour for giving the status of 'island' to these shoals; arguing that the man-made installations on Jaradah was suffice to describe the shoal as an 'island'. An argument which fails to attract the sympathy of British Admiralty. Even more bizarre is the suggestion of the Foreign Office that since the belt of territorial waters defined for qeta'at ad-Jaradah overlapped by a few metres with the southernmost tip of fasht ad-Dibal, a three mile belt of territorial sea should be defined for Dibal, no matter themselves openly and officially referred to it as a 'shoal' not an 'island'.

As has been demonstrated in the text, official documents of the British Government in respect of these particular territorial differences are both partial and contradictory, with great confusion in views expressed on various individual cases. Just how much weight could such documents carry in the task of forming an opinion on the territories in dispute, is hard to say. Yet, the significance of these documents in respect of determining certain historical facts and/or certain geographical descriptions is undeniable.

It is in this situation that the task of forming an opinion on these particular territorial disputes cannot avoid the compelling necessity of determining all facts of history and geography through the works of impartial and independent researchers.

Factors of considerations based on geographical proximity of locational contiguity of national maritime jurisdiction do not confer entirely factors like proximity, however, do provide a basis for allotting an island to one state rather than another, either by agreement between the parties, or by a decision not necessarily based on law. The permanent Court of Arbitration at the Hague's award of 4 April 1928 on the island of Palmas between the United States and the Netherlands is perhaps a good example of this.[3] It is also noteworthy that the British had also based their decision of allotment of islands in the Persian Gulf some time on this principle. Moreover, in the case of the island of Greater Tunb, in dispute between Iran and Great Britain on behalf of the Shaikh of Ras-al-Khaimah in the first half of the 20th century, once a high ranking official of British Foreign Office rules that 'it (Great Tunb) is indeed geographically a Persian island'.[4]

Finally, it is worth noting that GCC mediation between Qatar and Bahrain succeeded in bringing about a rapprochement between the two states in early Spring of 1997, when Manamah and Doha established diplomatic ties by exchanging ambassadors for the first time in their history.

The Iranians claim that the question of Iran's sovereignty over the islands of Tunb and Abu Musa was settled through negotiations in 1970 and 1971 between Iran and Britain the latter acting officially on behalf of the Emirates. This was the outcome of about 68 years of Iranian protests and demands for the return of the islands. Otherwise Britain, still in charge of the Emirates' territorial and boundary interests and foreign relations in November 1971, would, at least, have issued a statement of protest against the signing of the Memorandum of Understanding between Iran and Sharjah concerning the status of Abu Musa island and against Iran's seizure of the two Tunbs.

Given the location of Abu Musa and the two Tunbs in the strategically sensitive Strait of Hormuz, and given that both the regional countries of the Persian Gulf and the oil-consuming countries of the industrial world depend heavily on peace and security in the

Strait of Hormuz, outside support for either side in this argument against the other could easily lead to a conflict potentially as explosive as the Kuwait crisis of 1990–1. The Iranians have warned the political leaders of the United States and Europe of the danger of hinting support for one side in the issue.

Territorial and boundary differences in the Persian Gulf have prevented proper and lasting Arab-Iranian cooperation in the region. At the same time, in any emergency involving the overall interests of both sides, cooperation between Iran and her Arab neighbours has materialized, the best example being the period between the years 1968 to 1978. This ten-year period of Arab-Iranian cooperation was prompted by a sense of emergency arising from the British Government's announcement in January 1968 of its intention to withdraw its forces from east of Suez and hand the safe guarding of security in the Gulf to its littoral powers, an announcement which coincided with President Nixon's declaration of the doctrine of non-interference in regional conflicts, leaving regional security around the world to friendly regional players. Hence, the urgency of regional cooperation in the Persian Gulf for the maintenance of peace and security became clear. A further factor in the situation was the meeting in Tehran between the Shah of Iran and King Faisal of Saudi Arabia in 1965, when they had agreed on extensive cooperation among Muslim states. These agreements not only put an end to years of Shi'ah-Sunni conflict in the region, but paved the way for the creation of the Islamic Conference.[5]

Iran and her Arab neighbours promptly realised that settlement of geographical differences was to be seriously considered as a necessary precondition for the promotion of cooperation amongst them in the region. It was under the influence of this state of strategic urgency that many and complex border issues were settled. Two of the most complicated border issues settled in this period were those of continental shelf boundary settlement of late 1968 between Iran and Saudi Arabia and the 1971 understanding between Iran and Sharjah on Abu Musa island. These were followed by a number of other settlements such as: continental shelf boundary settlement of 1970 between Iran and Qatar; 1972 between Iran and Bahrain; 1975 between Iran and Oman and the river and inland boundary settlement between Iran and Iraq in that same year. Maritime boundaries between Iran and Kuwait, at the head of the Gulf, was covered by a draft agreement between the two sides which came about in 1962, but it is not in force because of continued territorial and boundary disputes between Iraq and Kuwait. Also Iran delimited her maritime boundaries with Dubai in 1972, but official ratification of this agreement is prevented by uncertainties arising from the unclear terms of the 1971 arrangements between Iran and Sharjah over Abu Musa island. A draft agreement also came into being between Iran and Abu Dhabi in that period, but it too is rendered inoperative by other differences in that vicinity.

Other manifestations of Arab-Iranian cooperation in the period 1968–1978 include Iran's internationally praised withdrawal of historical claims to Bahrain and her swift and highly effective response in 1973 to Oman's call for assistance in defusing a Marxist-separatist conspiracy against her territorial integrity. That swift and extensive military assistance eradicated the 12 year old armed struggle of Communist separatists in Dhufar province of Oman in a short period of less than three years. It is noteworthy that while Iran was busy defending Oman's territorial integrity, almost all Arabs attacked her on the accusation of having territorial ambitions in Oman. These accusations continued against Iran after the Islamic revolution of 1979 in spite of the fact that one of the initial foreign policy undertakings of the Islamic Republic of Iran was to withdraw the remaining military units from Oman. These attacks reflected on a wider scale of growing mistrust between Arabs and Iranians in the region, the flame of which was being fanned by dubious sources in the West, especially after it became clear that Arab-Iranian cooperation in other fields, such as OPEC international oil policies, effectively tipped the balance of power in the international geopolitical system in favour of regional states of the Persian Gulf. Some Western accusations against Iran of having territorial ambitions against Arab states of the region successfully impressed some Arabs in spite of the fact that Iran had withdrawn territorial claims to Bahrain and defended territorial integrity of Oman. These accusations reached their climax in 1977 with the publication of Paul Erdman's inflammatory novelette 'The Crash of 79'.

These intrigues and propaganda, clearly aimed at destroying all prospects of Arab-Iranian cooperation, eventually resulted in the collapse of Iran's proposal for the creation of 'a collective security pact in the region with the participation of all states littoral to the Persian Gulf', [6] and put a final end to that short period of Arab-Iranian cooperation in the region. Today, it is not impossible to envisage a repeat of history and to reanimate the spirit of collective cooperation in the region. A major step forward in this direction will have to be the satisfactory settlement of remaining Arab-Iranian territorial differences. Of these, Iran's differences with Iraq can only be settled if and when Iraq sincerely separates geographical issues with Iran from her inter-Arab politics. Alternatively, the only interim solution left for the rest of the region for cooperation will be to go ahead without an active participation from Iraq, until she is able to give her immediate geographical interests priority over her old and long exhausted inter-Arab geopolitical ambitions and is able to identify her regional and global interests with those of the rest of the region.

Considering that the changing world order of our time necessitates rethinking in all regions, especially in the region of the Persian Gulf, for preparing to face the challenges of the new global geopolitical realities through creation of regional politico-economic structures for cooperation, continuation of Arab-Iranian territorial and other disputes will only benefit outside interests; the potential future rivals of the region. In other words, cooperation between Iran and Arab states of the region is possible primarily if national interests were to be put before the geopolitical considerations of the big powers.

However, should Iran decide to allocate a number of its many ports on the Persian Gulf to the exclusive use of the landlocked countries of the Caucasus, Caspian Sea and Central Asia, giving these countries the opportunity of direct access to the open seas, she would, at the same time, have provided the Arab states of the Persian Gulf with the opportunity of direct access to the said regions and countries. This will create an unprecedented situation which no country of the said regions can afford to miss. Multilateral investments on the expansion of roads, rail and air ways, and other means of communications will facilitate economic amalgamation of the Persian Gulf, the Caucasus, the Caspian Sea and Central Asia in a gigantic economic zone with huge possibilities for economic development and political harmony which, in turn, expands security throughout this huge economic zone to the benefit of all nations far and wide.

Appendices

UN SECURITY COUNCIL'S DECISION ON THE QUESTION OF BAHRAIN

At its 1536th meeting, on 11 May 1970, the Council decided to invite the representatives of Iran, Southern Yemen and Pakistan to participate, without vote, in the discussion of the item entitled The Question of Bahrain.

(a) Letter dated 4 May 1970 from the Permanent Representative of Iran to the United Nation addressed to the President of the Security Council (S/9779);[1]

(b) Letter dated 5 May 1970 from the Permanent Representative of the United Kingdom of Great Britain and Northern Ireland to the United Nations addressed to the President of the Security Council (S/9783).[1]

(c) Note by the Secretary-General (S/9772).[1]

UN RESOLUTION 278 (1970) ON BAHRAIN OF 11 MAY 1970

(As presented to the Iranian Majlis and Senate by the Iranian Government)

The Security Council,
Noting communication from the Secretary-General to the Security Council of 28 March 1970. Noting also the statements made by the representatives of Iran and United Kingdom of Great Britain and Northern Ireland in their letters to the Secretary-General of 9 and 20 March 1970, respectively,[2]

1 Endorses the report of the Personal Representative of the Secretary-General, which has been circulated to the Security Council, under cover of a note from the Secretary-General, on 30 April 1970.[3]
2 Welcomes the conclusions and findings of the report, in particular that 'the overwhelming majority of the people of Bahrain wish to gain recognition of their identity in a full independent and sovereign state free to decide for itself its relations with other nation.

Now, considering that the report of the personal representative of the Secretary General concerning the will of the people of Bahrain has been endorsed unanimously by the Security Council of the United Nations, the Government also reports for endorsement the results of the said efforts to the Senate in Pursuance of their report 9 Farvardin 1349.

Prime Minister
Amir Abbas Hoveida

Locum Minister of Foreign Affairs
Abbas-Ali Khalatbari[4]

APPENDIX II

Original Persian text of the Iranian government's report of the finding of the United Nations Secretary-General's Personal Representative in Bahrain and the UN Security Council's Resolution 278, to the Iranian parliament which was ratified by the Lower House of the Majlis on 14 May, and by the Senate (Upper House) on 18 May, 1970[5]

وزارت امور خارجه

۱۴۵

متن گزارش جناب آقای عباسعلی خلعتبری قائم مقام وزیر امور خارجه درمورد گزارش نماینده ویژه دبیر کل سازمان ملل متحد
راجع به بحرین

۱۳۴۹/۲/۲۸ (۱۹۷۰۵۱۸)

بطوریکه سناتورهای محترم بخاطر دارند درجلسه مورخ
نهم فروردین ماه ۱۳۴۹ آقای وزیر امور خارجه گزارش اقدامات
دولت را درمورد بحرین باستحضار محلسین رسانیدند .
در گزارش مزبور اشاره شده بود که دولت شاهنشاهی
ایران از دبیر کل سازمان ملل متحد تقاضا کرده است که مساعی
جمیله خودرا برای کسب تمایلات واقعی مردم بحرین نسبت به
سرنوشت خود بهر نحوی که مقتضی میداند اعمال نماید .
در گزارش آقای وزیر امور خارجه همچنین تصریح شده بودکه
هر گاه نتیجه تحقیقات دبیر کل سازمان ملل متحدبه تأیید شورای
امنیت برسد، دولت ایران نیزمفاد آنرا محترم خواهد شمرد .
اینک بطوریکه سناتورهای محترم اطلاع دارند نماینده
اعزامی دبیر کل سازمان ملل به بحرین گزارش خودرا درباره
تمایلات اهالی بحرین به دبیر کل سازمان تسلیم نموده و این
گزارش در جلسه مورخ دوشنبه ۲۱ اردیبهشت ماه ۱۳۴۹
(برابر با ۱۱ ماه مه ۱۹۷۰) از طرف شورای امنیت طی
قطعنامه ای بشرح زیر تأیید شده است :

و با توجه به نامه مورخ ۲۸ مارس دبیر کل سازمان ملل متحد
به شورای امنیت و با توجه به نظرات نمایندگان ایران و انگلستان که ضمن

نامه های آنها در تاریخ ۹ مارس ۱۹۷۰ و ۲۰ مارس ۱۹۷۰ به ترتیب به
دبیر کل سازمان ملل متحد تسلیم شده است :
۱ ـ گزارش نماینده شخص اولیانت که ضمن یادداشت دبیر کل در
تاریخ ۳۰ آوریل ۱۹۷۰ بین اعضای شورای امنیت توزیع شده است ؟ أیید
میشود .
۲ ـ از نتیجه گیری و استنباطات گزارش ، بخصوص اینکه اکثریت
قاطع مردم بحرین آرزومند استقلال و تعیین سرنوشت خود در کمال آزادی
هستند ، ومیخواهند بعنوان یک دولت مختار و حاکم درباره آینده روابط
خود با دولتهای دیگر تصمیم بگیرند، استقبال میشود.۹
اینک با توجه باینکه گزارش نماینده دبیر کل در بار
تمایلات مردم بحرین به اتفاق آراء مورد تأیید شورای امنیت
سازمان ملل متحد قرار گرفته است، دولت نیزپرو گزارش مورخ
۹ فروردین بماه ۱۳۴۹ ، در نتیجه اقدامات مزبورقطعنامه شورای
امنیت را جهت تأیید به استحضار سنا میرساند .

قائم مقام وزیر امور خارجه   نخست وزیر
عباسعلی خلعتبری   امیر عباس هویدا

مستخرج از مذاکرات مجلس سنا شماره ۹۹۴
جلسه ۱۲۰ ـ مورخ ۱۳۴۸/۲/۲۸

TRANSLATION

Text of report by His Excellency Mr. Abbas-Ali Khalatbari, Locum Minister of Foreign Affairs on the report of the personal Representative of UN Secretary General concerning Bahrain.

28/2/1349 (18 May 1970)

As honourable Senators remember, Mr Minister of Foreign Affairs reported to the Houses of the Majlis on the ninth of Farvardin 1349 of the undertaking of the government regarding Bahrain. It was indicated in the said report that the Imperial Government of Iran had requested Secretary General of the United Nations to use his good offices to determine by whichever method he deems fit, the true will of the people of Bahrain about their own destiny. It was also emphasised in the report of Mr Foreign Minister that should the results of the UN Secretary General's research be endorsed by the Security Council, the Government of Iran will respect its contents.

Now, as the honourable Senators are aware, the representative of the UN Secretary General, despatched to Bahrain, has submitted to the Secretary General his report on the will of the people of Bahrain and this report was endorsed by the Security Council in the meeting of Monday 21 Ordibehesht 1349 (corresponding with 11 May 1970) in the form of the following resolution:

The Security Council, noting the communication from the Secretary General to the Security Council of 28 March 1970, noting also the statements made by the representatives of Iran and England in their letters to Secretary General of 9 and 20 March 1970, respectively:

1. Endorses the report of the Personal Representative of the Secretary General, which has been circulated among members of the Security Council on 30 April 1970.
2. Welcomes the conclusions and findings of the report, in particular that ' the overwhelming majority of the people of Bahrain wish to gain recognition of their identity in a full independent and sovereign state free to decide for itself its relations with other nations.

Now, considering that the report of the personal representative of the Secretary General concerning the will of the people of Bahrain has been endorsed unanimously by the Security Council of the United Nation, the Government also reports for endorsement the results of the said efforts to the Senate in Pursuance of their report of 9 Farvardin 349.

Prime Minister
Amir Abbas Hoveida

Locum Minister of Foreign Affairs
Abbas-Ali Khalatbari[6]

APPENDIX III

The 1971 Iran-Sharjah Memorandum of Understanding and related documents.[7]

1 Ruler of Sharjah asks British Foreign Secretary for Iranian acceptance of the MOU.

Khalid bin Mohamed Al Qasmi
Ruler of Sharjah & Its Dependencies

Date 18 November 1971

The Secretary of State for
  Foreign and Commonwealth Affairs,
The Foreign and Commonwealth Office,
London.

After Greetings,

With reference to our discussions about the arrange-
ments between Sharjah and Iran on the Abu Musa question,
I confirm that I accept the arrangements set out in the
Memorandum of Understanding annexed to this letter. I
should be grateful for confirmation that the Iranian
Government for its part accepts the arrangements.

Finally, please accept our highest regards and respects.

KHALID BIN MOHAMMED AL-QASIMI
Ruler of Sharjah and Its Dependencies

2 Full text of the Memorandum of Understanding as attached to the letter of 18 November 1971 from the Ruler of Sharjah to the British Foreign Secretary.

MEMORANDUM OF UNDERSTANDING
_____

Neither Iran nor Sharjah will give up its claim to Abu Musa nor recognise the other's claim. Against this background the following arrangements will be made:

1. Iranian troops will arrive on Abu Musa. They will occupy areas the extent of which have been agreed on the map attached to this memorandum.

2(a) Within the agreed areas occupied by Iranian troops, Iran will have full jurisdiction and the Iranian flag will fly.

 (b) Sharjah will retain full jurisdiction over the remainder of the island. The Sharjah flag will continue to fly over the Sharjah police post on the same basis as the Iranian flag will fly over the Iranian military quarters.

3. Iran and Sharjah recognise the breadth of the island's territorial sea as twelve nautical miles.

4. Exploitation of the petroleum resources of Abu Musa and of the seabed and subsoil beneath its territorial sea will be conducted by Buttes Gas and Oil Company under the existing agreement which must be acceptable to Iran. Half of the governmental oil revenues hereafter attributable to the said exploitation shall be paid directly by the company to Iran and half to Sharjah.

5. The nationals of Iran and Sharjah shall have equal rights to fish in the territorial sea of Abu Musa.

6. A financial assistance agreement will be signed between Iran and Sharjah.

3 Official map of Abu Musa Island attached to the Memorandum of Understanding of November 1971.

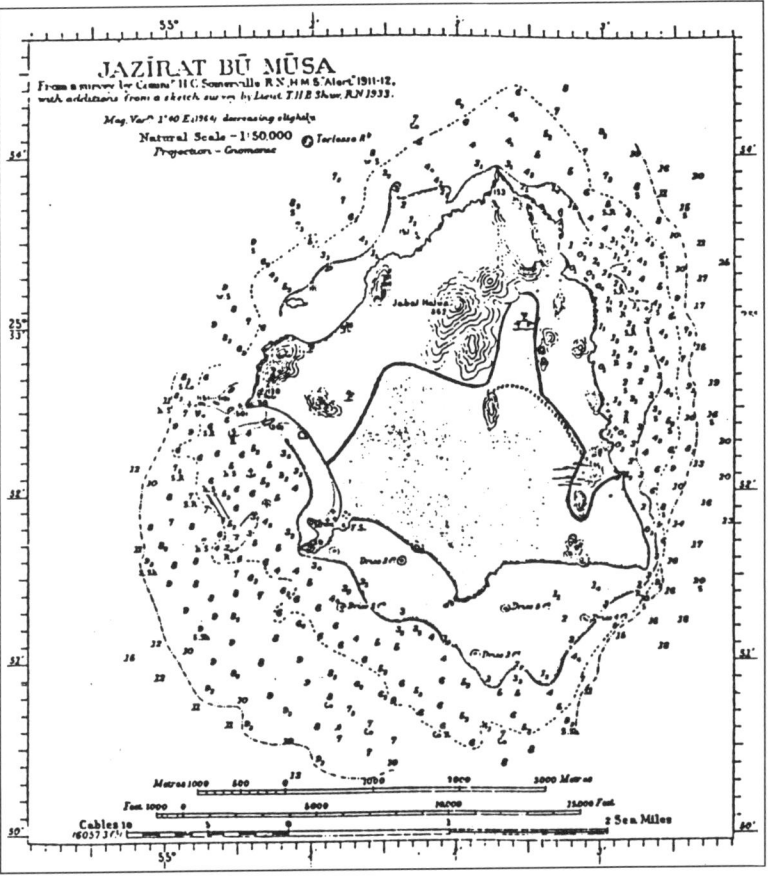

4 Letter of 24 November 1971 from British Foreign Secretary to the Iranian Minister of Foreign Affairs asking for Iranian acceptance of MOU.

Foreign and Commonwealth Office

London S.W.1

24 November, 1971

My dear Colleague

I enclose a copy of a letter addressed to Her Majesty's Government from the Ruler of Sharjah, in which the Ruler asks for confirmation that the Iranian Government accepts the arrangements for Abu Musa set out in the Annex to his letter. I would be grateful for confirmation that the Iranian Government accepts the arrangements.

Yours sincerely

(ALEC DOUGLAS-HOME)

His Excellency
    Dr. Abbas-Ali Khalatbari.
        Minister for Foreign Affairs, Iran.

5 Letter of 25 November 1971 from the Iranian Foreign Minister to the British Foreign Secretary spelling out Iran's conditions and warnings relevant to Iran's acceptance of the MOU.

IMPERIAL MINISTRY
OF FOREIGN AFFAIRS

Tehran, 25th November, 1971.

No. M/21284

Your Excellency,

With reference to my letter No. M/21282 of today's date and in reply to yours of 24th November, 1971, I am instructed by my Government to inform you that Iran's acceptance of the arrangements relating to Abu Musa set out in the enclosure to your aforesaid letter is given on the understanding that nothing in the said arrangements shall be taken as restricting the freedom of Iran to take any measures in the Island of Abu Musa which in its opinion would be necessary to safeguard the security of the Island or of the Iranian forces.

I would be grateful for confirmation that this understanding has been conveyed to the Ruler of Sharjah.

Abbas Ali Khalatbari
Minister for Foreign Affairs

The Principal Secretary of State
for Foreign and Commonwealth Affairs,
London.

6 Letter of 25 November 1971 from Iranian Foreign Minister to the
British Foreign Secretary concerning Iran's acceptance of the MOU.

IMPERIAL MINISTRY
OF FOREIGN AFFAIRS

Tehran, 25th November, 1971.

No. W/21282

Your Excellency,

I confirm that my Government accepts
the arrangements for Abu Musa as set out in the
enclosure to your letter of 24th November, 1971.

A copy of the Memorandum of Understanding
in which the arrangements are set out is annexed to
this letter.

Abbas Ali Khalatbari
Minister for Foreign Affairs

7 Letter of 26 November 1971 from British Foreign Secretary to the
Iranian Foreign Minister informing him that Iran's conditions and
warnings were conveyed to the Ruler of Sharjah.[8]

Foreign and Commonwealth Office

London S.W.1

26 November, 1971

My dear Colleague

With reference to your letter
number M/21284 of 25 November, 1971 I have taken note
of the understanding on which your government's
acceptance of the arrangements relating to
Abu Musa is given and have conveyed that
understanding to the Ruler of Sharjah.

Yours sincerely

Alec Douglas-Home

(ALEC DOUGLAS-HOME)

Text of financial assistance agreement between Iran and the Emirate of Sharjah.

Khalid bin Mohamed Al Qasmi
Ruler of Sharjah & Its Dependencies

خالد بن محمد القاسمي

حـم سكام الشارقة وملحقاتنا

Date 1st December 1971.

التاريخ ....

Your Excellency,

I have the honour to acknowledge receipt of Your Excellency's letter of the 30th November 1971, the text of which is as follows:

" I have the honour, on behalf of the Imperial Iranian Government, and in accordance with the agreed mutual intention of Iran and Sharjah to develop and strengthen their relations to the benefit of each State in as many fields as possible, to make the following proposals in relation to financial assistance.

a.   The Imperial Iranian Government will assist Your Highness by making semi-annual contributions of £ 750,000 Sterling on 21st April and 21st October of each year, beginning in 1972, provided that

(i) such a contribution shall not be made in any period of six months in which the revenue received by Your Highness from the commercial exploitation of oil, gas or mineral deposits on the Island of Abu Musa and beneath its territorial waters exceeds £1.5 million Sterling, or

(ii) in any period of six months in which the revenue received by Your Highness from the commercial exploit-ation of oil, gas or mineral deposits on the Island of Abu Musa and beneath its territorial waters is less than £1.5 million Sterling but exceeds £ 750,000 Sterling, the contribution shall be reduced by the amount of that excess.

b.   If this Agreement enters into force before 21st April, 1972, the Imperial Iranian Government will make to Your Highness on the date on which this Agreement enters into force an additional contribution equal to a total of as many monthly contributions of £ 125,000 Sterling as could be made on the 21st day of each month between the date of such entry into force and the first contri-bution under paragraph (a) above.

c.   The provisions of paragraph (a) above shall remain in force for an initial period of nine years beginning 21st April, 1972. At the end of the eighth year the provisions shall be reviewed and it will be open to either the Imperial Iranian Government or Your Highness to give notice that the provisions shall be terminated at the end of the ninth year.

التاريخ ....

d.   The sum mentioned under (a) above shall be payable, at
the choice of Your Highness, in United States of America
Dollars or in Federal Germany's Deutche Marks instead
of Pounds Sterling, in which case the amount payable
shall be calculated according to the parity prevailing
on the date when this agreement enters into force.

    If the foregoing proposals are acceptable to Your Highness,
I have the honour to suggest that the present Note and Your Highness's
reply to that effect shall be regarded as constituting an agreement
between the Imperial Iranian Government and Your Highness in this matter
which shall enter into force on the date of Your Highness's reply".

    I have the honour to inform Your Excellency that the
statement in Your Excellency's letter is acceptable to me and hence
that Your Excellency's letter and this reply shall be regarded as
constituting an agreement between Iran and myself in this matter
which shall enter into force on to-day's date.

Khalid bin Mohamed al Qasimi.

His Excellency, Mr. Abbas Ali Khalatbari,
Minister for Foreign Affairs,
Imperial Ministry of Foreign Affairs,
Iran.

APPENDIX IV

A list of some of the official, semi-official and unofficial maps from the eighteenth, nineteenth and twentieth centuries, confirming the islands of Greater Tunb, Lesser Tunb and Abu Musa as belonging to Iran. These maps are to be found in the India Office Library and Records (London), British Library (London), Public Record office (London), US Argosy Library (New York), French Foreign Ministry (Paris), Russian Foreign Ministry (Moscow), Iranian Foreign Ministry (Tehran), SOAS Library (London) and other document centres of the world.

A. OFFICIAL MAPS

- *Carte du Golphe persique*: compiled in 1764 by French Foreign Ministry, in colour, the islands coloured as Iranian territories.
- *The Gulf of Persia*: compiled in 1829 by Captain G.B. Brucks on the instructions of East India Company, the islands coloured as Iranian territories and named in the covering note as Iranian owned.
- *The Persian Empire*: compiled in 1813 by John Macdonald Kinner, Political Adviser to Sir John Malcolm in his mission to Iran, in black and white; printed in colour in 1832 by J. Arrowsmith, showing the islands and Iran in the same colour.
- *Central Asia comprising Cabool, Persia, the River Indus and countries Eastward of it*: compiled in 1834 by Lieut. Alexander Burnes on the basis of 'Authentic Maps', printed by Arrowsmith in colour, showing the islands in the colour of Iranian territories.
- *Limits of the activities of the Tribes of Pearl Coast*: compiled in 1835 by Captain S. Hennell, showing the islands in the Iranian side of the dividing line of the Persian Gulf.
- *Limits of the activities of the Tribes of Pearling Coasts*: compiled in 1838 by Major Morrison, British Political Resident in the Persian Gulf, showing the islands within Iranian jurisdiction.
- *Map of the Persian Gulf*, compiled by Captain C.B.S. St. John, under the auspices of the Indian Government, Bombay 1876, in which the Tunbs and Abu Musa were depicted in the same colour as the Iranian mainland.
- *The Persian Gulf*: compiled in 1886 by the Intelligence Division of the War Office. A copy of this map was presented to Naser ad-Din

Shah Qajar of Iran in 1888 on the instruction of Lord Salisbury, British Foreign Secretary. When Sir Drummond Wolff, British Minister-plenipotentiary in Tehran, expressed regret that the map had been presented to the Iranian monarch precisely because it confirmed Iran's territorial possessions in the Persian Gulf, including the three islands in question, Lord Salisbury remarked: 'Take note that maps shall never be presented in future'. Nevertheless, as it was already too late for that, the map was published again in 1891 in colour, showing the three islands in the colour of Iran.

- *Official Map of Persia (in six sheets)*: compiled in 1897 in the Simla Drawing Office, Survey of India, Administration of Topography of the Indian Foreign Office. The Tunbs and Abu Musa are shown in the colours of the Iranian mainland.

- *Map of Iran, Afghanistan, and West Pakistan*, in *World Atlas*, plate nos. 143–4, compiled under the supervision of the Council of Ministers of the Soviet Socialist Republics in 1967 on the occasion of the 50th anniversary of October Revolution. The name 'Iran' appears next to the islands in question.

- *Map of Persia*: compiled in 1897 by Colonel T.H. Holdich, Superintendent, Survey of India, British India Office Library W/L PS/21/B22, the three islands shown in Iranian colour.

B. SEMI-OFFICIAL MAPS

- *A Map of the Empire of Persia*: compiled in 1770 by Mr D'Anville; the islands are coloured like Iran's mainland.

- *A New Map of the Empire of Persia*: compiled in 1794 by Mr D'Anville, first Geographer to the Most Christian King, showing the three islands in the same colour as the rest of the Iranian territories.

- *Map of Persia and Cabul*: compiled in 1837 by Mr J. Arrowsmith in London; the three islands are coloured as Iranian.

- *Persia, Afghanistan and Baluchistan*: compiled in 1891 by the Royal Geographical Society under the supervision of Lord George Curzon MP, and attached to Curzon's *Persia and the Persian Question* (1892). The islands are coloured the same as the rest of Iran. Lord Curzon was Viceroy of India at the time when the islands in question were given to Sharjah in 1903 by the British.

C. UNOFFICIAL MAPS

- *The Map of Persia*: compiled in 1818 in England for *Thomsons New Grand Atlas*; the three islands are coloured like the Iranian mainland.
- *Map of Persia*: compiled in 1828 by Sidney Hall in London; the three islands are coloured as belonging to Iran.
- *Persia and Part of the Ottoman Empire*: compiled in 1831 by G. Long and published by the Society of Expanding Useful Education in England; the three islands are coloured as Iranian owned.
- *Map of Persia*: compiled in 1840 for the *Black Atlas* and published in London; the three islands are shown as belonging to Iran.
- *Map of Persia*: compiled in 1844 for the *Black Atlas* and published in London; again the three islands are coloured as Iranian.
- *Map of Persia & Cabul*: compiled in 1844 by A.K. Johnston for the *National Atlas*, published in England; the three islands are coloured like the rest of Iran.
- *Map of Persia*: compiled in 1851 by J. Rapkin for the *John Tallis Atlas* in London; the three islands are shown as Iranian.
- *Persia and Afghanistan*: compiled in 1854 by A.P.C. Black for the University of Edinburgh; the three islands are shown as Iranian.
- *Persia and Afghanistan*: compiled in 1860 for Keith Johnston's *General Atlas*; the three islands are coloured like the rest of Iran.
- *Map of Persia, Afghanistan, Baluchistan*, in Hammond's *Modern Atlas of the World*, C.S. Hammond & Co., 1909, p. 96 which depicts the islands of Tunb and Abu Musa as Iranian territory.
- *The Map of Iran*, in Rand McNally's *Cosmopolitan World Atlas*, Centennial Edition: 1856–1956, compiled by Rand McNally & Co., 1956, p. 157A. Here the islands are indexed as Iranian.
- *Map of South West Asia*, in *Atlas International Larousse*, *(Politique et Economique)*, I. De Janchy & S. Rado eds, Paris: Librairie Larousse 1965, map no. 13A in which the islands are depicted in the same colour as the Iranian mainland.
- *Map of Iran, Afghanistan, West Pakistan*, in *Atlante Internazionale*, 8th edition, Touring Club Italiano, Milan 1968, map no. 92, in which the islands are depicted in the same colour as the Iranian mainland.

APPENDIX V

Summary of debate at the UN Security Council Meeting of 9 December 1971 on the issue of Arab complaint against the seizure of Tunbs and Abu Musa islands by Iran.

COMPLAINT AGAINST IRANIAN OCCUPATION OF GULF ISLANDS

The Security Council on 9 December began consideration of a complaint by four Arab states – Algeria, Iraq, the Libyan Arab Republic and the People's Democratic Republic of Yemen – about 'the dangerous situation in the Arabian Gulf area arising from the occupation by the armed forces of Iran' on 30 November of three islands in the Gulf. The Council decided to defer further consideration of the matter while third-party efforts by 'states friendly to Iraq and Iran' were taking place.

Following the adoption of the agenda, the President of the Council, Ismael Byne Taylor-Kamara (Sierra Leone), drew attention to the requests to participate from the following states: Algeria, Iran, Iraq, Kuwait, the Libyan Arab Republic, People's Democratic Republic of Yemen, and the United Arab Emirates.

Talib El-Shibib (Iraq) said that what had happened in the Arabian Gulf had 'resulted in a tense and serious situation potentially threatening the peace and security of the entire area, and endangering the vital interests of my own country'. On 30 November, his government had received a cable from the ruler of Ras al Khaima stating that the two islands of Tunb had been invaded by Iran and that of the six policemen there, four had been killed and two injured. The cable stated that the islands had been, since ancient times, an indivisible part of Ras al Khaima and that the Iranian occupation was aggression against all Arab people. The cable asked for submission of the case to the Security Council.

The Greater and Lesser Tunb were at the exit of the Straits of Hormuz, connecting the Arab Gulf to the Gulf of Oman and the Arabian Sea. Iran's action was indefensible and a flagrant violation of the Charter. Any 'agreement' alleged by Iran to exist with the Shaikh of Al-Sharja regarding Abu Musa was contrary to commitments with the United Kingdom, which prevailed at the time.

Invasion of the Tunb Islands and partial occupation of Abu Musa was the latest step of a policy of expansion by the government of Iran and a blatant demonstration of the collusion between Iran and the United Kingdom government to bequeath to Iran the colonial role played in the area by Britain for more than three centuries. At one time, he said, Iran had claimed the whole Gulf Area, but 'such ludicrous blanket claims' had been reduced to claims on Bahrain and later to the Tunbs and Abu Musa. Those islands were sparsely inhabited, but strategically located.

The representative of Iraq said that Iran, with the aid and connivance of the United Kingdom and the United States, had referred to 'historical' claims and a 'power vacuum' after British withdrawal. He said Iran had been chosen by the United States and the United Kingdom to replace the latter in exercising hegemony over the area. Communications and oil were involved. Security and stability could only be assured through co-operation of the states situated in the Gulf. Security and stability were the vital concern of all Gulf states, including Iraq.

He rejected the appointment of Iran or any other single state as the sole guardian and guarantor of the continuation of the flow of Gulf oil to the outside world, and rejected the control by Iran of the only outlet for Iraqi commerce to the high seas.

The representative of Iraq said recent reports suggested that Iran had put sophisticated missiles in the occupied islands. Huge military, air and naval power was being built up to support the expansionist policy of Iran, to threaten every neighbouring country that resisted that policy, and to impose a self-proclaimed hegemony over the area. The old imperialist interests were to be preserved through imperialism by proxy.

In 1969, he said, Iran had unilaterally declared the 1937 treaty between Iran and Iraq null and void. That violation of the sanctity of treaties had been accompanied by a show of force. Iran had refused Iraq's request to the Secretary General for a special mission to investigate the troop concentrations on the borders.

Mr El-Shibib said Iranian occupation of the islands was designed to strengthen its expansionist policy vis-à-vis Iraq. His government reserved its right to take any and every action regarding both of Iran's illegal acts to protect Iraq's territorial integrity and its vital interests in the Arabian Gulf.

In all agreements with the Trucial States, the representative of Iraq continued, the United Kingdom was committed to respect and preserve the territorial integrity of the states concerned. The United Kingdom had reneged and must be condemned for not living up to its international obligations.

It was reported that Iranian forces had deported the 400 persons of the Greater Tunb to the Arabian mainland. The Iranian government by its armed aggression had created an extremely critical situation. Iraq had shown extreme self-restraint because of its overriding concern for peace in the area.

Mr El-Shibib appealed to the Council to shoulder its responsibilities and to take all effective measures to condemn the aggressors and their British collaborators, and to ensure the withdrawal of the forces of occupation. If the Council did not act, it left 'no option to others, like ourselves, but to believe that force is the only answer to aggression and to act accordingly'.

Abdullah Yaccoub Bishara (Kuwait) said contrary to all Iranian traditions in solving problems peacefully, Iran had launched on 30 November a completely unprovoked attack on the Arab islands of Greater Tunb and Lesser Tunb, that belonged for centuries to Ras al Khaima. Kuwait had spent tireless efforts to assist the emirates to lay the foundations of a federation of the nine Gulf emirates. The federation had not stood on its feet because Iran blocked the road to federation. It had said 'no islands, no federation'.

Kuwait had tried to persuade Iran not to resort to force, Mr Bishara said. Iran had not agreed. In a visit to Iran, the Foreign Minister of Kuwait had suggested the sovereignty of the Arab Emirates. Iran had categorically rejected the proposal.

Iran 'threatens unnecessarily the security of the Gulf' by its occupation of the Arab islands, declared Mr Bishara. The occupation had been planned and carried out with complete disregard of the Charter. One of the most sacred of United Nations principles was inadmissibility of territorial acquisition by force. Kuwait regarded the islands as Arab islands, historically and demographically. Kuwait had strongly protested to the United Kingdom about its ignoble role in the tragedy.

Kuwait had suggested that Iran refer its case to the International Court of Justice or to arbitration, but Iran had turned down all proposals for a peaceful solution. Iran could not accept that free passage through the Straits of Hormuz was not only essential to Iran's economic life but equally essential and vital to Kuwait, Iraq and the other littoral states. The Gulf was Kuwait's sole economic lifeline.

The United Kingdom's history was 'characterised by a chronic disease of pulling out and leaving behind explosive situations' and it 'deserves severe condemnation'. The United Kingdom, by treaties, was bound to defend the territorial integrity of the Emirates. The same United Kingdom policy had been pursued in Palestine when the

Zionists, working in collusion with the British administration, had taken over and expelled the indigenous Palestinians.

Mr Bishara said that Sir William Luce, on behalf of the United Kingdom government, had tried to get Kuwait to satisfy Iran at the expense of the territorial integrity of the Emirates. Kuwait had rejected that approach. The Council should call on Iran to withdraw its troops from the Arab islands immediately. It should adopt a resolution calling for such a withdrawal. Kuwait would not recognise any change in the status of the islands.

Abdellatif Rahal (Algeria) said that the military occupation by Iran of the three islands introduced a new element of tension in the area. There had been conflicting claims to those islands over the years, but it was undeniable that during the whole period of British control the islands had been part of the territory that had become the United Arab Emirates. That was a problem to be settled by all concerned, not unilaterally and by force. Territorial acquisition by force could not be recognised as legal or valid. Iran had violated the principles of the Charter. That resort to force was unjustified and called for condemnation by the Security Council. The United Kingdom also bore responsibility, for it was up to the United Kingdom to ensure that the Emirates suffered no territorial dismemberment. The United Kingdom as administering power, had an obligation to hand over to the federation its 'entire heritance'.

Abdul Malek Ismail (People's Democratic Reppublic of Yemen) said any discussion of the islands concerned the whole Gulf area. The islands were extensions of the Arab mainland, politically, economically and culturally. The responsibility for the invasion by Iran had to be assumed by the United Kingdom under the prevailing treaties.

Mr Ismail said the United Kingdom had not fulfilled its legal, political or social responsibilities to the area. The United Kingdom had lived in the area 'like parasites' and then left it in a weakened state, as easy prey for the Iranians. The United Kingdom had, however, failed to silence the voice of the people. Since 1955 the popular liberation movement had fought to liberate the whole area as a single area. That fight would continue. The United Kingdom remained the power in the Gulf area through the Shaikhs. They were 'puppet rulers'.

Mr Ismail said the United Kingdom had allowed recent violations of agreements in order to pursue its interests and those of its allies. That explained Iran's actions. Iran intended to interfere also in the domestic affairs of Oman and destroy the revolution elsewhere. The Shah of Iran had always said that he would occupy the Tunbs and Abu

Musa when the British left. Mr Ismail stated that Iran must immediately withdraw from the islands.

Amir-Khosrow Afshar (Iran) said a full-scale war was reported in South Asia. There was fighting in Vietnam and Cambodia. There was danger of war in the Middle East. And yet the Council had been convened to discuss a matter like this. The valuable time of the Council was being taken up not by real or threatened acts of war, but by the wanton and fanciful preoccupations of a few. He rejected the charges against Iran as baseless, and said the question was essentially an internal matter for his country. However, he would deal with some of the points raised.

The area concerned was the Persian Gulf, not the Arabian Gulf, a term used by certain states to distort historical reality and to give the area an Arab character. The riparian states of the Persian Gulf should work together, without outside interference, he said. Iran had no territorial ambitions. Iran was peace-loving and had a policy of trying to settle disputes peacefully, as shown by its actions in the case of Bahrain, for which his country had been praised here.

Mr Afshar said that Iraq had created a tense situation in the area in 1961 by its hostile acts against Kuwait, and had carried on a provocative campaign. Iraq had laid claim to Kuwait and had brought the matter to the United Nations. In this case, too, Iraq was taking up the Council's time for baseless claims.

The islands were Iranian territory. Iran's title to them was long-standing and they were shown in maps hundreds of years old as Iranian. The islands were part of a group forming a virtual archipelago that had always been Iranian. One of the islands was only 17 miles offshore; another was 22 miles offshore. The nearest Arab land was much farther and the Libyan Arab Republic, for instance, was thousands of miles away. He mentioned the Libyan Arab Republic because it was reported to have threatened to send troops to the area. Iraq had also said it might send troops. Iran, Mr Afshar said, would not allow its sovereignty, or a single inch of its territory, to be violated.

Sir Colin Crowe (United Kingdom) said that on 1 March 1971, his Foreign Minister had said that existing treaties in the area were to be terminated and British troops withdrawn by the end of the year. That confirmed a decision of the previous government in January 1968.

The United Kingdom had wanted to see stability in the area through a federation and settlement of outstanding territorial differences. That had been a unanimously acclaimed policy in the

Arab world. A federation had been created and had been welcomed into the United Nations today, and he hoped that an enduring political structure had been laid.

As for territorial claims, the aim had been largely achieved. Of the islands in question, Bahrain was the largest involved, with a population of 200,000 and it was able to take its place in the family of nations. A second problem island had been Abu Musa, with a population of 800, and an agreement had been reached between Iran and the Ruler of Sharjah. As for Tunbs, they had a population of 150. The United Kingdom had advised it could not protect them if agreement was not reached by the time of withdrawal. The United Kingdom had terminated its defence agreements with all the protected states.

The ending of Britain's special position and responsibilities with the Gulf had inevitably meant the striking of a balance between the conflicting claims of neighbouring states, and the taking into account of realities. It would have been better if agreed solutions to all outstanding problems could have been reached, Sir Colin said. But that was not for lack of trying. The over all outcome represented a positive achievement and a contribution to peace. That outcome represented a reasonable and acceptable basis for the future of the area, which should in time be based on co-operation between all states of the Gulf, Arab and non-Arab.

Mahmood Suleiman Maghribi (Libyan Arab Republic) said his delegation was on the point of losing respect for some of the United Nations institutions, especially the Security Council, after observing its deliberations for many years. His delegation had seen that 'a big power can do anything it wishes' and that the small States were powerless in such cases. His delegation had seen other states, with the support of a big power, take similar liberties in violation of the Charter. The Iranian military aggression and occupation of the islands, with the complicity of the British, was an example.

There was hardly a major conflict in the world for which the British were not responsible, the representative of Libya declared. He cited the case of Palestine, Britain followed a policy of treachery and 'divide and rule'. It had failed miserably and intentionally to live up to its responsibilities in this case.

The Libyan Arab Republic had reacted in the only way it could, by nationalising British oil interests in Libya, and by withdrawing its deposits from British banks. The small states of the third world should unify their efforts so that their voice would be heard. The United

Nations lent a deaf ear to the weak but listened to even the whispers of the big powers. The small states should hit the aggressors and their partners where it hurt instead of merely complaining to the Security Council.

Mr El-Shibib (Iraq) said Iran had still not presented any documents to support its claims. Iraqi troops were not stationed anywhere except in Iraqi territory. Iraq had not invaded anybody. Yet, Iran said it had territorial and expansionist ambitions. Every Arab capital had denounced the Iranian aggression. There was not the calm that had been mentioned by the United Kingdom representative. It was traditional British policy, the representative of Iraq said, 'to barter Arab lands'. Palestine was an example.

Mr El-Shibib said Iran had claimed the whole of the Gulf. He wondered whether there was an end to its claims after taking over the islands. The United Kingdom representative had not answered the questions as to whether the islands were Arab and whether the United Kingdom was responsible for their defence until the agreements ran out. The situation was potentially very dangerous. Iraq wanted to apprise the Council of that fact.

Adnan Pachachi (United Arab Emirates) said the problem was of immediate concern to his country and affected its vital interests. On the occasion of his country's admission to the United Nations, he had expressed the regret of his country at Iran's use of force to occupy those Arab islands. Iran's claim to them was untenable historically or juridically.

The six emirates had decided to join together in a strong union and had expected to establish the new state much earlier, but official statements emanating from responsible quarters in Iran had warned that they would prevent the union from coming into being unless Iran got sovereignty over the islands. The emirates had sought negotiations to settle the territorial dispute, but Iran had refused, and the United Arab Emirates had had to wait until now to proclaim their independence under the shadow of Iranian military occupation over the islands.

Mr Pachachi declared that, in his delegation's view, the islands were Arab, and always had been. The British had recognised them as Arab. Iran had claimed them, but had never presented any convincing evidence or brought its claims before the International Court of Justice or anywhere else. It had refused to negotiate the matter with the United Arab Emirates. It had chosen the method of force to settle its claims, although thousands of Iranians lived and worked in the

United Arab Emirates and the two countries should have friendly, neighbourly relations.

Mr Pachachi said that his country hoped Iran would reconsider its position regarding the islands and would find it possible to settle the matter in a way that befitted neighbours. Iran's action in using force and inflicting humiliation on the peoples of the Gulf was contrary to the principles of the Charter and threatened to substitute a feeling of enmity and hostility for the friendly relations that should exist in the area.

Abdulrahim Abby Farah (Somalia) said that unresolved territorial disputes often given rise to intractable problems. The region needed to be assured of peace, stability and security. The Council must act in strict conformity with the Charter. Chapter VI provided for a peaceful settlement of disputes. The Council could recommend procedures in that regard.

At this time, he said, action under Article 36 would be precipitate since states friendly to Iraq and Iran were attempting a discussion at the government level. The Council should adjourn its consideration of the matter *sine die* while those third party efforts were taking place.

The Council agreed without objection to that course.

Notes

INTRODUCTION

1 Charles Krauthammer, *The Unipolar Moment*, Foreign Affairs, Vol. 70, No.1, Spring 1991, p 33.

2 Samuel Huntington, *The Clash of Civilizations*, Foreign Affairs, Vol. 72, No.3, Summer 1993, pp 22–49.

3 Russell Kirk, (1918–1994), *The Politics of Prudence*, Intercollegiate Studies Institute, US, 1993.

4 Dr Antony T. Sullivan, 'Conservatism, Pluralism and Islam', *The Diplomat*, Vol. II, No.5, London June 1997, p. 10.

5 Peter Taylor, *Political Geography*, Longman UK, 2nd ed. 1989, p. 46.

6 Jean Gottmann, 'Geography and International Relations', *World Politics* 3, 1951, pp. 153–73.

7 Pirouz Mojtahed-Zadeh, *Evolution of Eastern Iranian Boundaries*, Unpublished PhD thesis in file at the University of London, 1993, General Introduction.

8 Peter J. Taylor, *Political Geography*, 2nd ed. Longman Group Ltd, London 1989, p. 135.

9 Jean Gottmann, 'Evolution of the Concept of Territory', *Social Science Information*, Paris 1976, Vol. 14, Nos. 3/4, p. 3.

10 Jean Gottmann, op. cit., p. 1.

11 Peter J. Taylor, op. cit., p. 145.

12 See for example; Arab Geographer of tenth century Abul Hassan Ali ibn Hussein al-Masudi, *Morravej az-Zahab*, Persian Trans by Abul- Qasem Payandeh, Tehran 1977, pp. 464–5–6–7.

13 Ferdosi (Hakim Abul-Qasem), *Shahnameh*, English translation by Arthur G. Warner and Edward Warner, London 1925, Vol. VIII pp. 92–160–161–164.

14 Saul B. Cohen, 1973. *Geography and Politics in a World Divided*, (2nd ed.), Oxford U.P. New York.

15 Pirouz Mojtahed-Zadeh, *The Changing World Order and the Geopolitical*

Regions of Caspian–Central Asia and the Persian Gulf. Published by Urosevic Foundation, London 1992.

16 Pirouz Mojtahed-Zadeh, *Political Geography of the Strait of Hormuz.* Joint Geography Department/Middle East Centre Publication, SOAS, University of London, 1990.

17 For a historical and geographical description of this Amirdom see: Pirouz Mojtahed-Zadeh's *Evolution of Eastern Iranian Boundaries*, Ph.D thesis, op. cit.

CHAPTER 1 – THE PERSIAN GULF

1 'Value of Uranium Deposits of Saghand Estimated at $150 billion', *The Echo of Iran*, London, Vol. 1, No.12, January 1989, p. 5.

2 Radio Cairo quoting Egyptian Foreign Minister, June 27, 1991, as appeared in the *Echo of Iran*, Vol. XXXVIV, No.7 (42), London, July 1991.

3 Pirouz Mojtahed-Zadeh, 'A Geopolitical Triangle in the Persian Gulf: Actions and Reactions Among Iran, Bahrain and Saudi Arabia', in the *Iranian Journal of International Affairs*, IPIS, Vol. VI, Nos. 1&2, Spring/ Summer 1994, pp. 47–59.

CHAPTER 2 – THE STRAIT OF HORMUZ

1 Gerald H. Blake, *Maritime Boundaries and Ocean Resources*, Croom Helm, London 1987, p. 137.

2 General Ali Razmara, *Joghraphiai-e Nezami-e Iran (Military Geography of Iran)*, Vol. on *Jazaier-e Iran Dar Khalij-e Fars (Iranian Islands in the Persian Gulf)*, Tehran (1941–42).

3 Ahmad Eqtedari, *Khlij-e Fars (The Persian Gulf)*, Tehran (1965–66), pp. 41–5.

4 See: Mohammad Hassan Khan Sani od-Doleh, *Mer'at ol-Boldan (Places in Mirror)*, text is Persian, no date of publication.

5 See: Sadeq Nash'at, (Mirdamad), *Tarikh-e Syiasi-e Khalif-e Fars (Political History of Persian Gulf)*, Tehran, (1966–67), pp. 402–411.

6 General Ali Razmara, op. cit.

7 Ibid.

8 Ibid.

9 Abdol Latif Bin Abdollah, *Latayef ol-Logat (Dictionary)*, 1854. Original manuscript copy in possession of this author.

10 The 1966 National Census puts Qeshm population at 23,957, Iran's Centre for Census Taking, General Census Taking 1966.

11 See: Sadeq Nash'at, op. cit., see also: Wilson, Sir Arnold T. *The Persian Gulf*, London, 1928.

12 General Ali Rezmara, op. cit.

13 Sadeq Nash'at, op. cit., p. 420.

14 See, for example, Ibn Batutah, *Rahelah*, Cairo 1287.

15 Sadeq Nash'at, op. cit., p. 419.

16 Razmara General, op. cit.
17 J.E. Peterson, 'Guerrila Warfare and Ideological Confrontation in Dhufar', *World Affairs*, Vol.139, No.4, Spring 1977, p. 206.
18 Ibid., see also: Alvin J. Cottrell, *Iran: Diplomacy in a Regional and Global Context*, 1975, p. 10.
19 J.E. Peterson, op. cit.
20 *An-Nahar Report*, Vol.6, No.14, April 7, 1975.
21 See: J.E. Peterson, *Guerilla Warfare and Ideological Confrontation in Arabian Peninsula*, op. cit., pp. 278–95. See also: Mojtahed-Zadeh, Pirouz, *Oman and its Significance for Iran*, op. cit.
22 Brian Bidham, 'Look Beyond the Oil', *The Economist*, May 1975, p. 55.
23 *Kayhan Hava'i* No. 1467, October 22, 1975.
24 J.E. Peterson, *Guerrilla Warfare and Ideological Confrontation in Arabian Peninsula*, op. cit.
25 Ibid.
26 Mohammad Reza Shah in an interview with As-Siyasah of Kuwait, reported in the *Middle East Economic Digest*, August 22, 1975. Early in 1977 reports emerged that Iran had reduced its military strength in Oman: *Financial Times*, January 14 and 21, 1977. When this author was touring around Dhufar in late 1977, there were still two Iranian military units stationed there. They were withdrawn after the Islamic revolution succeeded in Iran in 1979.
27 *International Herald Tribune*, March 24–25, 1973, p. 2.
28 Ibid.
29 J.E. Peterson, *Guerrilla Warfare and Ideological Confrontation in Arabian Peninsula*.
30 *Middle East Economic Digest*, January 10, 1975.
31 On the background to the joint Iranian–Omani naval operations at the Strait of Hormuz, see: J.E. Peterson *Twentieth Century Oman*, (1978), London, p. 192. It was reported that, following the Shah's state visit to Oman in late November 1977, Iran and Oman issued a joint communiqué declaring that they would be jointly responsible for the security of the Strait of Hormuz. See *The Middle East*, May 1978, No. 43, pp. 18 and 23.
32 G.H. Blake, op. cit., p. 137.
33 See: Pirouz Mojtahed-Zadeh, 'Arabestan Che Hodafha'i Ra Dar Khalij-e Fars Donbal Mikonad (What Aims Saudi Arabia is Following in the Persian Gulf)', *Masael-e-Jahan (World Affairs)*, Tehran 1977, Vol.5, No. 9, (November), pp. 36–48.
34 See for example, Paul Erdman, *The Crash 79*, Published in 1977.
35 Brian Beckett, 'Power Balance in the Gulf', *The Middle East*, No.25, November 1976, p. 15.
36 Report by US Senate Committee on Energy and Natural Resources, on *Access to Oil – United States Relations with Saudi Arabia and Iran*, December 1977.
37 Pirouz Mojtahed Zadeh, *What Aims Saudi Arabia is Following in the Persian Gulf, op.cit.*
38 Shahram Chubin, *Iran's Foreign Policy, 1960–76: an overview*, op. cit., p. 206.
39 BBC – SWB, ME/5085/A/3, 21 November 1975.

40 J.E. Peterson, *Guerrilla Warfare and . . .* op. cit., p. 288.
41 See: *The Times*, A Special Report, November 21, 1977. See also: *Events*, August 12, 1977.
42 Ibid.
43 *The Middle East*, No.43, May 1978, p. 18.
44 Ibid.
45 Pirouz Mojtahed-Zadeh, *What Aims Saudi Arabia is following in the Persian Gulf*, op. cit.
46 *Events*, August 27, 1977, p. 30.
47 See: 'Security Lies Behind Expensive Plans', *The Times*, (Special Report on Saudi Arabia), November 21, 1977, p. IV. See also: *Events*, August 12, 1977, pp. 38–39.
48 Ibid.
49 Ibid.
50 Ibid.
51 See Pirouz Mojtahed-Zadeh, 'Global Importance of the Persian Gulf', in *The Echo of Iran*, (London), Vol.1, No.12, January 1989, pp. 11–12.
52 Roger Vielvoye, quoting Saudi Arabian officials, 'Security Lies Behind Expensive Plans', *The Times* (Special Report), November 21, 1977, p. IV.
53 Judith Perera, 'Together Against the Red Peril', *The Middle East*, No.43, May 1978, p. 23.
54 *Facts About Shatt al-Arab Issue*, Foreign Ministry of Iran, May 1969, p. 3.
55 League of Nations, *Official Journal*, February 1935, pp. 201–202.
56 League of Nations, op.cit., pp. 196–208.
57 On the Shatt al-Arab issue, see: Richard Schofield, *Evolution of the Shatt al-Arab Boundary Dispute*, MENAS publication, London 1986. There is also masses of literature on the Shatt al-Arab dispute from both the governments and impartial individuals.
58 See: Jabir, Ibrahim Al-Rewi, *Hodud ad-Dowaliah wa Moshkilat el-Hodud al-Iraqiah wal-Iraniah (International Boundaries and the Iran-Iraq Boundaries Problems)*, a PhD thesis, Cairo University, 1970.
59 *The Times*, London December 17 and 19, 1969.
60 See: Facts about Shatt al-Arab, op.cit., p. 8.
61 Ibid.
62 Tarh-e Cham, or Project Cham: *cham* is a Persian abbreviation for Chahar Mantaqeh which means four regions.
63 See: R.K. Ramazani, *The Persian Gulf, The Role of Iran*, 1972.
64 *Ettela'aat Hava'i*, No. 5127.
65 *Kayhan International*, February 15, 1975, pp. 4–5.
66 Ibid.
67 *Middle East Economic Digest*, 10, No.15, April 22, 1966, p. 173.
68 *Ettela'at hava'i*, op.cit.
69 R.K. Ramazani, *The Persian Gulf*, (1972), op.cit., pp. 74–75.
70 See: Iranian Oil Operating Companies, Mahshahr Oil Products Export Terminal, Tehran 1967.
71 See for example, Alving J. Cottrell, *Iran Diplomacy in a Regional and Global Context*, Washington, (1975), p. 3.
72 R.K.Ramazani, *The Persian Gulf*, op. cit., p. 75.

73 *Kayhan International*, February 13, 1969.
74 The NPC was established in 1966 by an act of the Majlis as an affiliate of National Iranian Oil Company.
75 *Middle East Economic Digest 10*, No.15, April 22, 1966, p. 173.
76 R.M. Burrell, *The Persian Gulf*, the Washington Paper, No.1, p. 25.
77 Pirouz Mojtahed-Zadeh, Tahavvolat-e Eraq – Changes in Iraq, in *Masa'el-e Jahan (World Affairs)*, No.4, Vol.58, (1978), pp. 16–30.
78 Pirouz Mojtahed-Zadeh, 'Global Significance of the Persian Gulf', *The Echo of Iran*, Vol.1 in London, No. 12, pp. 11–13, January 1989.
79 R.M. Burrell, and Alvin J. Cottrell, *Iran, Arabian Peninsula, and the Indian Ocean*, New York, (1972).
80 Iran Foreign Policy Series, No.2, *The Echo of Iran* (Publisher), Tehran, January 1973, p. 23.
81 Ibid.
82 J.I. Clarke & W.B. Fisher, *Population of the Middle East and North Africa*, University of London Press, (1972), p. 101.
83 J. Kinsman, *Kurds and Iran, Iraq's Changing Balance of Power*, New Middle East, 22, pp. 25–27.
84 Iran's Foreign Policy No.2, op.cit., p. 23.
85 Kissing's *Contemporary Archives*, April 7–13, 1975, p. 27053.
86 *Kayhan Daily*, No. 9593, June 23, 1975, p. 2.
87 Keesing's *Contemporary Archive*, July 24, 1981, p. 30982.
88 *Keesing's*, February 26, 1982, p. 31353.
89 *Keesing's*, February 26, 1982, p. 31354.
90 *Keesing's*, February 26, 1982, p. 313563.
91 *Financial Times*, December 20, 1981.
92 *Keesing's*, June 25, 1982, p. 31563.
93 *Kuwait Times*, October 2, 1979.
94 R.K. Ramazani, *Revolutionary Iran*, 2nd ed. 1987, p. 49.
95 Jean Gottmann. See Introduction, Some Theoretical Backgrounds p. .
96 Jacques Ancel, *Les Frontieres*, Galliard, Paris, 1939, p. 196.
97 Associated Press quoting *Al-Sharq al-Ausat* quoting Prince Sultan bin Abdel-Aziz Al-Saud, *Ettelaat International of London*, No. 424, Friday 26 January 1996.

CHAPTER 3 – HISTORICAL FOUNDATIONS OF TERRITORIALITY IN THE PERSIAN GULF

1 Sir Arnold T. Wilson, *The Persian Gulf*, London 1954, p. 22.
2 Pirouz Mojtahed-Zadeh, *Evolution of Eastern Iranian Boundaries*, PhD Thesis, University of London, 1993, p. 23.
3 John Wilkinson, *Water and Tribal Settlement in South-East Arabia*, Oxford Clarendon 1977, p. 6.
4 R.H. Major, *India in the Fifteenth Century*, 1865, p. 10.
5 Pirouz Mojtahed-Zadeh, *The Changing World Order*, 1992, p. 10.
6 M.J. Tabari, *Tarikh Tabari*; Persian Translation, 1973, p. 462.
7 Abul-Hassan Masudi, *Moravvej az-Zahab*, 1977, p. 246.
8 Arnold T. Wilson, op. cit., p. 55.

9 John Wilkinson, *The Julanda of Oman*, in the Journal of Oman, Vol. 1, London, 1975, p. 98.

10 Donald Hawley, *The Trucial States*, London 1970, p. 38.

11 *Tu'am* in Middle Persian meant 'mixed'; *diba* in Old Persian (in use in Sassanid times) referred to flowery patterned silk clothes extensively worn by Iranians at the time.

12 Wilkinson, *The Julanda of Oman*, op. cit., p. 98.

13 Ibid, p. 99.

14 Ibid.

15 Ibn Huqal, *Surat al-Ardh*, London 1938, p. 244.

16 Maqdasi al-Beshari, *Ahsan at-Taqasim*, Tehran 1982, p. 18.

17 Abbasee was the currency unit of the Safavid Iran, introduced by and named after Shah Abbas The Great, the most famous Safavid Shahs in whose memoirs Port Ganbrun was named Bandar Abbas.

18 *Brief Notes* of Captain R. Taylor, Bombay New Series No. XXIV–1856/27.

19 Arnold Wilkinson, op. cit.

20 *Oman* published by the government of Oman, Muscat 1976, p. 26.

21 Walter Dastal, 'The Shihuh of Oman', in the *Geographical Journal*, No. 628, March 1972.

22 Abul Hassan Masudi, op. cit., p. 240.

23 Ian Skeet, *Muscat and Oman*, London 1974.

24 *Oman*, op. cit.

25 Pirouz Mojtahed-Zadeh, *The Islands of Tunb and Abu Musa*, CNMES/SOAS Publication, University of London, 1995, p. 25.

26 Pirouz Mojtahed-Zadeh, *Keshvarha va Marzha*, IPIS Publication, Tehran, 1993, p. 164.

27 Sawaheli (a mixture of Persian and Arabic with some Indian vocabularies). The Swahili language of East Africa is an extension and a more developed form of this language.

28 Pirouz Mojtahed-Zadeh, *The Islands of Tunb and Abu Musa*, op. cit., p. 9.

29 Pirouz Mojtahed-Zadeh, *Sheikh Neshin-ha-ye Khalij-e Fars*, Ataei Publication, Tehran, 1970, pp. 35–6.

30 Claus Michael Röhrborn, *Provinzen Und Zentrlgewalt Persiens*, Persian Translation, Tehran 1978, pp. 2–3.

31 FO 371/45507, *Persian Frontiers*, Confidential E. 10136/4029/34, 31.1.1947, p. 13.

32 Arnold Wilson, op. cit., pp. 245–6.

33 M.T. Lesan al-Molk Sepehr, *Nasekh at Tavarikh*, Tehran 1974, Vol. 1, p. 206.

34 Rupert Hay, *The Persian Gulf States*, Washington 1959, p. 148.

35 J.A. Kechichian, History of (Bahrain's) Political Relations with Iran, in the *Encyclopaedia Iranica*, Ehsan Yorshater, ed., Vol. III, Fascimile 5, Routledge & Kegan Paul, 1988, p. 508.

36 Donald Hawley, op. cit., p. 314.

CHAPTER 4 – MARITIME BOUNDARIES IN THE PERSIAN GULF

1 Pirouz Mojtahed-Zadeh, *Political Geography of the Strait of Hormuz*, Geography Department Publication, London University, January 1991, p. 59.

2 Confidential from National Iranian Oil Company to the Ministry of Foreign Affairs, dated 21.7.1344 (13 October 1995). 1539/84, in Persian.

3 Confidential, from British Embassy in Tehran to Imperial Iranian Government dated 4 May 1966.

4 Pirouz Mojtahed-Zadeh, *Sheikh Neshinshay-e Khalij-e Fars (The Sheikhdoms of the Persian Gulf*, Ataei Publications, Tehran 1970, p. 22.

5 Iranian Foreign Ministry *Book of Documents*, IFM Ninth Political Bureau, Tehran 1976, pp. 97, 100, 102, 104.

6 See appendix to the chapter for the documents.

7 G.H. Blake and R.N. Schofield, *Boundaries and State Territory in the Middle East and North Africa, MENAS Press Ltd, 1987 London, p. 123.*

8 *Limits in the Sea*, US Department of State, No. 94, Continental Shelf Boundaries in the Persian Gulf, 1981, p. 4.

9 *Limits in the Sea*, op. cit., No. 108, Maritime Boundaries of the World, 1990, p. 34.

10 Letter of 7 May 1957 from the British Resident in Bahrain, FO 371/126934.

11 FO 371/140194, from Given of British Residency in Bahrain to A.R. Walmsey of Arabian Department of Foreign Office, Confidential BA 1971/3, dated 20 August 1958, paragraph 3.

12 Extract from letter of 13.12.1336 (12.3.1958), No. 2682, from Moshfeq Kazemi, Ambassador of the Imperial Government of Iran in India, to the Ministry of Foreign Affairs, *Gozideh-e Asnad-e Khalij-e Fars, A Selection of Persian Gulf Documents*, IPIS publication, Vol. III, Tehran 1994, p. 187.

13 Richard Young (1970), Equitable Solutions for Offshore Boundaries, *The American Journal of International Law*, Vol. 64, pp.#146;125 to 157.

14 Pirouz Mojtahed-Zadeh, *Political Geography of the Strait of Hormuz*, op. cit., pp. 58–59.

15 Archive of Iran's *Binding Treaties with Other States* (Persian), Iranian Ministray of Foreign Affairs, Tehran 1976, p. 33.

16 *Limits in the Sea*, 1981, op. cit., p. 7.

17 *Limits in the Sea*, 1981, op. cit., p. 8.

18 Article 2 and 3 of Iran–Qatar Continental Shelf Boundary Treaty of 1969, Iranian Foreign Ministry, *Relations with UAE, Oman, Qatar*, Tehran 1976, pp. 109–111.

19 Confidential from National Iranian Oil Company to the Ministry of Foreign Affairs, dated 21.7.1344 (13 October 1965): No. 7539/84, p. 1.

20 Report (in Persian) from the Legal Department of the Ministry of Foreign Affairs to the Locum Minister of that Ministry, dated Tehran 3.12.1347 (21.11.1968), No. 7193/18, page 2, paragraph 4, Iranian Foreign Ministry documents, File 34, No. 4–12, titled *The Iran–Qatar Petroleum*.

21 Ibid.
22 National Legislative Series, UN Document No. ST/LEG/SER. B/16, p. 416 (1974).
23 Pirouz Mojtahed-Zadeh, *Political Geography of the Strait of Hormuz*, op. cit., p. 60.
24 *Limits in the Sea*, op. cit., pp. 2–3.
25 National Legislative Series, UN Document No. ST/LEG/SER. B/16, p. 428 (1974).
26 Iranian Foreign Ministry, *Documents and Treaties*, op. cit., p. 110.
27 Ibid.
28 National Iranian Oil Company, internal memorandum to the President of the Board of Directors, dated 28.9.1349 (19 December 1970), No. 90504/4922/Sh. W.
29 Ibid.
30 *Limits in the Sea*, No. 94, op. cit., pp. 8–9/
31 Ibid.
32 Iranian Foreign Ministry, *Documents and Treaties*, op. cit., p. 116.
33 Pirouz Mojtahed-Zadeh, *Political Geography of the Strait of Hormuz*, op. cit., p. 61.
34 Article 1 of the treaty of Iran–Oman Continental Shelf Boundary, Iranian Foreign Ministry's *Documents and Treaties*, op. cit., p. 177.
35 A draft agreement signed in 1962 governs unofficial Iran–Kuqait maritime boundary arrangements.
36 Pirouz Mojtahed-Zadeh, *Political Geography of the Strait of Hormuz*, op. cit., p. 60.
37 From Ministry of Foreign Affairs to National Iranian Oil Company, No. 119/18 dated 9/1/1352 (30/3/1973), selection of *Persian Gulf Documents*, Vol. 4, Document No. 331 34, IPIS, Tehran, 1995, pp. 93–6.
38 *Limits in the Sea*, No. 94, op. cit., p. 3.
39 Daily Ettelaat, in Persian, Tehran, Monday 4 Sahahrivar 1354, (26 August 1975), 'Bazar-e Syasat', p. 4.
40 Ettelaat International, London, 18 June 1997, p. 10.
41 The text of Decree No. 2/250–67 dated 31 Tir 1352 (22 July 1973) is not annexed to this Act; it has already been reproduced in: United Nations Legislative Series, National Legislation and Treaties relating to the Law of the Sea (ST/LEG/SER.B/19), p. 55.
42 This list is not attached.

CHAPTER 5 – EMERGENCE AND EVOLUTION OF TERRITORIAL STATES IN QATAR AND BAHRAIN

1 International Court of Justice at the Hague, Unofficial Communiqué No. 91/21, dated 8 July 1991.
2 Priouz Mojtahed-Zadeh, *Sheikh Neshinhay-e Khalij-e Fars (Emirates of the Persian Gulf)*, Ataei Publications, Tehran, 1970, p. 178.
3 E.A. Wallis, *A History of Egypt*, London 1902, p. 64.
4 Sadeq Nashat (Mirdamad), *Tarikh-e Syasi-e Khalij-e Fars* (The Political History of the Persian Gulf, Tehran 1966, p. 567.

5 Ibid.
6 Pirouz Mojtahed-Zadeh, *Sheikh Neshinhay-e . . .*, op. cit., p. 179.
7 Donald Hawley, *The Trucial States*, London 1970, p. 34.
8 Hawley, op. cit., p. 34.
9 Ibid.
10 Arnold T. Wilson, *The Persian Gulf*, London 1954, p. 85.
11 Shaikh Abdullah bin Khalid Al Khalifah, The State of Avounis, in *Al-Watheeka*, No.3, Vol. 2, July 1983, pp. 14–38.
12 Dr Ali Aba Hussain, Juboor – Were They Arabs of Bahrain or the Arabs of the East?, *Al-Watheeka*, op. cit., pp. 39–58.
13 Sadeq Nashat (Mirdamad), op. cit., pp. 317–8.
14 Extract from *Brief Notes* of Captain Robert Taylor, Assistant Political Agent in Turkish Arabia, Section on Bahrain, pp. 26–7, Selection from the Records of the Bombay Government, New Series, No. XXIV.
15 *Notes* of Captain Robert Taylor, op. cit., pp. 26–7.
16 A.T. Wilson, op. cit., p. 246.
17 Captain George Bruck's Memoir, *Descriptive of the Navigation of the Gulf of Persia*, 21 August 1829, page 563, Bombay Selection, Vol. XXIV.
18 Iranian Ministry of Foreign Affairs (IMFA), *Collection of the Iranian Government Documents*, Series No. 6207.
19 Colonel Jahangir Qaem-Maqami, *Bahrain and the Problems of the Persian Gulf*, Tehran 1962, text in Persian, p. 49.
20 Extract from the *Letter of 20 Ramazan 1276 (12 April 1860) from Shaeikh Mohammad bin Khalifah to Nasser ad-Din Shah Qajar, in Arabic and Persian*, IMFA'S Collection of Iranian Government Documents, Series No. 6044, p. 339.
21 Extract from *Letter* of 18 Shavval 1276 (10 June 1860) from Shaikh Mohammad bin Khalifah to Mirza Mehdi Khan, Foreign Minister of Iran, in Arabic and Persian, collection of Iranian Government Document, No. 6044, p. 269.
22 Iranian Government Document Collection, No. 6044, p. 274.
23 *Document* related to Iran, French Foreign Ministry Archive, Documents from French Consulate at Bushehr, pp. 58–60. Also, British FO 248/245.
24 *Document* related to Iran, French Foreign Ministry, ibid., also, FO 248/246.
25 Qatar Ministry of Information, *Glimpse of Qatar*, prepared, designed and produced by Gulf Public Relations (Qatar) WL.L, Doha 1985, p. 48.
26 *Note* on Qatar by Hajji Abdullah Williamson of Anglo-Persian Oil Company, dated 13 January 1934, p. 18, FO 371/17799.
27 Qaran was the currency unit of Iran in the nineteenth century also in circulation in the shaikhdoms of the Persian Gulf.
28 Extract from an Iranian Foreign Ministry report (of no description), section 5 on *The Emirate of Qatar*, dated 1348 (1969), p. 174, No. 2–2 of File 2 of the Ninth Political Bureau of the Military of Foreign Affairs, Tehran.
29 Ibid., p. 50.
30 Extracts from the *Memorandum* of 14 January 1934 by Hajji Abdullah Williamson of Anglo-Persian Oil Company, FO 371/17799, pp. 18–19.

31 Colonel Jahangir Qaem-Maqami, op. cit., p. 61.
32 *Letter* from Mirza Ali Khan, Governor of Fars, to Colonel Lewis Pelly, dated Safar 1284 (1867), FO 248/247.
33 *Iranian Government Documents*, Series No. 6044, p. 273.
34 Qaem-Maqami, op. cit., p. 61.
35 IMFA's *Collection of Iranian Government Documents*, Series No. 6044, p. 263.
36 Freydun Adamiyat, *Bahrain Island*, New York 1955, pp. 177–8.
37 Collection of *Iranian Government Documents*, No. 6044, dated Jamadi al-Awal 1288 (1871).
38 Adamiyat, op. cit., pp. 189–190.
39 French Foreign Ministry Documents, Vol. 4, Documents of the Consulate at Tabriz and Bushehr, p. 200.
40 French Foreign Ministry Documents, op. cit., pp. 208 to 212.
41 Ibid.
42 FO in India Office, L/P, L/S10/606, p. 8.
43 Documents 32 and 33 of *A Selection of Persian Gulf Documents* op. cit., pp. 87–8 and 91–2 respectively.
44 Documents 32 and 33 of *A Selection of Persian Gulf Documents* op. cit., pp. 87–8 and 91–2 respectively.
45 (British) House of Commons Debate, Vol. 578, 27 November 1957, Cols. 115–6.
46 Iranian Foreign Ministry, *Green Book*, Tehran 1967, pp. 38–40.
47 Iranian Ministry of Foreign Affairs, First Political Bureau, *Book of Documents*, Tehran 1976, p. 85.
48 Alinaghi Alikhani, ed. *The Shah and I*, Asadollah Alam's Confidential Diary of Iran's Royal Court 1969–77, 1991, p. 38.
49 Ibid.
50 Piere Shammas, *Border Disputes in the Greater Middle East*, Royal Institute of International Affairs, Chatham House, 1991, p. 38.
51 See Iran–Saudi Arabian Continental Shelf boundary delimitation in Chapter 4 for details.
52 Saudi Arabian government was suspected to have been involved.
53 *Al-Ahram* of Cairo. November 10, 1968.
54 Alinaghi Alikhani, ed., *The Shah and I*, op. cit., p. 44.
55 Denis Wright, 'Ten Years in Iran – Some Highlights', in *Asian Affairs*, Vol. XXII, Pt. III, October 1991, p. 269.
56 Alinaghi Alikhani, ed. *Yad-Dashthay-e Alam*, Confidential Diary of Asadollah Alam, Vol. I for the years 1347–8 (1968–9), original Persian text, New World Ltd, USA, 1992, p. 158.
57 *The Shah and I*, op. cit., p. 58.
58 See for example, Denis Wright's statements in *Ten Years in Iran*, op. cit., p. 268.
59 Pirouz Mojtahed-Zadeh, *Shaikh Neshinhay-e Khlij-e Fars*, op. cit., quoting news media, p. 187.
60 Confidential letter of 2 September 1966, from D.A.H. Wright, British Ambassador in Tehran, to Sir Roger Allen, KCMG, Foreign Office, P. 1, Paras. 1 and 2, and P. 2, Para. 7, FO 371/185331.
61 Abbas Aram, Iran's Minister of Foreign Affairs at the time.

62 Confidential from H.G. Balfour-Paul of British Residency in the Persian Gulf to T.F. Brenchley of Foreign Office, dated 29 September 1966, P. 1, Para. 2, FO 371/185331.

63 Ibid. P. 3, Para. 7.

64 Iranian Ministry of Foreign Affairs, *Book of Documents*, Ninth Bureau, Tehran 1976, p. 21.

65 Ibid.

66 Ibid.

67 *Bahrain*, published by the Ministry of Foreign Affairs of the Imperial Government of Iran, Ninth Political Bureau, Ordibehesht of 1354 (April–May 1975), p. 1.

68 *Bahrain*, published by the Ministry of Foreign Affairs of the Islamic Republic of Iran (The Green Book), Tehran 1368 (1989), pp. 1, 2 and 3.

69 Bahrain, 'Geography', *Encyclopaedia Iranica*, Ehsan Yarshater ed., Vol. III, Fascicle 5, Routledge & Kegan Paul, Columbia University 1988, p. 506.

70 Hamdollah Bin Abi-Baker Mostofi al-Qazvini, *Nozhat al-Qolub* in Persian, edited by Dabir-Siaqui, Tehran 1336 (1957), p. 164.

71 Sadeq Nashat (Mirdamad), *Political History of the Persian Gulf* Tehran 1345 (1966), section on Bahrain, p. 469.

72 Extract from letter of Safar 1261 (1845) from the Iranian Ministry of Foreign Affairs to the British Legation in Tehran, *Iranian Government Documents* series 6044, p. 329.

73 Pirouz Mojtahed-Zadeh, *Keshvarha va Marzha dar Mantaqeh-e Jeopolitik-e Khalij-e Fars* (*Countries and Boundaries in the Geopolitical Region of the Persian Gulf*), a collection of several articles in English, translated into Persian by Hamid-Reza Malek-Mohammadi Nouri, published by the Institute of Political and International Studies (IPIS) of the Iranian Ministry of Foreign Affairs (first published in 1993), 4th publication 1966, pp. 204–5.

74 Letter from Mohammad-Ali, Chief of Passport Office of the Southern Ports to the Ministry of Foreign Affairs, dated 5.12.1306 (24 February 1937), No. 425, enclosure No. 1. *A Selection of the Persian Gulf Documents*, published by IPIS of the Foreign Ministry of the Islamic Republic of Iran, Tehran 1993, Vol. 1, pp. 102–4.

75 *Letter* of 15.7.1335 (16.10.1956) from the Ministry of Justice, Legal Affairs, to the Ministry of Foreign Affairs, No. 4938, Third Political Bureau. Also, *letter* of 21.7.1335 (12.10.1956) from the Ministry of Foreign Affairs to the Ministry of Justice, Third Political Bureau, No. 24614/1198.

76 Said Zahlan, Rosemarie, *The Creation of Qatar*, London 1979, p. 84.

CHAPTER 6 – QATAR–BAHRAIN DISPUTES IN THE TWENTIETH CENTURY

1 Sir Charles Belgrave, *The Pirate Coast*, Bell 1968, pp. 123–4–5.

2 Charles D. Belgrave, *Personal Column*, Hutchison, 1960, p. 159.

3 According to the *Handbook of Arabia*, Vol. II, p. 17, the Manasir lives 'South of the Murrah on the edge of the great desert'.

4 Extracts from *Memorandum* of 14 January 1934 from Hajji Abdullah Williamson of Anglo-Persian Oil Company, pp. 18–19, FO 371/17799.

5 From Mr Longrigg to Mr Clauson (India Office), dated London 11 September 1936, Enclosure 1 to E6114/260/91 of FO 371/19974, p. 61.

6 Ibid.

7 Ibid.

8 From Mr Clauson to Mr Longrigg, dated India Office 14 September 1936, Enclosure 2 to E6114/260/91 of FO 371/19974–5415, p. 62.

9 Letter of 1 Shahrivar 1316 (22 August 1937) from the Iranian Ministry of the Interior's Political Department, to the Office of Prime Minister, No. 964/330K, Documents of the Office of Prime Minister, series 8165.

10 *Telegraph* of April 28, 1937 from Political Resident to India Office, L/P and S/12/3883.

11 *Telegraph* of May 21, 1937 from Political Resident to India Office L/P and S/12/3883.

12 Message enclosed in Political Agent to Bahrain's letter of 12 August 1937, to Mr Fowle, Political Resident, R/15/137.

13 See original copy of the agreement, signed and dated 24 June 1944, FO 1016/266, p. 33.

14 Extract from letter of 25 January 1950 from British Political Agent in Bahrain to the ruler of Qatar, No. C/Q - 23, FO 1016/154, pp. 2–3 of 63 and 64.

15 Extract from letter of January 17, 1954 of British Political Agent in Bahrain, J.W. Wall, to the ruler of Bahrain, No. 1010/3/54, FO 1016/332, pp. 1–3 (15–17).

16 Original and Arabic translation of letter of 14 May 1954 from the ruler of Qatar to the British Political Resident in the Persian Gulf, Bahrain, FO 1016/384, p. 19.

17 Ibid.

18 From Sir Bernard Burrows, British Political Resident in the Persian Gulf, Bahrain, to Shaikh Salman bin Hamad Al Khalifah, ruler of Bahrain, dated 10 August 1957, FO 371/26935.

19 Extract from the report of 24.3.1349 (14 June 1970) from Hassan Faramarzi of the Iranian Foreign Ministry to the Minister of Foreign Affairs, paragraph 5, No. 2–1 of File 2 of the Ninth Political Bureau of the Ministry of Foreign Affairs.

20 See Pirouz Mojtahed-Zadeh, 'Iran, Bahrain va Arabestan-e Saudi; Yek Mosllas-e Jeopolitik', *Ettelaat-e Siyasi - Eqtesadi*, Vol.7, Nos. 71–72, Tehran July–August 1993.

21 J.G. Lorimer, *Gazetteer of the Persian Gulf*, Vol. IIB, Section on Qatar, Calcutta 1908, reprinted London 1970, pp. 1513–14.

22 British Political Resident, No. 191, of May 19, 1938, as appeared in Arabic text of *Demarcation of Boundaries between Bahrain and Qatar in British Archives*, by Dr Walid Hamid Al-Adami, London, 1992, pp. 45–6.

23 From Mr Clauson of India Office to Mr S H Longrigg of Petroleum Concession Limited, dated 14 September 1936, Enclosure 2 of India Office to Foreign Office of 29 September 1936, Eastern (Arabia), Confidential, FO 371/19974, p. 3.

24 From British Political Agent to Political Resident at Bushehr, dated 15 May 1938, India Office Library R/15/2/547.

25 From C.W. Boxter of Foreign Office to Under Secretary of State in Indian Office, No. 3812196/91, dated 13 June 1939, FO 371/21825.

26 From Mr Prior to Mr Peal of India Office, dated September 1939 India Office Library R/15/2/547.

27 Extract from secret letter of British Political Agency to H.H. Shaikh Sir Salman bin Hamad Al Khalifah, ruler of Bahrain, No. C/L - 151, dated 30 April 1949, FO 1016/13, p. 19.

28 Unofficial Communiqué of International Court of Justice, No. 91/21, dated 8 July 1991, p. 2.

29 Unofficial Communiqué, op. cit., p. 2.

30 Part-quotation of Article 10 of Geneva Convention of 1958 as appeared in confidential letter of 8 July 1959 from British Foreign Office to Bahrain Residency, FO 371/140194.

31 From Foreign Office to E.F. Given Bahrain, Confidential BA 1271/1, dated 8 July 1959, FO 371/140194.

32 From Foreign Office to Kennedy of Admiralty, Confidential BA 1271/1, dated 16 July 1959, FO 371/140194.

33 Ibid.

34 Ibid, paragraph 3. From the largest scale chart of the area (Admiralty Chart 3790) the north east extremity of the coral formation of Jaradah is less than three miles from the Southwest corner of extent of Dibal shoal as shown on that chart. The survey was based on the latest information held by the Hydrographic Department of Admiralty in 1957, FO 371/1409194.

35 From R.N. Kennedy of HD of Admiralty to the Foreign Office, Confidential BA 1271/2, dated 25 August 1959, FO 371/140194.

36 From Admiralty, op. cit., No. iii of paragraph 4, FO 371/140194.

37 From Hydrographic Department of Admiralty to Foreign Office, Confidential BA 1271/2, No. iv of paragraph 4 and paragraph 5, FO 371/140194.

38 *Report* by HMS *Loch Fyne*, dated July 24, 1959 as quoted in Confidential No. BA 1271/3 from Bahrain British Residency to Foreign Office FO 371/140194, dated 20 August 1959.

39 Bahrain, No. C/L–151, dated 30 April 1949, FO 1016/13. Pirouz Mojtahed-Zadeh, *Keshvarha*, op.cit., p. 215.

40 J.B. Allcock, and others, *Border and Territorial Disputes*, 3rd edition, Longman Current Affairs, England 1992, p. 368.

41 Pirouz Mojtahed-Zadeh, *Keshvarha*, op. cit., p. 212.

42 Pirouz Mojtahed-Zadeh, *Keshvarha*, op. cit., p. 213.

43 From Foreign Office to H. Kennedy, Hydrographic Department of the Admiralty, Confidential No. BA 1271/1, dated 16 July 1959, FO 371/140194.

44 Unofficial Communiqué of the International Court of Justice, No. 91/21, dated 8 July 1991, p. 1.

45 Ibid.

46 Unofficial Communiqué, op. cit., p. 2.

47 Confidential from British Political Agency to Sir William Luce, British Political Resident in the Pursian Gulf, Bahrain, dated 23 February 1966, P. 1, Para. 2, FO 371/185335.

48 Confidential from British Political Residency in the Persian Gulf to R.H.M. Boyle, Esq., Doha, dated 17 September 1966, P. 1, Para. 2, FO 371/185335.

49 Dated 23 February 1966, op. cit., P. 1, Para. 2, FO 371/18533.

50 Ibid.
51 For the original copy of the declaration see Al-Adami, Dr W.H., *Tarsim al-Hodud Bain al-Bahrain wa Qatar fi Wathaeq al-Britaniyat*, London 1992, pp. 223–4.
52 Pirouz Mojtahed-Zadeh in interview with BBC Persian Service, News Bulletin, 16 April 1992.
53 Al Adami, op. cit., pp. 225–6.
54 Mojtahed-Zadeh, *Keshvarha*, op. cit., p. 215.
55 Unofficial Communiqué of ICJ, op. cit., p. 1.
56 BBC Summary of world broadcasts; Gulf States; ME/1438/A8-A/9, 21 July 1992.
57 Pirouz Mojtahed-Zadeh in interview with BBC Persian Service, News Bulletin, Monday 28 February 1994.
58 International Court of Justice, Unofficial Communiqué No. 94/16, dated 1 July 1994, p. 1.

CHAPTER 7 – DISPUTES OVER TUNBS AND ABU MUSA

1 James Morier, *A Second Journey Through Persia, Armenia and Asia Minor*, Longham, Hurst, Rees etc., London 1818, p. 30.
2 J.G. Lorimer, *Gazetteer of the Persian Gulf*, Vol. IIB, Geography and Statistical, India 1908, p. 1276.
3 For more details of the geographical description of the island of Abu Musa, see Pirouz Mojtahed-Zadeh, Masud Mohajer, Admiral Ebrahim Shah-Husseini, Malek-Reza Malekpour, 'Special Report on Abu Musa', *San'at-e Haml-o Naghl (Transport Industry) Monthly of Tehran*, No.1474, November 1992.
4 Arnold T. Wilson, op. cit., p. 55.
5 Arnold T. Wilson, op. cit., pp. 245–6.
6 Article 3 of General Treaty for the Cessation of Plunder and Piracy by Land and Sea, dated 5th February 1820, as appears in Donal Hawley's *The Trucial States*, London 1970, p. 314.
7 J.G. Lorimer, *Gazetteer of the Persian Gulf*, Vol. I India 1908, p. 625.
8 J.B. Kelly, *Eastern Arabian Frontiers*, London 1964, p. 18.
9 Rupert Hay, *The Persian Gulf States*, Washington 1959, pp. 3–4.
10 Lorimer, op. cit., p. 625.
11 From Reverend G P Badger to the government of Bombay, No.10, dated June 5th 1861, FO 60/385.
12 See Pirouz Mojtahed-Zadeh, *Sheikh-Neshinhay-e Khalif-e Fars (Sheikhdoms of the Persian Gulf)*, Ataei Publications, Tehran 1970.
13 J.C. Wilkinson, *Water and Tribal Settlement in South-East Arabia*, Oxford Research Studies in Geography, Oxford 1977, p. 6.
14 Donald Hawley, op. cit., p.93.
15 Esmail Naurizadeh Bushehri, *Iran-e Konuni va Khalij-e Fars*, Tehran 1946, p. 129.
16 Dr Dukes apparently died before reaching Tehran (Nayer-Nuri, Hamid, Fath-e Bandar Abbas va Jazayer-e Qeshm va Hormuz, 1968, in Vahid Monthly, vol. 5(4), pp. 18–31, & vol. 5(5), pp. 433–42.

17 Donald Hawley, op. cit., p. 114.
18 A great-grandfather of the author.
19 Jahangir Qaem-Maqami, *Bahrain va Masael-e Khalij-e Fars*, Tehran 1462, p. 117.
20 Bombay Selection XXIV.
21 Kazem Vadiei, *Moqadameh-I bar Joghrafiyay-e Ensani-e Iran*, Tehran University 1974, p. 192–3.
22 J.G. Lorimer, *Gazetteer of the Persian Gulf*, Bombay 1908, p. 2086.
23 Extract from the Persian text of letter from William Doria to Iranian Foreign Minister, 3 Shavval 1275 (7.5.1858), *Iranian Government Documents* (Vol.6180).
24 Colonel Jahangir Qaem-Maqami, op. cit., pp. 120–1.
25 *Iranian Government Documents* (Vol. 6044: 108)
26 *Iranian Government Documents* (Vol. 6044: 263)

CHAPTER 8 – RECENT DEVELOPMENTS

1 Foreign Broadcast Information Service, FBIS-NES-92-076, 20 April 1992
2 See for example: R.N. Schofield, ed., *Territorial Foundation of the Gulf States*, UCL Press, London 1994, pp. 71–2.
3 Ibid.
4 *Echo of Iran* 40 (5, 52), London, 13.5 1992, p. 9, quoting *Abrar* 13.5.1992.
5 BBC Persian Service, *News Bulletin*, 25.8.1992.
6 *Echo of Iran*, 30 (8/9, 55/56), London August/September 1992, pp. 3–4.
7 Ibid.
8 Dr Hassan Al-Alkim's presentation in the Round Table Discussion on the Dispute over the Gulf Islands, London, January 1993, p. 32.
9 *The Times*, London, 22.9.1992, p. 11.
10 Press release, Embassy of the UAE, London, October 1992.
11 *Iran Focus*, November 1992.
12 Summary of World Broadcasts: the Middle East ME/1573/A/7, 29.12.1992.
13 *Middle East Economic Survey*, C3, 11.1.1993.

CHAPTER 9 – LEGAL AND HISTORICAL ARGUMENTS

1 British Minister in Tehran to Iranian Ministry of Foreign Affairs, 26 Rabi ath-Thani 1322 (10.7.1904), Persian text, document 84 in *Gozideh-e Asnad-e Khalij-e Fars (A Selection of Persian Gulf Documents)*, Iranian Ministry of Foreign Affairs, Tehran 1989, p. 268.
2 See for example: J.B. Kelly, *Eastern Arabian Frontiers*, Faber & Faber, London 1964.
3 See also: Rupert Hay *The Persian Gulf States*, George Allen & Unwin, London 1959.
4 See: J.C. Wilkinson, *Water and Tribal Settlement in South-East Arabia*, Oxford Research Studies in Geography, Oxford Clarendon 1977, p. 6.

5 Abbas Eqbal Ashtiani, *Motaleati dar bareh-e Bahrain va Jazaier va Banader-e Khalij-e Fars (Some studies on islands and ports of the Persian Gulf)*, The Majlis Printing House, Tehran 1328 (1949), p. 144.

6 Hamdollah Ahmad ben Abi-Baker Mostofi, *Nozhat al-Qolub*, ed. Guy le Strange, Leiden, Brill 1928 (original 730s AH), pp. 171, 186, 234.

7 Memorandum of 24 August 1928, pp. 4512–28, L/P & S/18/B397.

8 171546: E10136/34, *Persian Frontiers*, Confidential document (17188) of H.B.M. Government, 31.1.1947, Section VI, paragraph 72, p. 13, FO 371/45507.

9 Arabia E982/52/91, Letter No. F160 - N/28 of 29 January 1929 from the secretary of the Government of India to the India Office, Enclosure 3, reports of private letters of Shaikh Yusof of Lengeh to Mohammad Hassan Khan, Governor General at Bandar Abbas and Lengeh, FO 371/13721.

10 D.H. Bavand, 'Bar-rasi-ye Mabani-ye Tarikhi va Hoghughi-e Jazayer-e Tunb va Abu Musa (The Study of Historical and Legal Backgrounds to the Islands of Tunbs and Abu Musa), *Jame'eh-e Salem monthly*, Vol. II, No.7, Tehran December 1992–January 1993, pp. 6–19.

11 Persia and Arab States, Order in Consul Jurisdiction 1857 to 1882, part II, Further Correspondence respecting Consular jurisdiction in Persia 1874–76, Mr Reilly's Correspondence and Memoranda, p. 19, FO 60/451.

12 Abdullah Mohammad Morsy, *The United Arab Emirates*, Croom Helm, London 1978, pp. 234–5.

13 Document No.53 of *Gozideh-e Asnad-e Khalij-e Fars*, op.cit., Vol. I, Tehran 1989, pp. 168–9.

14 Abdullah, op.cit., pp. 234–5.

15 Sir E. Beckett's Memorandum, dated 12 March 1932, FO 371/18901.

16 Hassan H. Al-Alkim's contribution to *Round Table Discussion on the Disputed Gulf Islands*, Farid et al., November 1992; Published by Arab Research Centre, London, January 1993, pp. 28–38.

17 The United Arab Emirates expanded its territorial sea to 12 miles in 1993.

18 Mohammad Reza Dabiri, 'Abu Musa: a binding understanding or a misunderstanding?', *Iranian Journal of International Affairs*, Vol. V, Nos. 3 and 4, Fall 1993/Winter 1994, pp. 575–583.

19 A.D.McNair, *The Law of Treaties*, Oxford, Clarendon Press, Oxford 1961, p. 185.

20 Sir Denis Wright, *The English Amongst the Persians*, London 1977, p. 66.

21 Ibid., p. 67.

22 Abbas Eqbal Ashtiani, *Motaleati dar Bab-e Bahrain va Jazayer va Savahel-e Khalij-e Fars*, Tehran 1949, p. 144.

23 The term *Banader-e Khalij-e Fars* (ports of the Persian Gulf), in official documents of the Qajar period, normally included the islands of the Gulf.

24 Iranian MFA to British Legation, letter no. 26, 26 Jamadi ath-Thani 1305 (10.3.1888), Persian text in *Iranian Government Documents* (Vol. 6180).

25 British Minister to Iranian MFA, letter of 5 Rajab 1305 (18.3.1888), Persian text in *Iranian Government Documents* (Vol. 6180).

26 Qaem-Maqami, op. cit., p. 125.

27 Iranian MFA to British Legation, letter no. 44 of 12 Ziqadeh 1305 (21.7.1888), Persian text in *Iranian Government Documents* (Vol. 6180).

28 Sir Denis Wright, op. cit., p. 68.

29 Iranian MFA to British Minister, letter of 24 Rabi ath-Thani 1312 (30.11.1894), Persian text in *Iranian Government Documents* (Vol. 6180).

30 Confidential from India Office to Foreign Office, dated 1 November 1900, enclosure No. 2, FO 60/733.

31 From George Hamilton to the Governor-General of India in Council, dated 23 November 1900, secret No.30, FO 60/733.

32 *Most Secret Persia*, War Office Memorandum on Sir A. Hardinge's letter of 14 October 1902, signed by Alton A.Q.M.G., FO 60/733.

33 Confidential Memorandum by Sir T. Sanderson, 14 July 1902, FO 416/10.

34 See Government of India to Mr Brodrick, Enclosure in No.130, 16 April 1904, No.154, FO 416/17, p. 191.

35 See Horace Walpole of India Office to Foreign Office, dated 16 April 1904, No.154, FO 416/17, p. 191.

36 See Lord G. Curzon *Persia and the Persian Question*, London 1892, map enclosed in Vol. I.

37 Extract from the Confidential Document (17188) of H.B.M. government *Persian Frontiers*, 31 January 1947, FO 371/45507, par. 72.

38 Donald Hawley, *The Trucial States*, London 1970, p. 287.

39 Telegram No.49, from Sir A. Hardinge to the Marquess of Lansdowne, dated Tehran 20 April 1904 enclosure No.165, FO 416/17, p. 197.

40 From Foreign Office to India Office, No.174, dated 23 April 1904, FO 416/17, p. 201.

41 Extract from A. Hardinge's telegram to Foreign Office, dated May 1904, FO 416/18, p. 160.

42 Government of India to Mr Brodrick, dated 13 April 1904, enclosure No.130, FO 416/17, p. 142.

43 Ibid.

44 Ibid.

45 From India Office to Foreign Office, dated 2 December 1908; to Viscount Morely of India Office, dated 24 November 1908; in reply to the inquiry of India Office of 20 October 1908, Enclosure to No.1: G.I., Persia E 34/42315, FO 371/506.

46 Hawley, op. cit., p. 162.

47 From First Agency of the ports of the Persian Gulf and coasts of Baluchistan to the Ministry of Foreign Affairs, dated 14 Shavval 1328 (1910), No. 64, in *A Selection of Persian Gulf Documents*, Foreign Ministry of the Islamic Republic of Iran's Institute of Political and International Studies, Tehran 1989, No. 91, p. 280.

48 From the Customs Office of Ministry of Finance to the Ministry of Foreign Affairs, No.11469, dated 5 Mordad 1306 (27 July 1927).

49 49, *Annual Confidential Report of British Legation in Tehran for the year 1928*, paragraph 147, pp. 23-4, FO 416/113.

50 Op. cit., paragraphs 150–4.

51 91, *Annual Confidential Report of British Legation in Tehran for the year 1929*, paragraph 156, p. 23, FO 416/113.

52 Extracted from Sir Robert Clive to Sir A. Chamberlain, Confidential Report of 8.1.1929, *Collection of British Political Documents* No. 420; quoted in Shaikh al-Eslami (1988: 213).

53 Ministry of War to MFA, enclosure in confidential despatch of 5 Esfand 1308 (24.2.1930), in MFA (1989: 351).

54 MFA to British Legation, same date, in MFA (1989: 355).

55 MFA to War Ministry, 26 Khordad 1310 (16.6.1931), quoting Hengam headman's report No. 182, in MFA (1989: 363).

56 Minister of Imperial Court (Taimurtash) to MFA, 29 Khordad 1310 (19.6.1931), No. 113 in MFA (1989: 269).

57 Persia E/284/19/34, Sir Robert Clive to Austen Chamberlain, No. 1.0 of 16.2.1929, FO 371/13776.

58 Hoare to Oliphant, 15.7.1932, FO 371/16070.

59 FO Confidential Report, Status of the islands of Tunb (Tamb) Sirri and Bu Musa, (1961), FO 371/157031.

60 Knatchbull-Hugessen to FO, 9.4.1935, FO 371/18980.

61 Foreign Office confidential report (1961), FO 371/157031.

62 From Mr Knatchbull-Hugessen to Mr Eden, Confidential Annual Report, 1935, E 1147/1147/34, dated Tehran 28 January 1935. See also the same to Foreign Office, dated 9 April 1935, FO 371/18980.

63 See, for example, the statement made by Richard Scholfield and Hassan Al-Alkim at the Arab, Iranian, British seminar of 18 November 1992 *Round Table Discussion on the Disputed Gulf Islands*, Arab Research Centre, London January 1993.

64 Ministry of Finance to MFA, 18 Esfand 1315 (9.3.1937), in MFA (1989: 379).

65 Captain R.M. Owen, Confidential Report on Visit of HMS *Lash Insh* to Tunb Island, on 24.8.1961, FO 371/157031, p. 1.

66 Ibid.

67 Sir A. Hardinge to Mushireed-Doleh, Iranian Foreign Minister, 2. 7. 1904, FO 60/734.

68 Farsi island is situated in the middle of the Persian Gulf parallel to Arabyah island, half-way between the coasts of Iran and Saudi Arabia.
Iran's sovereignty over this island has been officially recognised by the 1968 Iran-Saudi Arabian continental shelf boundary agreement, in return for recognition of Saudi Arabian sovereignty over Arabyah island. These two islands have never had anything to do with Kuwait and her sovereignty rights in the Persian Gulf, nor are they situated anywhere near Kuwait.

69 Confidential from Foreign Office to G.E. Millard, Tehran, November 2, 1961, FO 371/15703.

70 Ibid.

71 Ibid., p. 2.

72 FO to British Political Resident Bahrain, No. 227 of 24.8.1961; British Political Resident Bahrain, to FO, No. 1085/1 of 25.8.1961; British Embassy, Tehran to Iranian MFA, Note No. 487 – 1084/61 of 5.9.1961, FO 371/157031.

73 Sixth Political Department of MFA to HM Embassy, Extract from Note 3052 of 21.9.1961, FO 371/157031.

74 FO to Millard, No. BT 1083/7 of 2.11.1961, FO 371/150731.

75 Millard to Geven, Confidential of 13.1.1962; First Political Department of MFA to HM Embassy in Tehran, No. 5724 of 20.1.1962, FO 371/163032.

76 'Persia Seeks New Links', *The Scotsman*, 7.9.1962.

77 British Embassy Tehran, to FO, No. BT 1083/10-1084/61 of 20.11.1961, FO 371/157031.

CHAPTER 10 – SEIZURE OF THE TWO TUNBS AND RESTORATION OF SOVEREIGNTY IN ABU MUSA

1 Saudi Arabian government was suspected to have been involved.
2 *Al-Ahram* of Cairo, November 10, 1968.
3 Alinaghi Alikhani, ed. *Confidential Diary of Alam*, Vol. I – 1347 and 1348 (1969 and 1970). Text in Persian, published in USA 1992, p. 130.
4 D.F. Hawley, *The Trucial States*, London 1970, pp. 287–8.
5 Iran, Foreign Policy Series, No. 2, January 1973, *The Echo of Iran*, p. 26.
6 Mohammad Reza Shah in interview with the Associated Press, *Kayhan* No. 8278, 20 February 1971, p. 27.
7 *Kayhan of Tehran*, No. 8381, 25 June 1971.
8 Amir Abbas Hoveida in Bandar Abbas, *Ettlelaat of Tehran*, 27 June 1971.
9 *Middle East Journal* (MEJ), Vol. XXV, No. 2, 1971, pp. 234–5. Quoting Ardeshir Zahedi.
10 R.K. Ramazani, *The Persian Gulf*, USA, pp. 56–8.
11 Extract from the text of the original copy of the Memorandum of Understanding as appears in Appendix III of this book.
12 Pirouz Mojtahed-Zadeh, *Political Geography of the Strait of Hormuz*, op. cit., p. 12.
13 Alvin J. Cottrell, *Iran Diplomacy in a Regional and Global Context*, Washington, 1975, p. 6.
14 *Al-Ahram*, Cairo 8 December 1971.
15 *Ettelaat* and *Kayhan*, Tehran 30 November 1971.
16 See: UN *Monthly Chronicle*, January 1972, Vol. IX, No.1, Record of the Month of December 1971, p. 46.
17 Ibid.
18 Ibid.
19 Ibid, p. 50.
20 Ibid, p. 47.
21 International News Agencies quoted by *Kayhan* (London) Thursday 1992.
22 UN *Monthly Chronicle*, op. cit., p. 48.

CONCLUSION

1 See numerous official and confidential documents of British Foreign Office in this respect for the years of the 1950s and 1960s, under P.R.O. references FO 1016/154, FO 1016/260, FO 1016/332, FO 1016/384, FO 1016/476, FO 1016/148965.
2 International Court of Justice, Unofficial Communique No. 92/19, dated 29 June 1992.
3 Island of Palmas (United States/Netherlands), Permanent Court of Arbitration at the Hague, reprinted in J.B. Scott ed., *The Hague Court Reports*, 2nd ser. 1932, p. 111.

4 Persia E4369/19/34; Minutes of G.W. Rendel of Eastern Department, dated 10 September 1929, FO 371/13777.

5 The idea of the Islamic Conference was seriously considered after the incident of fire in the Al-Aqsa Musque in August 1969 and the organization came into being in the wake of that incident.

6 Pirouz Mojtahed-Zadeh, 'Political Geography of the Strait of Hormuz', Middle East Centre/SOAS Publications, London: 1990, pp. 5 and 46.

APPENDICES

1 Supplement for April, May and June 1970 of UN *Monthly Chronicle*.

2 Supplement for January, February and March 1970, document S/9726 of UN *Monthly Chronicle*.

3 Ibid., supplement for April, May and June 1970, Document S/9772.

4 Extracted from the debate of the Majilis of Senate, No. 994 meeting 120, dated 28/2/1349.

5 Document 994 of the Debate of the Senate, Meeting 120 – dated 28/2/1349 (18 May 1970). Iranian Foreign Ministry's *Book of Documents*, the Ninth Political Bureau, Tehran 1976, p. 145.

6 Extracted from the debate of the Majilis of Senate, No. 994 meeting 120, dated 28/2/1349.

7 Original documents as appeared in *Majalleh-e Siasat-e Khareji (The Journal of Foreign Policy)*, Vol. VI, No.4, winter of 1993, p. 194.

8 It was agreed that no reply from the Ruler of Sharjah to this letter would amount to his acceptance of Iran's conditions and warnings.

9 (UN *Monthly Chronicle*, Volume IX, Number 1, January 1972, Records of the Month (of) December 1971, pp. 46 to 50).

Bibliography

MANUSCRIPTS AND DOCUMENTS

Author's personal notes of his visits to the region of the Persian Gulf and of his talks with government officials in the region and in the West.

British Foreign Office confidential records and correspondence. Files from series Nos. FO 60/371/248/416, and 1016.

British India Office Library and Records, files series Nos. W/LPS, L/P & S, L/P, L/S – L/P, S/12 and R/15.

French Foreign Ministry Documents Vol. 4 of Tabriz and Bushehr Consulates.

International Court of Justice, Unofficial Communiqués; No. 91/21, dated 8 July 1991, No. 92/19, dated 29 June 1992 and No. 94/16, dated 1 July 1994.

Iranian Ministry of Foreign Affairs: Document Series 6044.

Iranian Ministry of Foreign Affairs: *Green Book of Documents*, Tehran 1976 and The Green Book on Bahrain (1989).

Iranian Ministry of Finance, document No. 11469, 27 July 1927.

Iranian Foreign Ministry files of Ninth Political Bureau, series 2, 3, 4, and the Bureau's *Green Book* on Bahrain, Tehran 1975.

Mojtahed-Zadeh, Pirouz, *Evolution of Eastern Iranian Boundaries*, Ph.D thesis, University of London, 1993.

Mojtahed-Zadeh, Pirouz, *Political Geography of the Persian Gulf (Iran's Role)*, Ph.D thesis, being prepared for the University of Oxford (1976–1979).

National Iranian Oil Company documents: 90504/4922/Sh.W. and 38/1–2/1780 also, 4611/509/4, also 38/1/1-M/15, also 7539/84 – 7205/84, and 38/1–1/60276.

Office of Prime Minister, Iranian Document Series 8165.

Records of Bombay Government, New Series No. XXIV, *Brief Notes of Captain Robert Taylor, Assistant Political Agent in Turkish Arabia of the same series* Memoir of Captain George Brucks, *Descriptive of Navigation of the Gulf of Persia*, 21 August 1829.

Selection of Persian Gulf Documents, Foreign Ministry of the Islamic Republic of Iran, Tehran 1989 to 1995, four volumes.

Shammas, Pierre, *Border Disputes in the Greater Middle East*, Paper presented to the Royal Institute of International Affairs, Chatham House, 1993.
UN National Legislative Series, Document No. ST/LEG/SER. B/16, 1974.
Wilkinson, J.C., *Arab Settlement in Oman*, DPhil thesis, University of Oxford 1969.

PERIODICALS AND ARTICLES

The American Journal of International Law, Equitable Solutions for Offshore Boundaries', by Richard Young, Vol. 64, 1970.
Asian Affairs, 'Ten Years in Iran – Some Highlights', by Denis Wright, Vol. XXII, Part III, October 1991.
BBC Summary of World Broadcast; Gulf States; ME/1438/A/8-A/9, 21 July 1992.
Encyclopaedia Iranica, edited by Ehsan Yarshater, published by Routledge & Kegan Paul, Vol. III, Columbia University 1988.
Ettelaat-e Siyasi va Eqtesadi monthly, article by Pirouz Mojtahed-Zadeh, Tehran, August/September 1992.
Financial Times, 20 December 1981.
Foreign Broadcast Information Service, FBIS-NES-92-076, 20 April 1992.
House of Commons' Debate, Vol. 578, 27 November 1957.
Iran Almanac 1972, ed. *The Echo of Iran*, Tehran 1972.
Iran Focus, Monthly News Bulletin, November 1992.
Iran Foreign Policy Series, No. 2, January 1973, ed. *The Echo of Iran*, Tehran 1974.
Journal of Oman Studies, Vol. I, London 1975, Wilkinson, J.C., 'The Julanda of Oman'.
Keesing's Contemporary Archive; 24 July 1981–25 July 1982–26 February 1982.
Siasat-e Khareji (The Journal of Foreign Policy), IPIS publication in Persian, Vol. VI, No.4, winter of 1993.
UN *Monthly Chronicle*, January 1972, Records of December 1971.
UN *Monthly Chronicle*; of February and March 1970; and Supplement of April, May and June 1970.
US Department of State, Bureau of Intelligence and Research, 'Limits in the Sea', No. 94 Continental Shelf Boundaries in the Persian Gulf, 1981; and No. 108 Maritime Boundaries of the World, 1990.

NEWS MEDIA

Al-Ahram of Cairo, 10 November 1968.
Al-Ahram of Cairo, 8 December 1971.
BBC Radio, Persian Service, *News Bulletin*, Tuesday 25 August 1992.
BBC Persian Service, *News Bulletin*, 16 April 1992, and 28 February 1994.
The Echo of Iran, London, Vol. XXXX, No. 5, May 1992.
The Echo of Iran, London, Vol. XXXX, August/September 1992.

Ettelaat Daily of Tehran, 27 June 1971.
The Geographical Journal, 'The Shihuh of Oman', by Walter Dstal, No. 628, March 1972.
Kayhan of Tehran, 20 February 1971.
Kayhan of Tehran, 25 June 1971.
Kayhan of Tehran, 30 November 1971.
Kuwait Times, 2 October 1979.
Sanat-e Haml va Naql (Transport Industry), Monthly Special Report on Abu Musa. Contributions from Pirouz Mojtahed-Zadeh, Masud Mohajer, Admiral Ebrahim Shah Husseini, Malek-Reza Malek-pour, No. 1474, Tehran November 1992.
The Times of London, 22 September 1992.
Vahid (Monthly) Vols. 5(4) & (5(5), Tehran 1968.

BOOKS IN ARABIC

Aba Hussain, Dr Ali, 'Jaboor – Were they Arabs of Bahrain or the Arabs of the East?', in *Al Watheeka*, No. 3, Vol. 2 Bahrain July 1983.
Al Adami, Dr Walid Hamid, *Tarsim al-Hodud Bain Bahrain wa Qatar fi Wathaeq al-Britaniyat* (*Demarcation of Boundaries Between Bahrain and Qatar in the British Archives*), London 1992.
Al Khalifah, Shaikh Abdullah bin Khalid, 'Dolat al-Ayouni (The Ayouni State)', in *Al Watheeka*, Vol. 2, No. 3, Bahrain July 1983.
Ibn Huqal, *Surat al-Ardh*, 4th century AH, published in London 1938.

BOOKS IN ENGLISH

Adamiyat, Freidun, *Bahrain Islands*, New York 1955.
Alinaghi Alikhani, ed., *The Shah and I*, Asadollah Alam's Confidential Diary of Iran's Royal Court, 1969–77, IB Tauris, London 1991.
Allcock, I.B. and others, *Border and Territorial Disputes*, 3rd ed., Longman Current Affairs, England 1992.
Belgrave, Charles D., *Personal Column*, Autobiography, Hutchison 1960.
Belgrave, Sir Charles, *The Pirate Coast*, Bell, London 1968.
Blake, G.H. and Schofield, R.N., *Boundaries and State Territory in the Middle East and North Africa*, MENAS Press Ltd., London 1987.
Cottrell, Alvin, J., *Iran: Diplomacy in a Regional and Global Context*, Washington 1975.
Curzon, Lord G., *Persia and the Persian Question*, London 1892, Vol.I.
Farid, A.M.; Schofield, Dr Richard; Moberly, Sir John; Mojtahed-Zadeh, Pirouz; Al-Alkim, Dr Hassan H., *Round Table Discussion on the Dispute over the Gulf Islands*, Arab Research Centre, London, January 1993.
Hawley, Donald, *The Trucial States*, George Allen & Unwin, London 1970.
Hay, Rupert, *The Persian Gulf States*, Washington 1959.
Kelly, J.B., *Eastern Arabian Frontiers*, London 1964.
Lorimer, J.G., *Gazetteer of the Persian Gulf*, two vols., India Superintendent Government Printing Press, 1908 and 1915.

Major, R.H., *India in the Fifteenth Century*, London 1865.

Mojtahed-Zadeh, Pirouz, *The Changing World Order and the Geopolitical Regions of the Persian Gulf and Caspian-Central Asia*, Urosevic Research Foundation, London 1992.

Mojtahed-Zadeh, Pirouz, *The Islands of Tunbs and Abu Musa*, CNMES/ SOAS Publication, University of London, 1995.

Mojtahed-Zadeh, Pirouz *Political Geography of the Strait of Hormuz*, Joint Geography Department and Middle East Centre Publication, SOAS, University of London 1991.

Oman, published by the Government of the Sultanate of Oman, Muscat 1976.

Oman 93, published by the Government of Sultanate of Oman, Muscat 1993.

Qatar Ministry of Information, *Glimpses of Qatar*, prepared, designed and produced by Gulf Public Relations (Qatar) W.L.L. Doha, 1985.

Ramazani, R.K., *The Persian Gulf*, USA 1972.

Ramazani, R.K., *Revolutionary Iran*, 2nd. ed. USA 1987.

Said-Zahlan, R., *The Creation of Qatar*, Croom Helm, London 1979.

Schofield, Richard N., *Territorial Foundation of the Gulf States*, UCL Press, London 1994.

Wallis, E.A., *A History of Egypt*, London 1902.

Wilkinson, J.C. *Water and Tribal Settlement in South-East Arabia*, Oxford Research Studies in Geography, Oxford Clarendon 1977.

Wilson, Sir Arnold T., *The Persian Gulf*, George Allen & Unwin, London 2nd ed. 1954.

Wright, Sir. Denis, *The English Amongst the Persians*, Heinemann, London 1977.

BOOKS IN PERSIAN

Alikhani, Alinaghi, ed., *Yad-Dashthay-e Alam* (Confidential Diary of Assadollah Alam), Vol. I for the year 1347–8 (1968–9), Original Persian Text, New World Ltd., USA 1992.

Ashtiani, Abbas Eqbal, *Motaleati dar Bab-e Bahrain va Jazayer va Savahel-e Khalij-e Fars* (*Studies on Bahrain and Islands and Coasts of the Persian Gulf*), Tehran 1949.

Gozideh Asnad-e Khalij-e Fars (*A Selection of Persian Gulf Documents*), IPIS publication, Vols I and III, Tehran 1993 and 1994 respectively.

Karim-Zadeh Tabrizi, Mohammad Ali *Asnad va Faramin-e Mantasher Nashadeh-e Qajari*, London 1989.

Maqdasi al-Bishani, *Ahsan at-Taqasim*, Persian translation, reprinted by SMM, Tehran 1982.

Masudi, Abul-Hassan Ali ibn Hussein, Arab Geographer/Historian of 4th Century AH, *Moravvej az-Zahab* (*Propagating the Way*), Persian Translation by Abul-Qasem Payandeh, Bongah-e Terjomeh va Nashr-e Ketab, Tehran 1977.

Mojtahed-Zadeh, Pirouz, 'Iran, Bahrain va Arabestan-e Saudi; Yek Mosallas-e Jeopolitik (Iran, Bahrain and Saudi Arabia, A Geopolitical Triangle)', in *Ettelaat-e Siyasi – Eqtesadi* Vol. 7, Nos. 71–72, July–August 1993.

Mojtahed-Zadeh, Pirouz, *Keshvarha va Marzha dar Mantaqeh-e Jeopolitike-e Khalij-e Fars (Countries and Boundaries in the Geopolitical Region of the Persian Gulf)*', Translated into Persian by Hamid Reza Malek-Mohammadi Nouri, IPIS Publication, Tehran 1993.

Mojtahed-Zadeh, Pirouz, *Shaikh Neshinhay-e Khalij-e Fars (The Sheikhdoms of the Persian Gulf)*', Ataei Publications, Tehran 1970.

Mostofi, Hamdollah Bin Abi-Baker al-Qazvini, *Nozhat al-Qolub*, edited by Dabir-Siaqi, Tehran 1336 (1957).

Nashat (Mirdamad), Sadeq, *Tarikh-e Siyasi-e Khalij-e Fars (Political History of the Persian Gulf), Tehran 1966*.

Nourizadeh Bushehri, Esmail, *Iran-e Konuni va Khalij-e Fars (Modern Iran and the Persian Gulf)*, Tehran 1325 (1946).

Qaem-Maqami, Colonel Jahangir, *Bahrain va Masael-e Khalij-e Fars (Bahrain and the Persian Gulf Problems)*, Tahuri publications, Tehran 1962.

Rohrborn, Claus-Michael, *Provinzen und Zentralgewalt Persiens (Provinces and Central Government in Iran)*. Translated into Persian by Kaykavous Jahandari, Bongah-e Tarjomeh va Nashr-e Ketab, Tehran 1978.

Sepehr, Mirza Mohammad Taqi Lesan al-Molk, *Nasekh at-Tavarikh*, ed. Mohammad Baqer Behbudi, Tehran 1974, Vol. I.

Sepehr, Mirza Mohammad Taqi Lesan al-Molk, *Nasekh at-Tavarikh*, ed. Jahangir Qaem-Maqami, Tehran 1958, Vol. III.

Sheikh al-Eslami, Dr Javad, *Qatl-e Atabak* (The Murder of Atabak), Kayhan Publications, Tehran 1988.

Tabari, Mohammad ben Jarir, *'Tarikh-e Tabari'*, translated into Persian by Abul-Qasem Payandeh, Bongah-e Tarjomeh va Nashr-e Ketab, Tehran 1973.

Vadiei, Kazem, *Moqadameh-i bar Joghrafiyay-e Ensani-e Iran (An Introduction to the Human Geography of Iran)*, Tehran University Press, No. 1280, Tehran 1974.

Index